# SUICIDE RESEARCH: SELECTED READINGS

## Volume 6

May 2011–October 2011

A. Milner, K.E. Kõlves, D. De Leo

Australian Institute for Suicide Research and Prevention

Griffith
UNIVERSITY

WHO Collaborating Centre for Research and Training in Suicide Prevention

National Centre of Excellence in Suicide Prevention

First published in 2011
Australian Academic Press
32 Jeays Street
Bowen Hills Qld 4006
Australia
www.australianacademicpress.com.au

ISBN: 9781921513930

# Contents

Non-fatal suicidal behaviour:

# Foreword

This volume contains quotations from internationally peer-reviewed suicide research published during the semester May 2011 – October 2011; it is the sixth of a series produced biannually by our Institute with the aim of assisting the Commonwealth Department of Health and Ageing in being constantly updated on new evidences from the scientific community. Compared to previous volumes, an increased number of examined materials have to be referred. In fact, during the current semester, the number of articles scrutinised has been the highest yet, with a progression that testifies a remarkably growing interest from scholars for the field of suicide research (718 articles for the first, 757 for the second, 892 for the third, and 1,121 for the fourth, 1,276 for the fifth, and 1,472 in the present volume).

As usual, the initial section of the volume collects a number of publications that could have particular relevance for the Australian people in terms of potential applicability. These publications are accompanied by a short comment from us, and an explanation of the motives that justify why we have considered of interest the implementation of studies' findings in the Australian context. An introductory part provides the rationale and the methodology followed in the identification of papers.

The central part of the volume represents a selection of research articles of particular significance; their abstracts are reported *in extenso*, underlining our invitation at reading those papers in full text: they represent a remarkable advancement of suicide research knowledge.

The last section reports all items retrievable from major electronic databases. We have catalogued them on the basis of their prevailing reference to fatal and non-fatal suicidal behaviours, with various sub-headings (e.g. epidemiology, risk factors, etc). The deriving list guarantees a level of completeness superior to any individual system; it can constitute a useful tool for all those interested in a quick update of what most recently published on the topic.

Our intent was to make suicide research more approachable to non-specialists, and in the meantime provide an opportunity for a *vademecum* of quotations credible also at the professional level. A compilation such as the one that we provide here is not easily obtainable from usual sources and can save a considerable amount of time to readers. We believe that our effort in this direction may be an appropriate interpretation of one of the technical support roles to the Government that the new status of National Centre of Excellence in Suicide Prevention — which has deeply honoured our commitment — entails for us.

The significant growth of our centre, the Australian Institute for Suicide Research and Prevention, and its influential function, both nationally and internationally, in the fight against suicide, could not happen without the constant support of Queensland Health and Griffith University. We hope that our passionate dedication to the cause of suicide prevention may compensate their continuing trust in our work.

**Diego De Leo**, DSc

Director, Australian Institute for Suicide Research and Prevention

# Acknowledgments

This report has been produced by the Australian Institute for Suicide Research and Prevention, WHO Collaborating Centre for Research and Training in Suicide Prevention and National Centre of Excellence in Suicide Prevention. The assistance of the Commonwealth Department of Health and Aging in the funding of this report is gratefully acknowledged.

# Introduction

## Context

Suicide places a substantial burden on individuals, communities and society in terms of emotional, economic and health care costs. In Australia, about 2000 people die from suicide every year, a death rate well in excess of transport-related mortality. At the time of preparing this volume, the latest available statistics released by the Australian Bureau of Statistics[1] indicated that, in 2009, 2,132 deaths by suicide were registered in Australia, representing an age-standardized rate of 9.6 per 100,000.

Further, a study on mortality in Australia for the years 1997–2001 found that suicide was the leading cause of avoidable mortality in the 25–44 year age group, for both males (29.5%) and females (16.7%), while in the age group 15–24 suicide accounted for almost a third of deaths due to avoidable mortality[2]. In 2003, self-inflicted injuries were responsible for 27% of the total injury burden in Australia, leading to an estimated 49,379 years of life lost (YLL) due to premature mortality, with the greatest burdens observed in men aged 25–64[3].

Despite the estimated mortality, the prevalence of suicide and self-harming behaviour in particular remains difficult to gauge due to the often secretive nature of these acts. Indeed, ABS has acknowledged the difficulties in obtaining reliable data for suicides in the past few years[4,5]. Without a clear understanding of the scope of suicidal behaviours and the range of interventions available, the opportunity to implement effective initiatives is reduced. Further, it is important that suicide prevention policies are developed on the foundation of evidence-based empirical research, especially as the quality and validly of the available information may be misleading or inaccurate. Additionally, the social and economic impact of suicide underlines the importance of appropriate research-based prevention strategies, addressing not only significant direct costs on health system and lost productivity, but also the emotional suffering for families and communities.

The Australian Institute for Suicide Research and Prevention (AISRAP) has, through the years, gained an international reputation as one of the leading research institutions in the field of suicide prevention. The most important recognition came via the designation as a World Health Organization (WHO) Collaborating Centre in 2005. In 2008, the Commonwealth Department of Health and Ageing (DoHA) appointed AISRAP as the National Centre of Excellence in Suicide Prevention. This latter recognition awards not only many years of high-quality research, but also of fruitful cooperation between the Institute and several different governmental agencies.

The new role given to AISRAP will translate into an even deeper commitment to the cause of suicide prevention amongst community members of Australia.

As part of this initiative, AISRAP is committed to the creation of a databank of the recent scientific literature documenting the nature and extent of suicidal and self-harming behavior and recommended practices in preventing and responding to these behaviors. The key output for the project is a critical bi-annual review of the national and international literature outlining recent advances and promising developments in research in suicide prevention, particularly where this can help to inform national activities. This task is not aimed at providing a critique of new researches, but rather at drawing attention to investigations that may have particular relevance to the Australian context. In doing so, we are committed to a user-friendly language, in order to render research outcomes and their interpretation accessible also to a non-expert audience.

In summary, these reviews serve 3 primary purposes:

1. to inform future State and Commonwealth suicide prevention policies;
2. to assist in the improvement of existing initiatives, and the development of new and innovative Australian projects for the prevention of suicidal and self-harming behaviors within the context of the Living is for Everyone (LIFE) Framework (2008);
3. to provide directions for Australian research priorities in suicidology.

The review is presented in 3 sections. The first contains a selection of the best articles published in the last 6 months internationally. For each article identified by us (see the method of chosing articles described below), the original abstract is accompanied by a brief comment explaining why we thought the study was providing an important contribution to research and why we considered its possible applicability to Australia. The second section presents the abstracts of the most relevant literature — following our criteria — collected between May 2011 and October 2011; while the final section presents a list of citations of all literature published over this time-period.

## Methodology

The literature search was conducted in 4 phases.

### Phase 1

Phase 1 consisted of weekly searches of the academic literature performed from May 2011 to October 2011. To ensure thorough coverage of the available published research, the literature was sourced using several scientific electronic databases including: Pubmed, Proquest, Scopus, Safetylit and Web of Science, using the following key words: *suicide* or *suicidal* or *self-harm* or *self-injury* or *parasuicide*.

Results from the weekly searches were downloaded and combined into 1 database (deleting duplicates).

Specific inclusion criteria for Phase 1 included:

- Timeliness: the article was published (either electronically or in hard-copy) between May 2011 and October 2011.
- Relevance: the article explicitly referred to fatal and/or non-fatal suicidal behaviour and related issues and/or interventions directly targeted at preventing/treating these behaviours.
- The article was written in English.

Articles regarding euthanasia, assisted suicide, suicide terrorist attacks, and/or book reviews, abstracts and conference presentations were excluded.

Also, articles that have been previously published in electronic versions (ahead of print) and included in the previous volumes (Volumes 1 to 5 of *Suicide Reseach: Selected Readings*) were excluded to avoid duplication.

## Phase 2

Following an initial reading of the abstracts retrieved in Phase 1, the list of articles was refined down to the most relevant literature. In Phase 2 articles were only included if they were published in an international, peer-reviewed journal.

In Phase 2, articles were excluded when they were:

- not particularly instructive or original;
- of a descriptive nature (e.g. a case-reports);
- of historical/philosophical content;
- a description of surgical reconstruction/treatment of self-inflicted injuries;
- concerning biological and/or genetic interpretations of suicidal behaviour, the results of which could not be easily adoptable in the context of the LIFE Framework.

In order to minimise the potential for biased evaluations, 2 researchers working independently read through the full-text of all articles selected to create a list of most relevant papers. This process was then duplicated by a third researcher for any articles on which consensus could not be reached.

The strength and quality of the research evidence was evaluated based on the *Critical Appraisal Skills Programme (CASP) Appraisal Tools,* published by the Public Health Resource Unit, England (2006). These tools, publically available online, consist of checklists for critically appraising systematic reviews, randomized controlled trials (RCT), qualitative research, economic evaluation studies, cohort studies, diagnostic test studies and case control studies.

## Phase 3

One of the aims of this review was to identify research which is both evidence-based and of potential relevance to the Australian context. Thus, the final stage of applied methodolgy focused on research conducted in countries with populations or health systems sufficiently comparable to Australia. Only articles in which the full-text was available were considered. It is important to note that failure of an article to be selected for inclusion in Phase 3 does not entail any negative judgment on its 'objective' quality.

Specific inclusion criteria for Phase 3 included:

- applicability to Australia;
- the paper met all criteria for scientificity (i.e. the methodology was considered sound);
- the paper represented a particularly compelling addition to the literature, which would be likely to stimulate suicide prevention initiatives and research;
- inevitably, an important aspect was the importance of the journal in which the paper was published (because of the high standards that have to be met in order to obtain publication in that specific journal). For this review, priority was given to papers published in high impact factor journals;
- particular attention has been paid to widen the literature horizon to include sociological and anthropological research that may have particular relevance to the Australian context.

After a thorough reading of these articles ('Key articles' for the considered timeframe), a written comment was produced for each article detailing:

- methodological strengths and weaknesses (e.g. sample size, validity of measurement instruments, appropriateness of analysis performed);
- practical implications of the research results to the Australian context, and
- suggestions for integrating research findings within the domains of the LIFE framework suicide prevention activities.

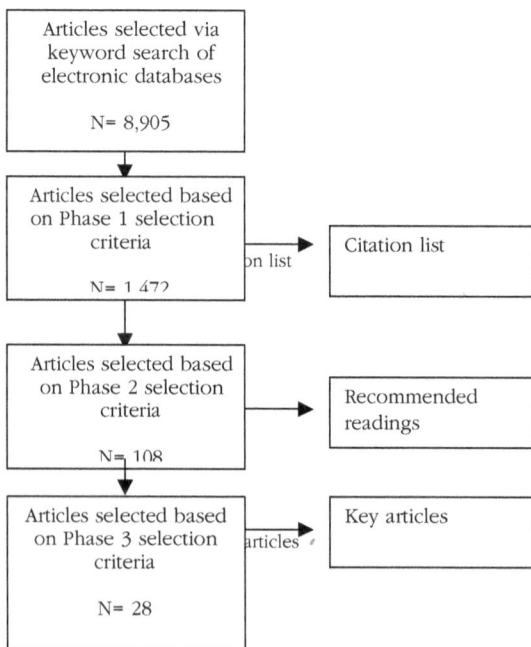

**Figure 1** Flowchart of process.

## Phase 4

In the final phase all selected articles were divided into the following categories:

- *Fatal suicidal behaviour* (Epidemiology, Risk and protective factors, Prevention, Postvention and bereavement).
- *Non-fatal suicidal behaviour* (Epidemiology, Risk and protective factors, Care and support).
- *Case reports* include reports of fatal and non-fatal suicidal behaviours.
- *Miscellaneous* include all articles which could not be classified into any other category.

Allocation to these categories was not always straightforwarded and where papers spanned more than 1 area, consensus of the research team determined which domain the article would be placed in. Within each section of the report (i.e. Key Articles, Recommended Readings, Citation List) articles are presented in an alphabetical order by author.

## Endnotes

1. Australian Bureau of Statistics (2011). *Causes of Death, Australia, 2009, Suicides.* Cat. No. 3303.0. ABS: Canberra.
2. Page A, Tobias M, Glover J, Wright C, Hetzel D, Fisher E (2006). *Australian and New Zealand Atlas of avoidable mortality.* Public Health Information Development Unit, University of Adelaide: Adelaide.
3. Begg S, Vos T, Barker B, Stevenson C, Stanley L, Lopez A (2007). *The burden of disease and injury in Australia 2003.* Australian Institute for Health and Welfare, Canberra.
4. Australian Bureau of Statistics (2009). *Causes of Death, Australia, 2007, Technical Note 1,* Cat. No. 3303.0. ABS: Canberra.
5. Australian Bureau of Statistics (2009c). *Causes of Death, Australia, 2007, Explanatory Notes.* Cat. No. 3303.0. ABS: Canberra.

# Key Articles

## Estimating risk for suicide attempt: Are we asking the right questions? Passive suicidal ideation as a marker for suicidal behavior

Baca-Garcia E, Perez-Rodriguez MM, Oquendo MA, Keyes KM, Hasin DS, Grant BF, Blanco C (USA)

*Journal of Affective Disorders* 134, 327–332, 2011

*Background:* Desire for death is not generally considered a harbinger of more severe suicidal behavior and is not routinely included in suicide research and assessment interviews. We aimed to compare desire for death and suicidal ideation as clinical markers for suicide attempts.

*Methods:* Using data from 2 nationally representative surveys ($n = 42,862$ and $n = 43,093$ respectively), we examined whether desire for death predicts suicide attempts. We compared the odds ratio (OR) and 'Number Needed to be Exposed for 1 additional person to be Harmed' [NNEH] for lifetime suicide attempts among those with desire for death but no suicidal ideation; those with suicidal ideation but no desire for death, and those with both desire for death and suicidal ideation, compared to those with neither desire for death nor suicidal ideation.

*Results:* The risk for lifetime suicide attempt was similar among those with life-time desire for death with no suicidal ideation and those with lifetime suicidal ideation with no desire for death. Respondents with both lifetime desire for death and suicidal ideation had the highest risk for lifetime suicide attempts.

*Limitations:* Cross-sectional design and self-reported suicidal ideation/ attempts are viewed as limitations of this study.

*Conclusions:* Querying individuals on desire for death has the same value as assessing suicidal ideation to examine risk for suicide attempt. A combination of desire for death and suicidal ideation is the best predictor for suicide attempts. This is of high clinical relevance since we suggest that desire for death should be included as a potential clinical marker of suicidality in clinical assessments.

### Comment

*Main findings:* The traditional continuum model of suicidal behaviour would suggest that the suicidal process begins with ideation, progresses to an attempt, and ends in the possibility of self-inflicted death. In accordance with this, research has suggested that a certain proportion of a population will have thoughts of suicide, a smaller proportion will make plans, and an even smaller proportion will engage in suicidal behaviours[1]. However, this continuum model does not account for cases of impulsive suicide[2]. The paper by Baca-Gracia and colleagues examines whether the emergence of a 'desire for death' may be an alternate onset point that influences whether an individual will progress to suicide attempt.

The sample for the study was drawn from 2 large general population surveys in the United States, conducted during 1991–1992 and 2001–2002. Both surveys included data from over 40,000 people. Lifetime desire for death and suicide ideation decreased slightly between the survey conducted in 1991–1992 and that conducted in 2001–2002 (11.3% to 10.2% and 9.7% to 8.4% respectively). The percentage of suicide attempts did not change over time (2.4%). The highest rates of lifetime suicide attempt were found among respondents with both lifetime desire for death and suicide ideation (25.9%). There were no significant differences in suicidal behaviours among those with lifetime desire for death but no suicide ideation (5.41%) and lifetime suicide ideation but no desire for death (2.75%), although prevalence of suicidal behaviour was markedly greater in the former. These results indicate that desire for death could be an alternative 'starting point' for a suicide attempt and lead Baca-Gracia and colleagues to question the validity of the traditional continuum model of suicide as a means for predicting suicide attempt. The main limitations of this study are that the survey materials are relatively old (particularly the first survey, which was conducted between 1991 and 1993) and are subject to participant recall bias. Further, it was not possible to actually assess the movement from ideation to attempt, which limits the extent to which discussion of the 'trajectory' is valid.

*Implications:* Considerations of 'passive' communications of suicidality are not new. In 2007, Silverman and colleagues[3] proposed that clinical definitions of suicide should be expanded to include a range of possible ideation and communications (including passive wishes and desire for harm or death) with the view that this expanded approach would improve surveillance and risk assessment. The research by Baca-Gracia et al., supports this perspectives by finding that a number of persons who attempted suicide, reported a desire for death but did not endorse suicide ideation. We suggest that clinical risk assessment should be widened to include 'passive' desire for death.

## Endnotes

1. Kessler RC, Borges G, Walters EE (1999). Prevalence of and risk factors for lifetime suicide attempts in the national comorbidity survey. *Archives of General Psychiatry* 56, 617–626.
2. Simon OR, Swann AC, Powell KE, Potter LB, Kresnow MJ, O'Carroll PW (2001). Characteristics of impulsive suicide attempts and attempters. *Suicide & Life-Threatening Behavior* 32, s49–s59.
3. Silverman MM, Berman AL, Sanddal ND, O'carroll PW, Joiner TE. (2007). Rebuilding the tower of babel: A revised nomenclature for the study of suicide and suicidal behaviours part 2: Suicide-related ideations, communications, and behaviours. *Suicide & Life-Threatening Behavior* 37, 264–277.

# Impact of screening for risk of suicide: Randomised controlled trial

Crawford MJ, Thana L, Methuen C, Ghosh P, Stanley SV, Ross J, Gordon F, Blair G, Bajaj P (UK)

*British Journal of Psychiatry* 198, 379–384, 2011

*Background:* Concerns have been expressed about the impact that screening for risk of suicide may have on a person's mental health.

*Aims:* To examine whether screening for suicidal ideation among people who attend primary care services and have signs of depression increases the short-term incidence of feeling that life is not worth living.

*Method:* In a multicentre, single-blind, randomised controlled trial, 443 patients in 4 general practices were randomised to screening for suicidal ideation or control questions on health and lifestyle (trial registration: ISRCTN84692657). The primary outcome was thinking that life is not worth living measured 10–14 days after randomisation. Secondary outcome measures comprised other aspects of suicidal ideation and behaviour.

*Results:* A total of 443 participants were randomised to early ($n = 230$) or delayed screening ($n = 213$). Their mean age was 48.5 years ($SD = 18.4$, range 16–92) and 137 (30.9%) were male. The adjusted odds of experiencing thoughts that life was not worth living at follow-up among those randomised to early compared with delayed screening was 0.88 (95% CI 0.66–1.18). Differences in secondary outcomes between the 2 groups were not seen. Among those randomised to early screening, 37 people (22.3%) reported thinking about taking their life at baseline and 24 (14.6%) that they had this thought 2 weeks later.

*Conclusions:* Screening for suicidal ideation in primary care among people who have signs of depression does not appear to induce feelings that life is not worth living.

## Comment

*Main findings:* There are growing calls for primary health care services to take an active role in suicide prevention[1]. However, the involvement of these facilities has been hindered by the belief that asking patients about their experiences of suicide leads to increased vulnerability.

This study reports results of a randomised controlled trial that investigated the effects of screening on patients attending 4 inner-city practices in London. All patients in the study responded 'yes' to a two-item screening instrument for depression and were randomised to a study or control group. Patients in the study group (i.e., the early screening group) were asked questions about suicide ideation and behaviour using items previously recommended as being helpful in assessing suicide risk. These were: 'In the last 2 weeks, have you felt that life was not worth living?' 'Have you ever wished that you were dead — for instance, that you would go to sleep and not wake up?' 'Have you ever seriously considered taking your own life?' and 'Have you ever attempted to take your own life?' The control group were asked questions about diet and lifestyle. Two weeks later, all participants in the control and study group were followed up and asked the same questions on suicide ideation and behaviour.

Results of the follow up indicated that approximately 26% of the total sample ($n$ = 351) experienced suicide ideation. However, there were no significant differences between the study (who had completed early screening at baseline) and control group. This result indicates that screening for suicidal behaviours was not associated with later adverse outcomes. Baseline reports of mental health problems and personality disorders were positively associated with feelings that 'life was not worth living'.

One limitation of this study is that people may conceal suicidality at follow-up due to shame and stigma, leading in under-reporting; another is that the study did not assess the potential for suicidality at a later time period (i.e., sometime after the follow up was conducted). Further, it is unknown whether these results could be generalised to other areas, as the study was conducted in a relatively confined geographical, social-economic and cultural area.

*Implications:* These results hold a number of potential implications for suicide prevention in the primary health care profession. For example, the study demonstrates that screening for suicidality was not associated with a subsequent increase in intentions or thoughts about self-inflicted harm or death. In this way, the research provides an answer to one of the most common problems raised by research ethics committees, which is that asking about suicide may increase vulnerability. Aside from this, the research revealed a significant number of persons experiencing suicide ideation who may not have been otherwise identified.

This study demonstrates the need to break down traditionally held beliefs about the harm associated with talking about suicide in the primary care setting. This could be tackled by familiarising general practitioners in Australia about empirically-validated screening tools and research on suicide. Attention is also warranted at the policy level in order to develop guidelines that inform general practitioners about how to effectively manage suicidality.

## Endnotes

1. Department of Health and Ageing (2007). *Living Is For Everyone (LIFE) Framework: A Framework for the Prevention of Suicide in Australia.* Canberra: Authors.

# Suicide in Indigenous people in Queensland, Australia: Trends and methods, 1994–2007

De Leo D, Sveticic J, Milner A (Australia)

*Australian and New Zealand Journal of Psychiatry* 45, 532–538, 2011

*Objective:* Suicide among Indigenous Australians is a well-recognised public health issue. Due to scarcity of epidemiological investigations in this area the exact size of this problem and its main characteristics remain uncertain. In this paper we present trends and methods of Indigenous suicides based on the Queensland Suicide Register for the period 1994–2007.

*Methods:* Trends of age-standardised suicide rates were calculated for Indigenous and non-Indigenous populations. Suicide methods were compared between the 2 groups, with particular focus on hanging. Discriminant analysis was used to ascertain the size of under-estimation of suicide rates due to a considerable number of cases with unknown ethnicity in the Queensland Suicide Register.

*Results:* Between 1994 and 2007, Indigenous populations had suicide rates 2.2 times higher than non-Indigenous Australians. Age-specific suicide rates for Indigenous men were highest in the 25–34 age group, while in women they were highest among 15–24 year olds. In children younger than 15 years, Indigenous suicide rate was almost 10 times higher than of non-Indigenous counterparts. More than 90% of Indigenous suicides occurred by hanging. It was estimated that lack of information about ethnicity for 7% of suicide cases might have caused an under-estimation of Indigenous suicide mortality for 15.4% in men and 9.1% in women in the period 1994–2007.

*Conclusions:* Suicide mortality of Indigenous Australians has reached alarming levels, particularly among youths. The unique profile of Indigenous suicides indicates the need for specifically tailored preventative programmes.

## Comment

*Main findings:* This article provides a time-series investigation of the burden of suicide among Australia's first peoples. Unlike past studies — which have been confined in both sample area and time covered — this paper is able to provide suicide data from across an entire state. It also attempts to tackle the issue of cases with 'unknown' ethnicity through canonical discriminant function analysis, which provides a way of estimating the probability of unknown cases being either Indigenous (defined as being Aboriginal or Torres Strait Islander) or non-Indigenous. Further, the article standardises suicide rates to the world population 2000 to 2025[1] to allow accurate comparison with the non-Indigenous population of Queensland.

The fluctuation in Indigenous suicide rates over the time period 1994 to 2007 may reflect the small numbers of suicides in some years. This problem aside, time trend analysis indicates that suicide rates among the Indigenous population were approximately 2.2 times higher than among the non-Indigenous population (i.e. Caucasian, Asian, European or other). Young Indigenous males had a particularly high burden of suicide, reaching a rate of 100 per 100,000 at some time points. Under-reporting of ethnicity was primarily found to impact analyses prior to 2001; after this year, only 1% of cases had no known ethnicity.

The authors offer several possible explanations for the markedly higher rates among Indigenous persons. First, the higher burden of youth suicide may be connected to the younger age-distribution of the Indigenous population, and social-economic factors such as poverty, lack of employment and adverse living conditions. Alcohol and drug use are also thought to influence the total burden of Indigenous suicides, as is the possible effect of 'contagion' and the use of hanging as a highly lethal suicide method.

*Implications:* There is increasing momentum for the development of culturally-specific strategies for Indigenous suicide prevention in Australia (i.e., the recent publication of the Victorian Aboriginal Suicide Prevention and Response). These prevention initiatives follow the publication of other strategies for first peoples in countries such as New Zealand[2]. These strategies emphasise the importance of community-based activities, built from the ground up, rather than from a top-down approach. The high rates of Indigenous suicide reported in this paper emphasises the need for similar types of targeted suicide prevention initiatives at a national, state, and community-based level.

## Endnotes

1. Ahmad O, Boschi-Pinto C, Lopez AD, Murray CJL, Lozano R, Inoue M (2001). *Age standardization of rates: A new WHO standard.* World Health Organization, Geneva.
2. Suicide Prevention Information New Zealand (2011). *Suicide Prevention, Intervention and Postvention Resources for Maori.* Retrieved: 16 October 2011 from http://www.spinz.org.nz.

## Where do youth learn about suicides on the Internet, and what influence does this have on suicidal ideation?

Dunlop SM, More E, Romer D (USA)

*Journal of Child Psychology and Psychiatry* 52, 1073–1080, 2011

*Background:* Young people are susceptible to suicidal behavior as a result of learning about the suicidal behavior of others. This study was designed to determine whether Internet sites, such as online news and social networking websites, expose young people to suicide stories that might increase suicide ideation.

*Method:* We reinterviewed 719 young people ages 14 to 24 who had participated in a prior nationally representative survey. Respondents reported knowledge of persons they knew who had committed or attempted suicide as well as personal experiences of hopelessness and suicidal ideation on both occasions. On the second occasion 1 year later, they also reported use of various Internet platforms and how often they had been exposed to suicide stories on those sites, as well as from personal sources. Changes in ideation as a function of exposure to different sources of suicide stories were analyzed holding constant prior hopelessness and ideation.

*Results:* While traditional sources of information about suicide were most often cited (79% were from friends and family or newspapers), online sources were also quite common (59%). Social networking sites were frequently cited as sources, but these reports were not linked to increases in ideation. However, online discussion forums were both cited as sources and associated with increases in ideation.

*Conclusions:* The Internet and especially social networking sites are important sources of suicide stories. However, discussion forums appear to be particularly associated with increases in suicidal ideation. Greater efforts should be undertaken to promote Internet sites directed to young people that enhance effective coping with hopelessness and suicidal ideation.

## Comment

*Main findings:* The sample used in this study was drawn from a telephone survey conducted with males and females aged between 14 and 21 years during the years 2008 and 2009. The survey covered topics such as beliefs and stigma about mental illness, media use, and engagement in risky and/or protective health behaviours. Dunlop and colleagues examined the association between knowledge about someone who died by suicide and the source this news was ascertained from.

Results suggest that while friends and family were the most common sources of information, a substantial proportion of young people also obtained news about suicide among those they personally knew from social networking sites. This supports the idea that young people use social networking websites to receive information previously only discussed in the bounds of friends and family. At the same time, it appeared that young people used social networking websites to provide and receive social support following the news of a death by suicide.

Those who participated in online forums more often experienced suicide ideation in the twelve-months leading to the survey. The authors of this paper suggest that these sites may 'facilitate' suicidal behaviours in young people by providing a platform through which harmful behaviours can be endorsed. However, it is likely that persons who used online forums experienced significant mental health issues and actively sought out like-minded persons. The paper reports no increase in suicide ideation in relation to newspapers.

This study is among the first to recognise the numerous ways in which young persons communicate information about suicidality. While the internet may be protective for some people, it could be associated with significant rise in suicide risk for other people. The limitations of this study were that it was entirely self-report and therefore unable to provide information on possible deaths or attempts in the sample group. Another issue was that the paper did not control for how many people experienced psychiatric problems or adverse life events, which would also influence suicidality in the group. An interesting topic of future research would be the conditions under which a young person may change their online behaviours (i.e., from seeking positive support from peers to visiting 'pro suicide' sites) over time or when experiencing adverse life events.

*Implications:* In Australia, it has been illegal to use the internet to promote the idea or provide practical details about suicide since 2006 (the *Suicide Related Materials Offences Act,* was passed by federal parliament in 2006). Presumably, this response reflects fears that greater use of the internet will lead to an increase in the behaviour. There is some research that supports this negative perspective. A review by Biddle et al.,[1] highlighted the role of the internet in providing ready and easy access to 'pro suicide' information. Another study by McCarthy[2] found a significant relationship between Google search engine activities for suicide-related terms and an increase in self-harm and death by suicide in the youth population. Expanding on this topic of research, the results of this study by Dunlop and colleagues show that the internet can be either used to seek emotional support or to endorse harmful behaviours. These results suggest the need for investment into easily accessible websites to promote suicide prevention and intervention efforts for young people. These resources need to appear in the primary list of websites resulting from searches in popular engines such as Google and Yahoo.

## Endnotes

1. Biddle L, Donovan J, Hawton K, Kapur N, Gunnell D (2008). Suicide and the internet. *British Medical Journal* 336, 800.
2. McCarthy MJ (2010). Internet monitoring of suicide risk in the population. *Journal of Affective Disorders* 122, 277–279.

## Suicide death and hospital-treated suicidal behaviour in asylum seekers in the Netherlands: A national registry-based study

Goosen S, Kunst AE, Stronks K, van Oostrum IE, Uitenbroek DG, Kerkhof AJ
(The Netherlands)

*BMC Public Health* 11, 484, 2011

*Background:* Several suicide and suicidal behaviour risk factors are highly prevalent in asylum seekers, but there is little insight into the suicide death rate and the suicidal behaviour incidence in this population. The main objective of this study is to assess the burden of suicide death and hospital-treated non-fatal suicidal behaviour in asylum seekers in the Netherlands and to identify factors that could guide prevention.

*Methods:* We obtained data on cases of suicide death and suicidal behaviour from all asylum seeker reception centres in the Netherlands (period 2002–2007, age 15+). The suicide death rate in this population and in subgroups by sex, age and region of origin were compared with the rate in the Dutch population; the rates of hospital-treated suicidal behaviour were compared with that in the population of The Hague using indirect age group standardization.

*Results:* The study included 35 suicide deaths and 290 cases of hospital-treated suicidal behaviour. The suicide death rate and the incidence of hospital-treated suicidal behaviour differed between subgroups by sex and region of origin. For male asylum seekers, the suicide death rate was higher than that of the Dutch population ($N$ = 32; RR = 2.0, 95%CI 1.37–2.83). For females, the suicide death rate did not differ from the Dutch population ($N$ = 3; RR = 0.73; 95%CI 0.15–2.07). The incidence of hospital-treated suicidal behaviour was high in comparison with the population of The Hague for males and females from Europe and the Middle East/South West Asia, and low for males and females from Africa. Health professionals knew about mental health problems prior to the suicidal behaviour for 80% of the hospital-treated suicidal behaviour cases in asylum seekers.

*Conclusions:* In this study the suicide death rate was higher in male asylum seekers than in males in the reference population. The incidence of hospital-treated suicidal behaviour was higher in several subgroups of asylum seekers than in the reference population. We conclude that measures to prevent suicide and suicidal behaviour among asylum seekers in the Netherlands are indicated.

## Comment

*Main findings:* Many persons who seek asylum in developed countries such as Australia have experienced past trauma or adversities. Additional to this, the process of settling in a new country is noted to be fraught with difficulties for some asylum seekers[1]. While there is increasing attention to mental health issues in this population[2], there has been limited research into experiences of suicidality.

This article seeks to provide evidence about the burden of suicide among asylum seekers in the Netherlands. The sample used in the study represented asylum seekers who were housed in residential reception centres. These persons are free to leave the centres, are permitted to work for a limited number of weeks per year, and are entitled full access to health care. Under the current system in the Netherlands, asylum seekers with mental health issues could be offered up to 5 consultations with a public health doctor specialised in refugee health, and can be referred to other mental health services or offered preventative interventions.

Across the sample of 125,026 asylums seekers, there were 35 cases of suicide. This corresponds to a suicide rate of 17.5 per 100,000. Male asylum seeker suicide rates were over 7 times higher than female suicide rates and were also markedly above the male suicide rates in the general population of the Netherlands. Males from Africa and Central, Eastern and Southern Europe had the highest risk of suicide. The authors suggest a number of reasons for the higher burden of suicide in male asylum seekers, including the perception that they will be in danger if forced to return to their country of origin. These fears are often compounded with social and economic problems experienced in the host country.

Cases of hospital-treated suicidal behaviours among asylum seekers were more often females who came from Central, Eastern and Southern Europe and Middle East/South West Asia. Most of those treated for hospital-based injuries (80%) had mental health problems. The asylum procedure, relationship issues, loss of a family member, transfer between centres, substance abuse, and living conditions were noted as the most pertinent stressors. This study is based on data from across an entire national population, which strengthens the generalisability of findings. However, a notable limitation of the study was its inability to include data on suicide behaviours treated in the primary care or in other settings. Data were also not available from those who did not seek any treatment after suicidal behaviours.

*Implications:* This study is particularly relevant in the Australian context given the recent consternation and legal arguments over the wellbeing of asylum seekers in the country. There have been several recent news articles on self-harm and mental health of refugees in detentions centres (*Self-harm 'on the rise' in detention camps.* Herald Sun, 29 September 2011), which has also sparked general interest to the issue. The results of this paper highlight the need for physicians to recognise possible risks associated with the asylum seeking process. The stresses associated with asylum seeking also need to be addressed at the wider policy and service provision level.

## Endnotes

1. Porter M, Haslam N (2005). Predisplacement and postdisplacement factors associated with mental health of refugees with mental health or refugees and internally displaced persons: A meta analysis. *The Journal of the American Medical Association* 294, 602–612.

2. Fazel M, Wheeler J, Danesh J (2005). Prevalence of serious mental disorder in 7000 refugees resettled in western countries: A systematic review. *Lancet* 365, 1309–1314.

# Problem-solving therapy for people who present to hospital with self-harm: Zelen randomised controlled trial

Hatcher S, Sharon C, Parag V, Collins N (New Zealand)
*British Journal of Psychiatry* 199, 310–316, 2011

*Background:* Presentations to hospital with self-harm are common, associated with suicide and have an increased mortality, yet there is no accepted effective intervention.

*Aims:* To investigate whether problem-solving therapy would improve outcomes in adults presenting to hospital with self-harm, compared with usual care.

*Method:* A Zelen randomised controlled trial was conducted in 4 district health boards in New Zealand. A second hospital presentation with self-harm at 1 year for all episodes, plus separate comparisons of first-time and repeat presentations at the index episode, were the a priori primary outcomes. The trial registration number was ACTRN12605000337673.

*Results:* In an intention-to-treat analysis of all randomised patients ($n = 1094$) there was no significant difference at 12 months in the proportion of people who had presented again with self-harm when comparing all episodes (intervention 13.4%, usual care 14.1%; relative risk reduction RR = 0.05, 95% CI -0.28 to 0.30, $p = 0.79$) or where the index episode was the first episode (intervention 13.4%, usual care 9.4%, RR = -0.42, 95% CI -1.17 to 0.08, $p = 0.37$). Where the index episode was repeated self-harm, those who received therapy were less likely to present again with self-harm (intervention 13.5%, usual care 22.1%, RR = 0.39, 95% CI 0.07 to 0.60, number needed to treat 12, $p = 0.03$).

*Conclusions:* Problem-solving therapy is not recommended for everyone who presents to hospital with self-harm. Among adults with a history of self-harm it may be an effective intervention.

## Comment

*Main findings:* Self-harm represents a significant burden on hospitals emergency departments (EDs) – particularly because people who engage in these behaviours are likely to make multiple presentations to health care facilities[1]. One continuing problem in suicide research is the lack of interventions found to effectively reduce these acts.

This study from New Zealand sought to implement problem-solving therapy for persons who have self-harmed and presented to a hospital. The authors provide open access to the manuals, client workbooks and training videos used in the study at the website: www.tractusgroup.ac.nz.

This study used a 'Zelen' design that randomised patients before they were approached to be involved in the project. This approach seeks to ascertain a larger and more representative sample of potential participants, provide information about the acceptability of the intervention (e.g., how many people actually agreed to be involved in the intervention), and takes participant treatment preferences into account.

Those in the intervention group received the problem solving therapy (PST) and follow up at 3 months and 12 months, while the control group (treatment as usual — TAU) received follow-up and routine care. The problem solving intervention consisted of up to 9 hour-long sessions conducted up to 3 months after the index episode. Approximately half of those persons approached consented to follow-up. Persons who refused were more likely to have presented only once for self-harm and less likely to be of New Zealand or European ethnicity.

While PST had little effect on overall repetition of self-harm, there were some significant differences within sub-groups. For example, results indicate that problem solving therapy may be most helpful to those persons who made repeat presentations for self-harm (14.7% of those in PST vs. 27.7% of those in TAU made a repeat presentation after 1 year). These people were also more likely to re-present earlier than those who had received TAU. The study also indicates that those consenting to PST had improvements in scores of hopelessness, suicidal thinking, problem-solving, anxiety and depression. Patients who had completed 4 or more sessions of PST had better outcomes than those who had fewer sessions. One of the main problems with this intervention is that it would be difficult to find people skilled enough to conduct PST. The intervention could also be expensive and time consuming to conduct.

*Implications:* The key finding of this study is that PST was reasonably effective for some participants (e.g., those who made frequent attendances to the Emergency Department [ED]) but not for others. This result provides further support for the argument that there may be multiple motivations and factors underpinning suicidal presentations to the ED[2]. Considering this, it is not surprising that there may be differences in treatment outcomes between suicidal persons. As indicated above, PST was not necessarily appropriate for all cases of self-harm. Following on from this, there is a need for more investigation into which treatment may be effective for other cases of self-harm. A potential area for research could be an investigation into multi-modal treatment, or treatment that uses a combination of approaches in the effort to reduce the suffering of those presenting with self-harm to the Hospital ED.

### Endnotes

1. Colman I, Dryden DM, Thompson AH, Chahal AM, Borden K, Rowe BH, Voaklander DC (2004). Utilization of the emergency department after self-inflicted injury. *Academic Emergency Medicine* 11, 136–142.
2. McAuliffe C, Arensman E, Keeley HS, Corcoran P, Fitzgerald AP (2010). Motives and suicide intent underlying hospital treated deliberate self-harm and their association with repetition. *Suicide and Life-Threatening Behavior* 37, 397–408.

# The social environment and suicide attempts in lesbian, gay, and bisexual youth

Hatzenbuehler ML (USA)

*Pediatrics* 127, 896–903, 2011

*Objective:* To determine whether the social environment surrounding lesbian, gay, and bisexual youth may contribute to their higher rates of suicide attempts, controlling for individual-level risk factors.

*Methods:* A total of 31,852 11th grade students (1,413 [4.4%] lesbian, gay, and bisexual individuals) in Oregon completed the Oregon Healthy Teens survey in 2006–2008. We created a composite index of the social environment in 34 counties, including (1) the proportion of same-sex couples, (2) the proportion of registered Democrats, (3) the presence of gay-straight alliances in schools, and (4) school policies (nondiscrimination and antibullying) that specifically protected lesbian, gay, and bisexual students.

*Results:* Lesbian, gay, and bisexual youth were significantly more likely to attempt suicide in the previous 12 months, compared with heterosexuals (21.5% vs 4.2%). Among lesbian, gay, and bisexual youth, the risk of attempting suicide was 20% greater in unsupportive environments compared to supportive environments. A more supportive social environment was significantly associated with fewer suicide attempts, controlling for sociodemographic variables and multiple risk factors for suicide attempts, including depressive symptoms, binge drinking, peer victimization, and physical abuse by an adult (odds ratio: 0.97 [95% confidence interval: 0.96–0.99]).

*Conclusions:* This study documents an association between an objective measure of the social environment and suicide attempts among lesbian, gay, and bisexual youth. The social environment appears to confer risk for suicide attempts over and above individual-level risk factors. These results have important implications for the development of policies and interventions to reduce sexual orientation-related disparities in suicide attempts.

## Comment

*Main findings:* Social environmental factors such as family, school connectedness and school safety have been recognised as important influences on lesbian, gay and bisexual (LGB) mental health[1,2]. A problem with past research is that it has been dependent on self-reported accounts of the social climate, which may be biased by personal conceptualisations and life circumstances.

This study sought to investigate the importance of the social environment on youth suicide across 34 counties of the United States using an objective index measurement. This index measure included: the proportion of same-sex couples in the county, proportion of democrats in the county, proportion of schools with gay-straight alliances, proportion of schools with anti-bullying policies to protect LGB students, and proportion of schools with antidiscrimination policies that included sexual orientation.

The sample of LGB youth came from the Oregon Healthy Teens survey conducted in 297 schools over the period 2006 to 2008. Confirming past research, results indicate a higher proportion of suicide attempts in the LGB population of students compared to heterosexual teens. The social environmental index was significantly associated with suicide attempts in both bi-variate analyses and in a model controlling for demographic factors. It appeared that teens living in positive social environments were less likely to attempt suicide than those living in negative environments, even after controlling for individual factors such as depressive symptoms, binge drinking, peer victimisation and physical abuse by an adult. The risk of attempting suicide was 20% higher among LGB youth who were living in a negative environment compared to those LGB youth living in a positive environment. Further, living in a negative environment was associated with a 9% increase in risk among heterosexual youth. These results suggest that positive social environments can have an attenuating influence on the risk of suicide in LGB (and non LGB) youth. The study was not able to control for possibly relevant risk factors such as age and level of stress at the time of disclosure about sexuality.

*Implications:* Past survey research in Australia found that LGB youth attempted suicide significantly more than those who are heterosexual[3]. This research supports the statements contained in Australia's senate report 'The Hidden Toll', which also draw attention to the need for appropriate service provision for the LGB community. The results of this study indicate specific environmental factors — such as bullying and supportive policies — that may place LGB at risk of suicide. This article finds that there is a lower risk of suicide in locations that have implemented proactive anti-discrimination policies. We suggest that similar anti-bullying and anti-discrimination policy approaches should be developed in Australia.

## Endnotes

1. Eisenberg ME, Resnick MD (2006). Suicidality among gay, lesbian and bisexual youth: The role of protective factors. *Journal of Adolescent Health* 39, 662–668.
2. Saewyc EM, Homma Y, Skay CL, Bearinger LH, Resnick MD, Reis E (2009). Protective factors in the lives of bisexual adolescents in North America. *American Journal of Public Health* 99, 110–117.
3. Mathy RM (2002). Suicidality and sexual orientation in five continents: Asia, Australia, Europe, North America, and South America. *International Journal of Sexuality and Gender Studies* 7, 215–225.

# Risk of suicide in medical and related occupational groups: A national study based on Danish case population-based registers

Hawton K, Agerbo E, Simkin S, Platt B, Mellanby RJ (UK)
*Journal of Affective Disorders* 134, 320–326, 2011

Suicide risk may be elevated in 'medical' occupational groups, although results of studies are inconsistent. National data are required to examine this issue. It is also important to investigate the possible contribution of psychiatric disorder and access to specific suicide methods. In a nested case-control design we used data from Danish national registers for 1981–2006 to examine risk of suicide in nurses, physicians, dentists, pharmacists and veterinary surgeons compared to teachers and the general population, and associations with psychiatric service contact and suicide methods. Crude age- and gender-adjusted rate ratios for suicide compared to teachers were significantly elevated in nurses (RR 1.90, 95% CI 1.63–2.21), physicians (RR 1.87, 95% CI 1.55–2.26), dentists (RR 2.10, 95% CI 1.58–2.79) and pharmacists (RR 1.91, 95% CI 1.26–2.87), but not veterinary surgeons. Risk was also elevated in nurses, physicians and dentists compared with the rest of the general population, the relative risk increasing following adjustments for psychiatric service contact, marital status, gross income and labour market status. Results were similar in both genders. The elevated risk in nurses and dentists decreased during the study period. Elevated risks were not associated with greater psychiatric service contact. Medicinal drugs were commonly used for suicide by nurses, physicians and pharmacists. The study was based in 1 country. Risk of suicide is increased in nurses, physicians, dentists and pharmacists in Denmark. This is not reflected in excess psychiatric service contact. Ready access to medicinal drugs may influence risk in nurses, physicians and pharmacists.

## Comment

*Main findings:* This Danish nested case-control study found that risk of suicide was significantly elevated in several medical occupations including nurses, physicians, dentists and pharmacists (compared to teachers). Contrary to previous studies[1], veterinary surgeons did not have an elevated risk of suicide. Suicide risk among medical professionals remained higher when adjusted for psychiatric service contact, marital status, gross income and labour market status. This finding was similar for both genders. Psychiatric service contact was used as a proxy for psychiatric disorder. The authors of this study suggested that the elevated risk in the medically-related occupational group was not explained by an excess of persons with psychiatric disorders; indeed, risk relative to the comparison groups (teachers and the general population) was somewhat greater in those without contact with psychiatric services. However, this proxy is likely to underestimate the true level of psychiatric disorders, as it only refers to those persons who have sought help for their problems. Findings of this study indicate that suicide risk in medically-related professions is associated with easier access to and knowledge about lethal methods. Thus, medical drugs were used considerably more frequently in suicides by nurses, physicians and pharmacists compared to both teachers and the general population.

*Implications:* Considering that access to and knowledge about lethal drugs is integral to the work of most medical professionals, it is not feasible to prevent suicide by restricting access to means. However, it is possible to improve emotional coping skills and stress management of medically-related occupations and medical students, who have been shown elevated risk of suicidal behaviours[2]. Detection and treatment of mental health disorders might also reduce suicide risk in medical occupations.

## Endnotes

1. Platt B, Hawton K, Simkin S, Mellanby RJ (2010). Systematic review of the prevalence of suicide in veterinary surgeons. *Occupational Medicine* 60, 436–446.
2. Tyssen R, Vaglum P, Grønvold NT, Ekeberg O (2001). Suicidal ideation among medical students and young physicians: A nationwide and prospective study of prevalence and predictors. *Journal of Affective Disorders* 64, 69–79.

# Impact of withdrawal of the analgesic co-proxamol on nonfatal self-poisoning in the UK

Hawton K, Bergen H, Waters K, Murphy E, Cooper J, Kapur N (UK)
*Crisis* 32, 81–87, 2011

*Background:* In early 2005 the UK Committee on Safety of Medicines (CSM) announced gradual withdrawal of the analgesic co-proxamol because of its adverse benefit/safety ratio, especially its use for intentional and accidental fatal poisoning. Prescriptions of co-proxamol were reduced in the 3-year withdrawal phase (2005 to 2007) following the CSM announcement.

*Aims:* To assess the impact of the CSM announcement in January 2005 to withdraw co-proxamol on nonfatal self-poisoning with co-proxamol and other analgesics.

*Methods:* Interrupted time series analysis of general hospital presentations for nonfatal self-poisoning (5 hospitals in 3 centres in England), comparing the 3-year withdrawal period 2005–2007 with 2000–2004.

*Results:* A marked reduction in the number of episodes of nonfatal self-poisoning episodes involving co-proxamol was found following the CSM announcement (an estimated 62% over the period 2005 to 2007 compared to 2000 to 2004). There was no evidence of an increase in nonfatal self-poisoning episodes involving other analgesics (co-codamol, codeine, co-dydramol, dihydrocodeine, and tramadol) in relation to the CSM announcement over the same period, nor a change in the number of all episodes of self-poisoning.

*Limitations:* Data were from 3 centres only.

*Conclusions:* The impact of the policy appears to have reduced nonfatal self-poisoning with co-proxamol without significant substitution with other analgesics. This finding is in keeping with that for suicide.

## Comment

*Main findings:* Co-proxamol was withdrawn in the UK over a 3-year period, following reports that the drug was involved in a large number of suicide deaths and attempts annually. This study examined the impact of this gradual withdrawal on hospital presentations of non-fatal self-poisoning involving co-proxamol and other analgesics. A decrease of 62% in non-fatal overdoses involving co-proxamol was estimated in 2005–2007 (average drop of 6.5 episodes per quarter). There was no evidence of a major increase in non-fatal overdoses involving other analgesics, whether prescription or over the counter drugs. However, in 2007, there was a substantial upturn in the number of episodes of self-poisoning involving other analgesics. Thus, ongoing examination will be essential to ascertain the possibility of method substitution. A limitation of this study was that it only provided data for 5 hospitals in the UK. Considering the contextual differences in health service provision, the results of this study cannot be necessarily generalised to the Australian context. Further, the authors were unable to control for other drugs taken or the level of co-proxamol in the overdose. This meant that co-proxamol was not always the drug taken in the largest amount.

*Implications:* The main ingredient of co-proxamol, dextropropoxyphene, can be rapidly fatal due to the small difference between treatment dose and a dose that could cause harm[1]. Because of this, the benefits of all medicines containing dextropropoxyphene, either on their own or in combination, do not outweigh their risks. In 2009, the Committee of European Medicines Agency recommended that the marketing authorisations for these medicines be withdrawn across the EU. Further, the US Food and Drug Administration requested that companies voluntarily withdraw drugs containing dextropropoxyphene from the US markets[2]. As early as 1995, Buckley et al.,[3] were concerned about dextropropoxyphene over-representation in self-poisoning in Australia. However, both pure dextropropoxyphene capsules and combination tablets and capsules (with paracetamol) continue to be available by prescription in Australia[4]. Withdrawal of dextropropoxyphene should be considered in order to prevent intentional and accidental overdoses of dextropropoxyphene.

## Endnotes

1. European Medicines Agency (2010). *Questions and answers on the withdrawal of the marketing authorisations for medicines containing dextropropoxyphene.* Retrieved: 14 October 2011 from http://www.ema.europa.eu/docs/en_GB/document_library/Referrals_document/ dextro-propoxyphene_31/WC500014076.pdf

2. US Food and Drug Administration (2010). *FDA Drug Safety Communication: FDA recommends against the continued use of propoxyphene.* Retrieved: 14 October 2011 from http://www.fda.gov/Drugs/DrugSafety/ucm234338.htm

3. Buckley NA, Whyte IM, Dawson AH, McManus PR, Ferguson NW (1995). Correlations between prescriptions and drugs taken in self-poisoning. Implications for prescribers and drug regulation. *Medical Journal of Australia* 162, 194–197.

4. Murnion BP (2010). Combination analgesics in adults. *Australian Prescriber* 33, 113–115.

# Lithium in drinking water and suicide mortality

Kapusta ND, Mossaheb N, Etzersdorfer E, Hlavin G, Thau K, Willeit M, Praschak-Rieder N, Sonneck G, Leithner-Dziubas K (Austria)

*British Journal of Psychiatry* 198, 346–350, 2011

*Background:* There is some evidence that natural levels of lithium in drinking water may have a protective effect on suicide mortality.

*Aims:* To evaluate the association between local lithium levels in drinking water and suicide mortality at district level in Austria.

*Method:* A nationwide sample of 6,460 lithium measurements was examined for association with suicide rates per 100,000 population and suicide standardised mortality ratios across all 99 Austrian districts. Multivariate regression models were adjusted for well-known socioeconomic factors known to influence suicide mortality in Austria (population density, per capita income, proportion of Roman Catholics, as well as the availability of mental health service providers). Sensitivity analyses and weighted least squares regression were used to challenge the robustness of the results.

*Results:* The overall suicide rate ($R(2) = 0.15$, $\beta = -0.39$, $t = -4.14$, $p = 0.000073$) as well as the suicide mortality ratio ($R(2) = 0.17$, $\beta = -0.41$, $t = -4.38$, $p = 0.000030$) were inversely associated with lithium levels in drinking water and remained significant after sensitivity analyses and adjustment for socioeconomic factors.

*Conclusions:* In replicating and extending previous results, this study provides strong evidence that geographic regions with higher natural lithium concentrations in drinking water are associated with lower suicide mortality rates.

## Comment

*Main findings:* Lithium enters drinking water as a natural trace element mobilised by rain from rock and soil. In some areas, the natural daily intake of lithium may be up to 10 mg/day. While this level is much lower than the one usually prescribed in therapeutic doses for clinical populations, the authors of this paper suggest potential protective effects associated with low-level consumption of lithium. The study extends earlier research in Japan by Ohgami et al.[1] by assessing the relationship between lithium and suicide mortality while controlling for regional socioeconomic conditions and the availability of mental health providers. Results of a Weighted Least Squared (WLS) regression analysis indicated that lithium remained a significant predictor of suicide mortality after controlling for population density, per capita income, proportion of Catholics in the population, and the density of psychiatrists, psychotherapists, and general practitioners. It appeared that higher levels of lithium in the population were associated with a decline in male and female suicide rates. These results concur with the earlier research conducted in Japan[1] but differ with another study also reported in this volume[2], which found no association between lithium levels in tap water and standardised suicide rates in 47 subdivisions in the east of England.

As in past investigations, this research was unable to control for other possible sources of lithium, such as bottled mineral water and vegetables. Aside from this, it is important to recognise that there may be several other factors responsible for variations in suicide rates not considered in this paper (such as variation in the levels of lithium between studies). In fact, lithium concentrations only explained about 3.9% of the variance in suicide rates in the adjusted and weighted model. These limitations are acknowledged by the study authors.

*Implications:* It is highly controversial whether lithium should be added to water, particularly because this has been found to have adverse effects on the development of fetuses[3]. Further, the pathways linking the effects of lithium to suicide in a population are still unclear, particularly when considered over time. Clearly, more research is needed before this should be considered in suicide prevention policies.

## Endnotes

1. Ohgami H, Terao T, Shiotsuki I, Ishii N, Iwata N (2009). Lithium levels in drinking water and risk of suicide. *British Journal of Psychiatry* 194, 464–465.
2. Kabacs N, Memon A, Obinwa T, Stochl J, Perez J (2011). Lithium in drinking water and suicide rates across the East of England. *British Journal of Psychiatry* 198, 406–407.
3. Gentile S (2010). Neurodevelopmental effects of prenatal exposure to psychotropic medications. *Depression and Anxiety* 27, 675–686.

# Declining autopsy rates and suicide misclassification: A cross-national analysis of 35 countries

Kapusta ND, Tran US, Rockett IR, De Leo D, Naylor CP, Niederkrotenthaler T, Voracek M, Etzersdorfer E, Sonneck G (Austria)

*Archives of General Psychiatry* 68, 1050–1057, 2011

*Context:* Suicides are prone to misclassification during death ascertainment procedures. This problem has generated frequent criticism of the validity of suicide mortality statistics.

*Objective:* To employ an external measure of the validity of cause-of-death statistics (ie, national autopsy rates) and to examine potential misclassification of suicide across countries from Europe to Central and Northern Asia.

*Design:* Cross-national analysis.

*Setting:* Thirty-five countries.

*Participants:* Aggregated mortality data.

*Main Outcomes Measure:* Data from 35 countries during the period from 1979 to 2007 were used to analyze the association of suicide rates with autopsy rates and death rates of undetermined and ill-defined causes, respectively. Analyses were cross-sectional and longitudinal.

*Results:* Cross-sectionally, a 1% difference in autopsy rates among nations was associated with a suicide rate difference of 0.49 per 100,000 population. Longitudinally, a 1% decrease in the autopsy rate aligned with a decrease of 0.42 per 100,000 population in the suicide rate. These cross-sectional and longitudinal associations were robust after adjustment for unemployment, degree of urbanization, and prevalence of undetermined or ill-defined deaths. Associations strengthened when analyses were confined to 19 European Union member countries.

*Conclusion:* Autopsy rates may spatially and temporally affect the validity of suicide mortality statistics. Caution should be exercised in comparing international suicide rates and evaluating interventions that target suicide rate reduction.

## Comment

*Main findings:* This study highlights deficiencies in supposing that suicides are hidden only in undetermined deaths and not in other possible categories, such as deaths due to ill-defined or unknown causes and unintentional poisoning. The authors argue that true extent of misclassification cannot be determined by comparing mutually exclusive causes of death (e.g. undetermined deaths). Instead, it would be more appropriate to use an external validation criterion, such as the autopsy rate, to assess possible under-reporting.

The study finds that the 'traditional' hypothesis (e.g., that suicides are misclassified as undetermined causes of death) does not consistently explain cross-national variation in suicide rates, even when mortality classified under symptoms, signs, ill-defined conditions, and unknown causes are considered. Instead, autopsy rates emerged as the major predictor of suicide rates in both cross-sectional and longitudinal analysis. This suggests that an increase in the autopsy rate of a country reduces the rate of misclassified deaths. Based on this, the authors argue that autopsy rates could impact suicide registration by influencing the overall validity of cause-of-death statistics. Countries with the highest autopsy rates in the study also had the highest suicide rates (Estonia, Latvia, Lithuania, and Hungary); further, countries with the most notable reductions in suicide also had decreases in the national rate of autopsies being conducted. The authors propose this apparent dose-response relationship as an alternate explanation for the reduction in suicide rates in several countries, and suggest the possibility that the effects of some national interventions are 'overstated'. Instead, reductions in official suicides may be a symptom of miscoding, rather than reporting a true decrease in deaths.

*Implications:* The findings of this paper challenge the held assumption that declines in suicides rates represent a genuine reduction in deaths. Instead, these may also be due to changes in the quality of death reporting. There has been considerable criticism of the official statistics in Australia (by one of the authors of this volume)[1]. The paper by Kapusta and colleagues offers another possible interpretation for fluctuations in suicides deaths in the country. These study results highlight the importance of users of suicide data in Australia to maintain a degree to skepticism when interpreting statistics over time.

## Endnotes

1. De Leo D, Dudley MJ, Aebersold CJ, Mendoza JA, Barnes MA, Harrison JE, Ranson DL (2010). Achieving standardised reporting of suicide in Australia: Rationale and program for change. *Medical Journal of Australia* 192, 452–456.

# Marital breakdown, shame, and suicidality in men: A direct link?

Kõlves K, Ide N, De Leo D (Australia)

*Suicide and Life-Threatening Behavior* 41, 149–159, 2011

The influence of feelings of shame originating from marital breakdown on suicidality is examined. The role of mental health problems as probable mediating factors is also considered. Internalised shame, state (related to separation) shame, and mental health problems were significantly correlated with the score for suicidality during separation in both genders. Tested structural equation model indicated that internalised shame was not directly linked to suicidality, but was mediated either by state shame or mental health problems in males in the context of separation. Our findings seem to indicate that separated males are more vulnerable to the experience of state shame in the context of separation, which might lead to the development of suicidality.

## Comment

*Main findings:* It is surprising that there is not much past research on the links between feelings of shame and suicidal behaviours, particularly as these are recognised as important influences on male help-seeking[1]. Potentially, the lack of in-depth investigation of this topic is connected to the conceptual complexity of shame as an area of research. As discussed by Kõlves and colleagues, shame may be experienced as an internal and/or external feeling. In the former, the person experiences strong negative self-judgment, while in the latter, negative perceptions from others are most salient. Aside from this, shame may be 'state-based' and connected to a specific circumstance, or 'trait- based', which implies that shame is an enduring individual factor.

The focus of this article is the shame and stigma that may follow separation from romantic partners. The authors seek to investigate the effect of both state-based shame associated with the separation event and underlying trait-based shame proneness. State-based shame is hypothesised to mediate the effect of trait-based shame on suicidality.

The data from this study came from a survey with a convenience sample of males (and females) that had recently separated from their partners and contacted relationship counselling services, help-lines, or a variety of other support and self-help groups. Results indicate that both males and females reported similar levels of internalised shame. However, separated males had higher levels of suicidality (thoughts/plans about suicide and suicide attempts) than separated females. Further, state-based shame was more strongly associated with mood disorders in separated males than females. Results also indicate the relevance of depression, anxiety and substance abuse in the 12 months previous to the survey as being highly associated with sucidality. Structural equation modelling indicated that internalised (trait-based) shame was not directly linked to suicidality among separated males, but was instead mediated by mental health problems or separation-related state-based shame. This analysis also revealed a direct relationship between state-based shame and suicidality among separated males; but no such relationship was found for females. This may indicate that males are more vulnerable to the experiences of separation than females. Some of the main limitations of this study were connected to the use of a sample obtained from those seeking help from counselling services, which makes it difficult to state if these results are applicable to the general population (who may not have sought help). Results were also likely to be influenced by the self-report nature of the questionnaire and relatively small sample size.

*Implications:* These limitations aside, the results of this study provide some clear directions for future research and intervention. Males who are estranged from partners appear to be at high levels of risk, particularly if they perceive shame associated with the separation. This indicates the need for efforts at multiple levels of society to encourage help-seeking. This could be achieved through general awareness and education campaigns at the national level, as well as in schools, workplaces and in community groups. Apart from this, the results of this study highlight the process of separation from a partner as a particularly stressful time and highlights the need for targeted intervention strategies, risk assessment and clear pathways of referral for separated males.

## Endnotes

1. Oliffe JL, Ogrodniczuk JS, Bottorff JL, Johnson JL, Hoyak K (2010). 'You feel like you can't live anymore': Suicide from the perspectives of men who experience depression. *Social Science & Medicine*. Published online: 24 May 2010. doi:10.1016/j.socscimed.2010.03.057.

# A systematic review of elderly suicide prevention programs

Lapierre S, Erlangsen A, Waern M, De Leo D, Oyama H, Scocco P, Gallo J, Szanto K, Conwell Y, Draper B, Quinnett P (Canada)

*Crisis* 32, 88–98, 2011

*Background:* Suicide rates are highest among the elderly, yet research on suicide prevention in old age remains a much-neglected area.

*Aims:* We carried out a systematic review to examine the results of interventions aimed at suicidal elderly persons and to identify successful strategies and areas needing further exploration.

*Methods:* Searches through various electronic databases yielded 19 studies with an empirical evaluation of a suicide prevention or intervention program designed especially for adults aged 60 years and older.

*Results:* Most studies were centred on the reduction of risk factors (depression screening and treatment, and decreasing isolation), but when gender was considered, programs were mostly efficient for women. The empirical evaluations of programs attending to the needs of high-risk older adults seemed positive; most studies showed a reduction in the level of suicidal ideation of patients or in the suicide rate of the participating communities. However, not all studies used measures of suicidality to evaluate the outcome of the intervention, and rarely did they aim at improving protective factors.

*Conclusions:* Innovative strategies should improve resilience and positive aging, engage family and community gatekeepers, use telecommunications to reach vulnerable older adult, and evaluate the effects of means restriction and physicians education on elderly suicide.

## Comment

*Main findings:* Globally, the suicide rates are found to be highest among males and females aged 75 and older[1]. However, there is a lack of knowledge and training about elderly suicide and its prevention. The systematic review by Lapierre and colleagues showed that only 19 of the 490 publications on elderly suicide presented an empirical evaluation of a prevention or intervention program focusing on older adults. In total, 19 studies presented 11 different interventions. Two of these were primary care interventions, both of which were efficacious in reducing suicide ideation and depression. Most community based outreach prevention and telephone counselling produced mixed effects, with females benefiting from depression screening and group activities more than males. Clinical treatment and intervention programs that specifically focused on strengthening protective factors also produced some positive results for elderly persons.

It is worth noting that only 3 studies in this review evaluated suicide rates, 4 assessed changes in suicidal ideation, and 4 studies were limited to measurement of depression levels (rather than suicidality). Most of the programs ($n = 9/11$) addressed risk predictors and were centred on depression screening and treatment, information about symptoms, treatment options, and use of medications, as well as reduction of social isolation. A few interventions were gender-specific and women appeared to benefit more than men. Women were more likely than men to use social resources and mental health services; so, workshops, telephone counselling, and group meetings were found to be more suitable for them than for males. Older males were less likely to seek medical advice and could prefer intervention programs that focus on action and problem solving rather than the expression of emotions or creating new relationships.

*Implications:* In order to meet the needs of the elderly who are suicidal, the content of suicide prevention programs must be multifaceted. Currently, key strategies for suicide prevention include the early detection of mental health problems and suicidality (with the help of family and community gatekeepers), the treatment of high-risk elderly individuals, physician education, and increased outreach to older adults. Improvement of detection, treatment, and management of mood disorders should remain the primary focus of suicide prevention, in view of the finding that these types of interventions were beneficial to elderly persons. Furthermore, risk assessment could be improved by addressing a range of issues experienced by suicidal older men, such as involuntary retirement, pain, dependency, daily hassles, sleep problems, loss of driver's license, bereavement, and, in particular, alcohol abuse.

The authors of this review recommend reaching out to those who fail to seek medical or psychological help. Considering the poor help-seeking in males, there is need for trials that demonstrate successful interventions aimed at older men. Future avenues for intervention should address attitudinal barriers to help-seeking and treatment by deemphasising labelling of depression and accentuating the focus on symptoms and stressors[2]. Future research should also seek new ways of reaching suicidal older men, for example by training community gatekeepers[3]. In addition, new programs should involve relatives and friends, as these persons play an important part in the lives of many elderly individuals. Protective factors such as development of positive aging, strengths, coping, and resilience should be studied in elderly suicide prevention and intervention.

## Endnotes

1. De Leo D, Krysinska K, Bertolote JM, Fleischmann A, Wasserman D (2009). Suicidal behaviours on all the continents among the elderly. In: D Wasserman and C Wasserman (eds). *Oxford Textbook of Suicidology and Suicide Prevention: A global perspective* Part 13, 693–701.

2. Hinton L, Zweifach M, Oishi S, Tang L, Unützer J (2006). Gender disparities in the treatment of late-life depression: qualitative and quantitative findings from the IMPACT trial. *The American Journal of Geriatric Psychiatry* 14, 884–892.

3. Matthieu MM, Cross W, Batres AR, Flora CM, Knox KL (2008). Evaluation of gatekeeper training for suicide prevention in veterans. *Archives of Suicide Research* 12, 148–154.

# Suicide categories by patterns of known risk factors: A latent class analysis

Logan J, Hall J, Karch D (USA)

*Archives of General Psychiatry* 68, 935–941, 2011

*Context:* Multiple risk factors contribute to suicides; however, patterns of co-occurrence among these factors have not been fully identified.

*Objectives:* To assess patterns of known suicide-related risk factors, classify suicide decedents by these patterns, track class proportions during a 6-year period, and characterise decedents across the classes to help focus prevention strategies.

*Design, Setting, and Participants:* Latent class analysis was conducted using 2003–2008 data from the National Violent Death Reporting System. The population included 28,703 suicide decedents from 12 US states.

*Main Outcome Measures:* The known risk factors included having the following: mental health conditions; a sad or depressed mood; substance abuse problems; medical problems; recent crises; financial, job, and legal problems; intimate partner and other relationship problems; and perpetrated interpersonal violence.

*Results:* Nine distinct patterns of risk factors emerged. Of these classes, one only endorsed mental health-related factors and one only endorsed alcohol- and substance abuse-related factors; however, 7 classes of decedents had distinct patterns of factors that spanned multiple domains. For example, 5 of these classes had mental health factors with other risks (eg, substance abuse, financial problems, relationship problems, a recent crisis, and medical problems). Two classes had recent crises with relationship problems; one of these classes also had high probabilities for criminal problems and interpersonal violence. Class proportions differed during the 6 years. Differences across classes by demographic and event characteristics were also found.

*Conclusions:* Most suicide decedents could be classified by patterns of risk factors. Furthermore, most classes revealed a need for more connected services across medical, mental health/substance abuse, and court/social service systems. Reducing fragmentation across these agencies and recruiting family, friend, and community support for individuals experiencing mental health problems and/or other stress might significantly reduce suicides.

## Comment

*Main findings:* This article investigates the complex set of life experiences that may contribute to suicide using latent class analysis (LCA). LCA uses statistical probabilities to classify the likelihood of certain and known risk factors being present in suicide cases. The sample used in this study was drawn from the National Violent Death Reporting System (NVDRS) in the United States over the period 2003 to 2008. The data in NVDRS was obtained from a range of sources, including coronial or medical reports, toxicology reports, law enforcement documents and death certificates. The final sample of suicide cases ($n = 28,703$) came from 12 states. The researchers classified each case of suicide according to health and life stress-related factors, demographic factors, military status, access to means (i.e., suicide method), location of death, and attendance at a mental health facility before death.

The LCA analysis identified a 9-class model representing patterns of known risk factors. These were: (1) mental health (MH) conditions with alcohol problems (8.9% of the sample); (2) MH with recent crisis (14.6% of the sample); (3) MH conditions only i.e., no other relevant risks (24.9% of the sample); (4) depressed mood with financial problems (12.5% of the sample); (5) alcohol problems with other life stress (4.4% of the sample); (6) medical problems with depressed mood (9.2% of the sample); (7) recent crisis with criminal legal problems (6.5% of the sample); (8) interpersonal problems with recent crisis (10.5% of the sample), and; (9) suspected alcohol use at the time of death (8.5% of the sample).

In addition to mental health conditions, results suggest a number of life-event related risks associated with suicide. For example, more than 4,000 decedents who had known MH issues also experienced a life crisis in the two-weeks before death. The proportion of cases with life-crises increased over the 5-year time period of the project. A substantial number of cases also experienced relationship problems or legal issues in the absence of known mental health conditions. Alcohol-related issues were also commonly identified as contributing factors to suicide, particularly among those cases that experienced a critical life event or other stressors prior to death. Those with serious medical issues and depression were generally in the older age groups, which indicate the need for adequate screening among those who are diagnosed with severe illness. Approximately 75% of suicides with mental health conditions or a depressed mood were receiving treatment at the time of death. This finding leads the authors to speculate that treatment for a MH problem alone may not be sufficient in the presence of significant life stressors. The limitations of this article are connected to the aggregate nature of the data analysis and the fact that it is unable to untangle the complex number of factors related to suicide, which may also stem from early life experience and biological factors.

*Implications:* As shown in this article, a death by suicide represents more than the outcome of a mental health disorder; instead, suicide was found to be related to wide range of life, relationship and legal issues. Considering this, suicide prevention should not be confined to the realm of mental health, as those who have died by suicide also experience a range of life experiences connected with employment and the legal system. This highlights the need for a holistic approach to suicide prevention that includes greater collaboration between connected medical, mental health, substance abuse, court and social services. More investigation is needed to deepen the results of this study by investigating the complex linkages through which life factors and mental and physical health are related to suicidal behaviour over time.

# Sadness, suicide, and their association with video game and internet overuse among teens: Results from the youth risk behavior survey 2007 and 2009

Messias E, Castro J, Saini A, Usman M, Peeples D (USA)
*Suicide and Life-Threatening Behavior* 41, 307–315, 2011

We investigated the association between excessive video game/Internet use and teen suicidality. Data were obtained from the 2007 and 2009 Youth Risk Behavior Survey (YRBS), a high school-based, nationally representative survey ($N = 14,041$ and $N = 16,410$, respectively). Teens who reported 5 hours or more of video games/Internet daily use, in the 2009 YRBS, had a significantly higher risk for sadness (adjusted and weighted odds ratio, 95% confidence interval = 2.1, 1.7–2.5), suicidal ideation (1.7, 1.3–2.1), and suicide planning (1.5, 1.1–1.9). The same pattern was found in the 2007 survey. These findings support an association between excessive video game and Internet use and risk for teen depression and suicidality.

## Comment

*Main findings:* There has been growing attention to the possibility that excessive internet and gaming may have negative consequences on youth wellbeing. A previous study in South Korea found that adolescents who met the criteria for 'internet addiction' had higher rates of depression and suicide ideation[1]. Another study found that youth diagnosed with 'video game addiction' experienced a range of adverse mental and physical outcomes[2]. The authors of this study argue that these addictive behaviours may be similar to other pathological behaviours such as gambling, also shown to be associated with higher suicide risk. However, outside these studies conducted in Asia, there has been little research linking internet and online gaming to suicide. This study was based on a large sample (13,817 in 2007 and 16,124 in 2009) of students aged 14 to 18 years who participated in a survey designed as part of regular surveillance of behaviours that influence youth health.

Young people who reported 5 or more hours of daily video and gaming use were significantly more likely to report 2 weeks of sadness over the previous year compared to those who reported no video game use. Results also indicate a strong and consistent association between the highest level of video game use/internet use with suicide ideation, planning and attempts. However, there was no association between video game use/internet use with suicide attempts severe enough to warrant medical attention (i.e., injury, poisoning, or overdose that had to be treated by a doctor or nurse). The authors find evidence of the potential protective effects of low use of video games compared to no video game use. The main limitation of this study was that it is impossible to attribute causality to the effects or identify whether the relationship between video gaming and suicidality signifies underlying mental illness or a coping strategy for adverse life events. Aside from these issues, the surveys are also likely to be subject to problems in self-report biases.

*Implications:* In 2009, approximately 80% of children in Australia had access to the internet[3]. Home was reported as the most common site of internet use (73%) followed by school (69%). Of the 2.0 million children accessing the internet at home, playing online games (69%) was among the most common activities. Less than half (42%) of children who used the internet at home did it for 2 hours or less per week, while 4% were online for 20 hours or more. Considering that past research has shown several adverse effects of excessive internet use, more research is needed in Australia in order to more fully understand the effects of children's online behaviours on their wellbeing.

## Endnotes

1. Kim EJ, Namkoong K, Ku T, Kim SJ (2008). The relationship between online game addiction and aggression, self-control and narcissistic personality traits. *European Psychiatry* 23, 212–218.

2. Chiu SI, Lee JZ, Huang DH (2004). Video game addiction in children and teenagers in Taiwan. *CyberPsychology and Behavior* 7, 571–81.

3. Australian Bureau of Statistics (2009). *Household use of information technology, Australia, 2008–09*. Cat. No. 8146.0. Canberra: ABS.

# Bereavement-related depressive episodes. Characteristics, 3-year course, and implications for the DSM-5

Mojtabai R (USA)

*Archives of General Psychiatry* 68, 920–928, 2011

*Context:* The DSM-IV criteria for major depressive episodes exclude brief episodes that are better accounted for by bereavement. However, a proposal has been made to remove this exclusion from the DSM-5.

*Objectives:* To compare the demographic and psychiatric characteristics of participants with bereavement-related, single, brief (< 2 months) depressive episodes and other types of depressive episodes and to compare the future risk of depression between these groups and participants without a history of depression at baseline.

*Design:* A longitudinal, community-based, epidemiologic study conducted from August 1, 2001, through May 31, 2002 (wave 1), and from August 1, 2004, through September 30, 2005 (wave 2).

*Setting:* The US general population, including residents of Hawaii and Alaska.

*Participants:* Participants in the National Epidemiologic Survey on Alcohol and Related Conditions waves 1 ($n$ = 43 093) and 2 ($n$ = 34 653).

*Main Outcome Measures:* Demographic characteristics, age at onset, history of depression in first-degree relatives, impairment in role functioning, psychiatric comorbidities, lifetime mental health service use, and new depressive episodes during the 3-year follow-up period.

*Results:* Compared with participants with other types of depression, those with bereavement-related, single, brief depressive episodes were more likely to experience later onset and to be black but less likely to have had impairment in role functioning, comorbid anxiety disorders, or a treatment history at baseline. Participants with bereavement-related, single, brief episodes were less likely than those with bereavement-unrelated, single, brief episodes to experience fatigue, increased sleep, feelings of worthlessness, and suicidal ideations. The risk of new depressive episodes during the follow-up period among participants with bereavement-related, single, brief episodes was significantly lower than among participants with bereavement-unrelated, single, brief episodes and other types of depression but similar to the risk among the participants from the general population with no baseline history of depression.

*Conclusions:* Bereavement-related, single, brief depressive episodes have distinct demographic and symptom profiles compared with other types of depressive episodes and are not associated with increased risk of future depression. The findings support preserving the DSM-IV bereavement exclusion criterion for major depressive episodes in the DSM-5.

## Comment

*Main findings:* Recently, the DSM-V committee has made recommendation to eliminate the DSM-IV's bereavement exclusion for major depressive episodes. Defending this recommendation, 1 of the DSM-V Work Group members, Kenneth S. Kendler, pointed to the failure of past studies to show consistent evidence supporting a distinction between bereavement-related and bereavement-unrelated depression. This longitudinal study in the US aimed to provide guidance for future revisions of the diagnostic criteria by investigating the distinction between bereavement-related and bereavement-unrelated brief depressive episodes and non-brief, recurrent depressive episodes in a general population. The author found that bereavement-related episodes were characterised by less frequent impairment in functioning, lower prevalence of co-morbid anxiety disorders and less frequent treatment seeking. Furthermore, bereavement-related and bereavement-unrelated brief depressive episodes and non-brief, recurrent depressive episodes differed with regard to demographic distribution and symptom profiles. Those with bereavement-related depressive episodes were less likely to express feelings of worthlessness, suicidal ideations, fatigue, or increased sleep. Overall, participants with bereavement-related episodes had fewer co-morbidities, less impairment in role functioning, and a lower rate of treatment seeking than participants with other types of depressive episodes. The strengths of this study were its large population-representative sample and use of a structured clinical interview to diagnose mental disorder (rather than being self-report). These features increase the generalisability of study findings and the reliability of diagnosed mental disorders.

*Implications:* The present study is particularly important in the context of the current developments of the DSM-V. Despite limitations in study design, significant differences between bereavement-related and bereavement-unrelated, brief depressive episodes, with regard to morbidity, symptom profiles, and future course were found. These results make the recommendation of the DSM-V committee questionable. Eliminating the bereavement exclusion inappropriately may expand the definition of major depression to include emotional reactions to loss that are self-limiting and not associated with future risk of depression. Furthermore, removing the bereavement exclusion may pathologise normal bereavement reactions and may lead to inappropriate medication treatment.

# Emergency treatment of deliberate self-harm

Olfson M, Marcus SC, Bridge JA (USA)

*Archives of General Psychiatry.* Published online: 5 September 2011. doi:10.1001/archgenpsychiatry. 2011.108, 2011

*Context:* Although concern exists over the quality of emergency mental health services, little is known about the mental health care of adults who are admitted to emergency departments for deliberately harming themselves and then discharged to the community.

*Objectives:* To describe the predictors of emergency department discharge, the emergency mental health assessments, and the follow-up outpatient mental health care of adult Medicaid beneficiaries treated for deliberate self-harm.

*Design:* A retrospective longitudinal cohort analysis.

*Setting:* National Medicaid claims data supplemented with county-level sociodemographic variables and Medicaid state policy survey data.

*Participants:* Adults aged 21 to 64 years who were treated in emergency departments for 7,355 episodes of deliberate self-harm, focusing on those who were discharged to the community (4,595 episodes).

*Main Outcome Measures:* Rates and adjusted risk ratios (ARRs) of discharge to the community, mental health assessments in the emergency department, and outpatient mental health visits during the 30 days following the emergency department visit.

*Results:* Most patients (62.5%) were discharged to the community. Emergency department discharge was directly related to younger patient age (21–31 years vs 45–64 years) (ARR, 1.18 [99% confidence interval {CI}, 1.10–1.25]) and self-harm by cutting (ARR, 1.18 [99% CI, 1.12–1.24]) and inversely related to poisoning (ARR, 0.84 [99% CI, 0.80–0.89]) and recent psychiatric hospitalisation (ARR, 0.74 [99% CI, 0.67–0.81]). Approximately one-half of discharged patients (47.5%) received a mental health assessment in the emergency department, and a similar percentage of discharged patients (52.4%) received a follow-up outpatient mental health visit within 30 days. Follow-up mental health care was directly related to recent outpatient mental health care (ARR, 2.30 [99% CI, 2.11–2.50]) and treatment in a state with Medicaid coverage of mental health clinic services (ARR, 1.13 [99% CI, 1.05–1.22]) and inversely related to African American (ARR, 0.86 [99% CI, 0.75–0.96]) and Hispanic (ARR, 0.86 [99% CI, 0.75–0.99]) race/ethnicity.

*Conclusions:* Most adult Medicaid beneficiaries who present for emergency care for deliberate self-harm are discharged to the community, and many do not receive emergency mental health assessments or follow-up outpatient mental health care.

# Comment

*Main findings:* Deliberate self-harm (DSH) is an important risk factor for repeated self-harm and suicide. The current study focused on adult (21 to 64 years) Medicaid patients who were admitted to the emergency department (ED) for deliberate self-harm in the 50 states of the US and the District of Columbia. In total, 62% of patients who were admitted to ED for DSH were discharged to the community. People who were hospitalised with DSH were more often older in age, had used highly lethal self-harm methods, and had a history of mental health treatment. Hospitalisation was not related to other known suicide risk factors such as male gender, history of self-harm, and mental health disorders (including depression, schizophrenia, or substance use disorder). Persons who injured themselves by 'cutting' were more often discharged to the community rather than being admitted for inpatient treatment. This is concerning, given findings from past research that death by suicide is higher among patients who presented to an ED with self-inflicted cutting compared to other methods[1].

Mental health assessments were conducted with half (47.5%) of patients presenting with DSH, while outpatient follow-up within 30 days was provided to 52% of those discharged to the community. Hispanic patients with DSH received an emergency mental health assessment significantly less often than their Caucasian counterparts. Furthermore, Hispanics and African Americans were less likely to receive follow-up outpatient mental health care. The authors suggest that this ethnic difference in service delivery might reflect language or cultural barriers. However, recent mental health treatment emerged as the most powerful predictor of follow-up outpatient mental health care.

*Implications:* Presentations for deliberate self-harm represent a heavy burden to EDs worldwide. However, the ED is an important setting to assess and treat this population in order to prevent repeated self-harm and suicides. The authors of the present paper recommend that more attention should be paid to the policies and procedures that promote ED mental health assessments and timely transitions to outpatient mental health care. Furthermore, triage scales, mental health screenings, educational efforts are needed to improve the attitudes of emergency department staff toward patients who engage in DSH. Systematic efforts to manage service transitions and coordinate care represent promising ways to help encourage mental health assessments and effective referrals. The authors also suggest providing specific outpatient appointments (rather than only contact information), shorter waiting times between emergency department discharge and the outpatient appointments, and telephone reminders of outpatient appointments in order to improve referral adherence. These recommendations align with brief phone-based interventions, such as those provided in the WHO/SUPRE-MISS Study[2] supported by DoHA in Australia. Furthermore, they could be provided over the mobile using SMS-es[3].

## Endnotes

1. Cooper J, Kapur N, Webb R, Lawlor M, Guthrie E, Mackway-Jones K, Appleby L (2005).

Suicide after deliberate self-harm: A 4-year cohort study. *American Journal of Psychiatry* 162, 297–303.

2. Fleischmann A, Bertolote JM, Wasserman D, De Leo D, Bolhari J, Botega NJ, et al. (2008). Effectiveness of brief intervention and contact for suicide attempters: A randomized controlled trial in five countries. *Bulletin of the World Health Organization* 86, 703–709.

3. Owens C, Farrand P, Darvill R, Emmens T, Hewis E, Aitken P (2011). Involving service users in intervention design: A participatory approach to developing a text-messaging intervention to reduce repetition of self-harm. *Health Expectations* 14, 285–295.

## Racism as a determinant of social and emotional wellbeing for Aboriginal Australian youth

Priest NC, Paradies YC, Gunthorpe W, Cairney SJ, Sayers, SM (Australia)

*Medical Journal of Australia* 194, 546–550, 2011

*Objective:* To explore the associations between self-reported racism and health and wellbeing outcomes for young Aboriginal Australian people.

*Design, Setting and Participants:* A cross-sectional study of 345 Aboriginal Australians aged 16–20 years who, as participants in the prospective Aboriginal Birth Cohort Study, were recruited at birth between 1987 and 1990 and followed up between 2006 and 2008.

*Main Outcome Measures:* Self-reported social and emotional wellbeing using a questionnaire validated as culturally appropriate for the study's participants; recorded body mass index and waist-to-hip ratio.

*Results:* Self-reported racism was reported by 32% of study participants. Racism was significantly associated with anxiety (odds ratio [OR], 2.18 [95% CI, 1.37–3.46]); depression (OR, 2,16[95% CI, 1.33–3.53]); suicide risk (OR, 2.32 [95% CI, 1.25–4.00]); and poor overall mental health (OR, 3.35 [95% CI, 2.04–5.51]). No significant associations were found between self-reported racism and resilience or any anthropometric measures.

*Conclusions:* Self-reported racism was associated with poor social and emotional wellbeing outcomes, including anxiety, depression, suicide risk and poor overall mental health.

### Comment

*Main findings:* Racism can be described as comprising of avoidable and unfair acts and behaviours that produce inequalities in power, resources and opportunities across racial and ethnic groups. This can be manifested interpersonally and systematically across various levels of society[1]. An increasing amount of research indicates the racism has real effects on health and wellbeing[2]. Racism is also thought to be related to the high rates of suicide among Indigenous persons in Australia[3]; however, previous to the paper by Priest and colleagues, there has been little empirical research on this relationship.

This article examines racism as determinant of social and emotional wellbeing of Indigenous youth using the Aboriginal Birth Cohort study, a prospective longitudinal study set in the Northern Territory from the years 1987 and 1990 onwards. Data used in the current paper came from the third wave of the study, conducted from December 2006 to January 2008, when participants were between 16 and 20 years of age. The main outcome of the study was social and emotional wellbeing, as measured through a 25-item survey and 4 main underlying factors: anxiety, depression, suicide risk (e.g., wish to be dead, harm self or kill self), and resilience.

Multivariate analyses indicate a strong association between racism and increased anxiety, depression, poor mental health and suicide risk. These associations remained after adjusting for substance use (alcohol, petrol, Gunja, tobacco and cigarettes) and socio-demographic factors (such as sex, age, high school attendance etc.). One potential problem with this research was the conceptual difficulties in separating racism from inequality. Participant self-report bias in data collection was another issue. Last, the research is unable to provide information on the casual pathways that explain how racism has a detrimental effect on Indigenous suicide.

*Implications:* The causes of Indigenous suicide are thought to be connected to various social, economic, political and cultural factors. Considering this, many researchers have suggested the importance of providing multi-dimensional, socially and culturally relevant strategies in Indigenous communities[3,4]. At the same time, there is growing pressure to provide culturally appropriate services that seek to eliminate racism in the health care setting[5]. The findings by Priest and colleagues adds weight to the argument that wider social and cultural phenomenon – such as racism – have observable effects on Indigenous wellbeing. This supports inclusion of such factors in Indigenous suicide prevention initiatives. These findings are the first of their kind in Australia and more research is needed to determine the various pathways through which racism impacts Indigenous wellbeing.

## Endnotes

1. Berman G, Paradies Y (2010). Racism, disadvantage and multiculturalism: Towards effective anti-racist praxis. *Ethnic and Racial Studies* 33, 214–232.

2. Paradies Y (2006). A systematic review of empirical research on self-reported racism and health. *International Journal of Epidemiology* 35, 888–901.

3. Elliot-Farrelly T (2004). Australian Aboriginal suicide: The need for Aboriginal suicidology? *Advances in Mental Health* 3, 138–145.

4. Tatz C (2004). Aboriginal, Maori and Inuit youth suicide: Avenues to alleviation? *Australian Aboriginal Studies* 2, 15–25.

5. Durey A (2010). Reducing racism in Aboriginal health care in Australia: Where does cultural education fit? *Australian and New Zealand Journal of Public Health* 34, s87–s92.

# The impact of psychiatric illness on suicide: Differences by diagnosis of disorders and by sex and age of subjects

Qin P (Denmark)

*Journal of Psychiatric Research.* Published online: 30 June 2011. doi:10.1016/j.jpsychires.2011.06.002, 2011

People with a psychiatric illness are at high risk for suicide; however, variation of the risk by patients' sex and age and by specific diagnosis needs to be explored in a more detail. This large population study systematically assesses suicide incidence rate ratio (IRR) and population attributable risk (PAR) associated with various psychiatric disorders by comparing 21,169 suicides in Denmark over a 17-year period with sex-age-time-matched population controls. The study shows that suicide risk is significantly increased for persons with a hospitalised psychiatric disorder and the associated risk varies significantly by diagnosis and by sex and age of subjects. Further adjustment for personal socioeconomic differences eliminates the IRRs associated with various disorders only to a limited extend. Recurrent depression and borderline personality disorder increase suicide risk the strongest while dementia increases the risk the least for both males and females. The influence of various disorders generally weakens with increasing age; however, there are important exceptions. Schizophrenia affects people aged $\leq 35$ years the strongest in terms of both IRR and PAR. Recurrent depression increases suicide risk particularly strong in all age groups and the associated PAR increases steadily with age. Borderline personality disorder has a strong effect in young people, especially those $\leq 35$ years. Alcohol use disorder accounts the highest PAR of suicides in males of 36–60 years old. For the elderly above 60 years old, reaction to stress and adjustment disorder increases the risk for suicide the most in both sexes. These findings suggest that approaches to psychiatric suicide prevention should be varied according to diagnosis and sex and age of subjects.

## Comment

*Main findings:* The relationship between mental illness and suicide is well established. This paper seeks to deepen understandings of this association by providing evidence on the burden of suicide in different psychiatric disorders. The author uses population attributable risk (PAR) — a measure that takes both effect size and the prevalence of exposure in the population.

The study is based several longitudinal registers in Denmark. Each suicide case was matched to 20 control cases by sex, age and date of suicide. Information on psychiatric disorders for both suicides and controls were retrieved from the Danish Psychiatric Central Register and were based on diagnosis given at most recent psychiatric hospitalisation. The nested-case control design also controlled for marital status, income level, and place of residence. Approximately 37% of male and 57% of female suicide cases had a recorded history of hospitalisation in the study population. Schizophrenia was the most common reason for hospitalisation for those under the age of 35 years, while recurrent depression was the most common reason above the age of 60 years. Alcohol use disorder was most commonly diagnosed in males, while other personality disorders were most common in females.

Conditional logistic regression confirmed the finding that suicide risk was significantly increased for all people with a history of psychiatric hospitalisation. There were however, several distinguishing factors based on psychiatric disorder, sex and age. For males, risk of suicide was higher among those diagnosed with recurrent depression, borderline personality disorders, other affective disorder, and reaction to stress and adjustment disorder. For females, the risk was substantially higher among those that received a diagnosis of bipolar disorder, borderline personality disorder, recurrent depression and substance and alcohol disorders. Dementia was also associated with increased risk for suicide. Population attributable risks (PAR) indicate that a hospitalised psychiatric illness accounted for 36.1% (under 35 years), 39.2% (between 35 and 60 years) and 22.3% (over 60 years) of male suicide cases. For females, PAR for psychiatric disorder were 55.7%, 62.3% and 43.3% for each of the age-groups mentioned above, respectively.

*Implications:* This study demonstrates that suicide risk in relation to psychiatric disorders varies across gender and age. This suggests that risk assessment and intervention should be tailored according to the demographic and psychiatric profile of the patient. At a broader level, the findings of this study support the long-held belief that psychiatric disorder raises the risk of suicide. However, it is necessary to assess the strength of these associations in the Australian context to establish if these findings are contextually specific or generalisable to other contexts.

# Relationship between household income and mental disorders: Findings from a population-based longitudinal study

Sareen J, Afifi TO, McMillan KA, Asmundson GJG (Canada)

*Archives of General Psychiatry* 68, 419–427, 2011

There has been increasing concern about the impact of the global economic recession on mental health. To date, findings on the relationship between income and mental illness have been mixed. Some studies have found that lower income is associated with mental illness, while other studies have not found this relationship. To examine the relationship between income, mental disorders, and suicide attempts. Prospective, longitudinal, nationally representative survey. United States general population. A total of 34,653 noninstitutionalised adults (aged ≥ 20 years) interviewed at 2 time points 3 years apart. Lifetime DSM-IV Axis I and Axis II mental disorders and lifetime suicide attempts, as well as incident mental disorders and change in income during the follow-up period. After adjusting for potential confounders, the presence of most of the lifetime Axis I and Axis II mental disorders was associated with lower levels of income. Participants with household income of less than $20,000 per year were at increased risk of incident mood disorders during the 3-year follow-up period in comparison with those with income of $70,000 or more per year. A decrease in household income during the 2 time points was also associated with an increased risk of incident mood, anxiety, or substance use disorders (adjusted odds ratio, 1.30; 99% confidence interval, 1.06–1.60) in comparison with respondents with no change in income. Baseline presence of mental disorders did not increase the risk of change in personal or household income in the follow-up period. Low levels of household income are associated with several lifetime mental disorders and suicide attempts, and a reduction in household income is associated with increased risk for incident mental disorders. Policymakers need to consider optimal methods of intervention for mental disorders and suicidal behavior among low-income individuals.

## Comment

*Main findings:* Income per capita has been found to be related to both suicide[1,2] and mental disorders[3] within a population. However, the ecological and cross-sectional design of most past research on this topic has created problems in disentangling whether these relationships are due to social causation (which posits that exposure to certain risk factors will increase the risk of suicide) or social selection (persons who are suicidal or with mental disorders have a pre-disposition to declining socioeconomic status). Other issues with past studies are that they have not been able to provide reliable assessments of mental disorder and suffer from rather small samples.

The research reported in this paper provides a more rigorous examination of the relationships between income, mental disorder and suicide attempts through its use of a longitudinal and population-based mental health survey. Unlike previous papers, information on mental disorders was collected through structured clinical interviews rather than self-report tools (using the *Alcohol Use Disorder and Associated Disabilities Interview Schedule-DSM-IV Version*), which increases the reliability of information provided on both Axis I and Axis II disorders. The sample consisted of 34,653 persons who were interviewed between 2001–2002 and 2004–2005.

The results of this study suggest that persons in the lowest income group had the greatest odds of lifetime suicide attempt. The most notable differences in the effect of income were noted for those in younger age groups (between the ages of 20 and 54 years). Compared to the reference category of high-income (over $70,000 per year), the odds of suicide attempt for those earning less than $19,999 was 3.66, while the odds were 2.03 and 1.52 for those earning between $20,000–$39,999 and $40,000 and $69,999, respectively. There were no significant income differentials for those aged over 55 years. Like other research on this topic, it is difficult to establish whether these relationships are causal. Further, analyses did not control for the possible influence of physical health problems.

*Implications:* There are several factors that may explain the higher frequency of suicide attempts in persons in lower income groups, such as hunger, violence, higher levels of social stress, and decreased capacity to afford treatment. Interventions need to be mindful of the potential role of these factors in raising suicide risk. Regardless, this study indicates the importance of developing and providing intervention for those persons in the lowest income groups of society. These results are particularly relevant in consideration of recent adverse developments in the world economic market and rising unemployment.

## Endnotes

1. Neumayer E (2003). Are socioeconomic factors valid determinants of suicide? Controlling for national cultures of suicide with fixed-effects estimation. *Cross-Cultural Research* 37, 307–329.
2. Sher L (2006). Per capita income is related to suicide rates in men but not in women. *The Journal of Men's Health & Gender* 3, 39–42.
3. Fryers T, Melzer D, Jenkins R (2003). Social inequalities and the common mental disorder: A systematic review of the evidence. *Social Psychiatry & Psychiatric Epidemiology* 38, 229–237.

## Attitudes and knowledge of clinical staff regarding people who self-harm: A systematic review

Saunders KE, Hawton K, Fortune S, Farrell S (UK)

*Journal of Affective Disorders.* Published online: 16 September 2011. doi:10.1016/j.jad.2011.08.024, 2011

*Background:* The attitudes held by clinical staff towards people who harm themselves, together with their knowledge about self-harm, are likely to influence their clinical practice and hence the experiences and outcomes of patients. Our aim was to systematically review the nature of staff attitudes towards people who engage in self-harm, including the factors that influence them, and the impact of training on attitudes, knowledge and behaviour of staff.

*Methods and Findings:* A comprehensive search for relevant studies was performed on 6 electronic databases. Two independent reviewers screened titles, abstracts and full reports of studies, extracted data and gave each paper a quality rating. Qualitative and quantitative studies published in English were included. A total of 74 studies were included. Attitudes of general hospital staff, especially doctors, were largely negative, particularly towards individuals who repeatedly self-harm. Self-harm patients were viewed more negatively than other patients, except those abusing alcohol or drugs. Psychiatric staff in community and hospital settings displayed more positive attitudes than general hospital staff. Negative attitudes were more common among doctors than nursing staff although this was only true of general hospital staff. Active training led to consistent improvements in attitude and knowledge in all groups.

*Conclusions:* Attitudes of general hospital staff towards self-harm patients are often negative, mirroring the experience of service users. Interventions can have a positive impact and improve the quality of patient care.

*Limitations:* Included only English language publications.

## Comment

*Main findings:* This systematic literature review identified 74 papers about the attitudes and knowledge of clinical staff regarding self-harm, 9 of which were from Australia. The results draw attention to the negative perceptions of medical and nursing staff towards those who self-harm, which aligns with past research on ED nurses in Qld[1]. The results of this review indicate that pessimistic attitudes towards suicide are still common, despite increases in awareness, guidance and publicity regarding the prevalence, risk factors and management of self-harm over time. This is concerning given that persons who self-harm are a group at higher risk of subsequent death by suicide. Gender specific differences indicate that female staff had more positive attitudes towards suicidal patients than male staff. Furthermore, the gender of patients influenced attitudes in some studies, with female patients being viewed more positively. Results indicate more negative attitudes among medical (such as doctors) and ED staff compared to nurses and those employed in psychiatric hospital and community settings. This may reflect self-selection of such staff to work with this patient group. These findings may also reflect greater understanding of the causes and nature of self-harm among sympathetic staff employed in psychiatric and community settings.

The review also highlights some of the practical difficulties with assessing self-harm patients in EDs, including waiting times and delays in a psychiatric service response.

*Implications:* Past research in Australia has found that nurses and doctors generally have negative attitudes toward patients that self-harm, particularly those persons who make repeat presentations for self-harming beahviours[1,2,3]. Considering this, formal training that aims to increase awareness and reduce negative attitudes should be made available to all clinical staff that regularly treat those who self-harm. An Australian randomised trial showed that attending targeted clinical education on borderline personality disorder had a positive influence on the attitudes of both emergency medicine clinicians and mental health clinicians[4]. This suggests that training should address knowledge, understanding, attitudes, self-awareness, communication and behaviour. In addition, there should be regular supervision and support available to staff who are in contact with self-harming patients. Furthermore, all hospitals should have agreed guidelines for the management of individuals who self-harm, and these should parallel national guidelines in other countries where these exist. However, there is still need for further studies, as we still know relatively little about how patient characteristics such as ethnicity or social status influence attitudes.

## Endnotes

1. McAllister M, Creedy D, Moyle W, Farrugia C (2002). Nurses' attitudes towards clients who self-harm. *Journal of Advanced Nursing* 40, 578–586.
2. Bailey S (1994). Critical care nurses' and doctors' attitudes to parasuicide patients. *Australian Journal of Advance Nursing* 11, 11–17.
3. Commons Treloar A, Lewis A (2008a) Professional attitudes towards deliberate self-harm in patients with borderline personality disorder. *Australian and New Zealand Journal of Psychiatry* 42, 578–584.
4. Commons Treloar A, Lewis A (2008b). Targeted clinical education for staff attitudes towards deliberate self-harm in borderline personality disorder: Randomized controlled trial. *Australian and New Zealand Journal of Psychiatry* 42, 981–988.

# Do suicides' characteristics influence survivors' emotions?

Schneider B, Grebner K, Schnabel A, Georgi K (Germany)

*Suicide and Life-Threatening Behavior* 41, 117–125, 2011

The suicide of a related person can often induce severe negative emotional reactions. The objective of this study was to explore the relationships between sociodemographic and diagnostic data of suicides and survivors' emotions and to close this substantial gap. The main outcome of this study was that survivors' severity of emotional disturbance was inversely correlated with age of suicides. In the multivariable approach, only age remained related to the majority of the assessed survivors' emotions, whereas other characteristics, such as gender, presence of psychiatric disorder, or suicide method were not associated with survivors' emotions. Age had a dominant impact on the relationship between suicides' characteristics and survivors' emotional reactions and supersedes the effect of most suicides' characteristics including diagnoses.

## Comment

*Main findings:* This German psychological autopsy (PA) study investigated whether survivors' emotional reactions to suicide differed depending on suicides' socio-demographic characteristics and psychiatric diagnoses. As the age of the deceased increased, the everyday life of survivors appeared to be less influenced by a range of specific emotions, such as depressed mood, lack of energy, guilt, abandonment, and anger towards others. Apart from the effect of age, most of the suicides' socio-demographic and diagnostic characteristics (including previous suicide attempts) did not predict survivors' emotional reactions in the final model. However, severe physical illness was related to a reduction in the occurrence of any kind of disturbed emotions, which may suggest that relatives might have been more prepared for a death if their loved one was severely ill. Substance use disorders and personality disorders predicted increased anger toward the deceased; this may have reflected the nature of these disorders before death. For example, the behaviours and life style choices associated with substance use and personality disorders may have led to increased conflicts with friends and family. Affective disorders were associated with increased admiration toward the deceased. Potential explanations for this result were not provided the study authors. Although the sample size was adequate for analysis, the reactions of survivors are likely to be influenced by pre-existing emotional problems and vulnerabilities.

*Implications:* Survivors of suicide often find it more difficult to talk about their grief than other bereaved people — which highlights the need for sensitive, private and easily accessible postvention services. While all survivors may require effective postvention following the death of a loved one, the authors of this study indicate that those who have lost a younger relative suffer more intensely than when suicide occurs in older age. Survivors also have stronger reactions if the deceased had suffered from an affective disorder, substance use disorder, or personality disorder, which indicates that these persons require special attention following the death. Postvention is an integral and indispensable preventive part of comprehensive suicide prevention. Support groups can greatly assist survivors as a lack of communication can delay the healing process[1]. There exist several support groups for suicide survivors in Australia. One community based program called StandBy Response Service[2] provides a 24 hour coordinated crisis response to assist people who have lost someone through suicide. Currently, their services are available in 9 sites around Australia. However, further large scale studies on long-term effects of people bereaving by suicide are needed.

## Endnotes

1. Andriessen K (2009). Can postvention be prevention? *Crisis* 30, 43–47.
2. Webpage of United Synergies: StandBy Response Service. Retrieved: 14 October 2011 from http://www.unitedsynergies.com.au/index.php?option=com_content&view=article&id=39&Itemid=23

## Genomewide association scan of suicidal thoughts and behaviour in major depression

Schosser A, Butler AW, Ising M, Perroud N, Uher R, Ng MY, Cohen-Woods S, Craddock N, Owen MJ, Korszun A, Jones L, Jones I, Gill M, Rice JP, Maier W, Mors O, Rietschel M, Lucae S, Binder EB, Preisig M, Perry J, Tozzi F, Muglia P, Aitchison KJ, Breen G, Craig IW, Farmer AE, Muller-Myhsok B, McGuffin P, Lewis CM (UK)

*PLoS One* 6, e20690, 2011

*Background:* Suicidal behaviour can be conceptualised as a continuum from suicidal ideation, to suicidal attempts to completed suicide. In this study we identify genes contributing to suicidal behaviour in the depression study RADIANT.

*Methodology/Principal Findings:* A quantitative suicidality score was composed of 2 items from the SCAN interview. In addition, the 251 depression cases with a history of serious suicide attempts were classified to form a discrete trait. The quantitative trait was correlated with younger onset of depression and number of episodes of depression, but not with gender. A genome-wide association study of 2,023 depression cases was performed to identify genes that may contribute to suicidal behaviour. Two Munich depression studies were used as replication cohorts to test the most strongly associated SNPs. No SNP was associated at genome-wide significance level. For the quantitative trait, evidence of association was detected at GFRA1, a receptor for the neurotrophin GDRA ($p = 2e-06$). For the discrete trait of suicide attempt, SNPs in KIAA1244 and RGS18 attained *p*-values of <5e-6. None of these SNPs showed evidence for replication in the additional cohorts tested. Candidate gene analysis provided some support for a polymorphism in NTRK2, which was previously associated with suicidality.

*Conclusions/Significance:* This study provides a genome-wide assessment of possible genetic contribution to suicidal behaviour in depression but indicates a genetic architecture of multiple genes with small effects. Large cohorts will be required to dissect this further.

## Comment

*Main findings:* This multicentre study aimed to identify genes that underlie suicidality by performing a Genome Wide Association Study (GWAS) and investigating candidate genes for susceptibility to suicidality. They carried out a GWAS for both suicide ideation and behaviour in 2,023 subjects with DSM-IV and/or ICD-10 diagnosis of Major Depressive Disorder in the RADIANT studies. However, they failed to detect significant evidence of an association at a genome-wide level for either suicidality measure. Even so, SNP (single-nucleotide polymorphism) in 3 genetic regions reached their threshold for suggestive evidence of association: in GFRA1, when analysing suicidality as a quantitative trait and 2 regions (in KIAA1244, and between RGS18 and FAM5C) when analysing the discrete trait of suicide attempt, but fell short of the required significance for multiple testing across genes.

*Implications:* The studies in search for vulnerability genes of suicidal behaviours have found several candidate genes in the past years. However, associations have been fairly weak and none have survived replication testing in different patient cohorts. The authors suggest that further studies with large samples of homogenous patients are needed in order to replicate these findings and to determine whether the suggestive signals detected are true effects or false positives. The findings also draw attention to the necessity of being replicated in large independent MDD cohorts to assess their reliability.

# The gender paradox in suicidal behavior and its impact on the suicidal process

Schrijvers DL, Bollen J, Sabbe BG (Belgium)

*Journal of Affective Disorders.* Published online: 6 May 2011. doi:10.1016/j.jad.2011.03.050, 2011

*Background:* An important gender difference has been reported regarding suicidal behavior with an overrepresentation of females in nonfatal suicidal behavior and a preponderance of males in completed suicide, also known as the 'gender paradox of suicidal behavior'. The concept of a 'suicidal process' classifies suicidal behavior chronologically; this process starts with suicidal ideation and then implies a progression of suicidality ranging from suicidal ideation over plans to suicide attempts and finally fatal suicide.

*Aims/Methods:* The current paper aims to deepen the knowledge on the gender paradox by collecting and discussing the recent literature on this topic: the most relevant, impacting gender-related factors will be discussed within the suicidal process concept.

*Results:* Several factors had a gender-dependent impact on suicidal behavior: psychosocial life stressors such as stressful life events but also sociodemographical or socio-economical factors, and sexual abuse. The gender differences in psychiatric (co)morbidity and in response to or attitude towards antidepressant treatment also appear to have an impact. Furthermore, not only suicide methods but also the gender-dependent variation in reporting suicide has an influence. Finally, the gender differences in help seeking behavior as well as region-dependent cultural beliefs and societal attitudes are discussed.

*Conclusions:* Especially life-events seem to exert an important influence at the beginning of a suicidal process, whereas the other factors occur at a further stage in the process, however without a fixed chronology. Also, the duration of the suicidal process is much shorter in male than in females. Finally, some implications with regard to clinical practice and suicide prevention are suggested.

## Comment

*Main findings:* The 'gender paradox' is a term used to describe the higher burden of fatal suicidal behaviour in males and the greater proportion of non-fatal suicidal behaviours in females[1]. The authors of this paper provide a review of published literature on the gender-specific biological, social and cultural factors that may underpin these differences. Relationship breakdown and job-loss are notable psycho-social factors that may place males at elevated risk of death, particularly as westernised norms of masculinity are tied to notions of economic success and emotional stoicism. The authors provide evidence that males who die by suicide more frequently have substance-related problems, personality disorders, and bipolar disorders, while a larger proportion of female suicides have suffered from conditions such as anorexia nervosa. A number of other factors may explain the higher number of suicide deaths in males; including the possibility of under-diagnosed depression, less than optimal treatment in psychiatric services, and poorer compliance in treatment. Last, males are more likely to use highly lethal suicide methods (such as hanging and firearms) that are less likely to be reported and miscoded as accidental deaths. To some extent, these gender differences may impact the length of the 'suicide process' from ideation, to attempt to death by suicide.

*Implications:* This paper suggests the need for better recognition of the range of gender specific risks associated with suicidal behaviours. This point has also been raised in a recent position statement by Suicide Prevention Australia[2] which calls for the development of a national health and wellbeing strategy for men that emphasises improved resources for help-seeking, removal of barriers to care, and the elimination of the negative aspects of gender stereotyping. Aside from this, it may be necessary to alter the environmental context of psychiatric care to increase the likelihood of males being more compliant to psychiatric treatment. These gender specific issues are particularly important considerations in Australia, which has a gender ratio of over 3.5 male suicides to 1 female suicide[3]. At the same time, it is necessary to invest research and intervention efforts into measures aimed at reducing the greater number of non-fatal suicidal behaviours among women.

## Endnotes

1. Cannetto SS, Sakinofsky I (1998). The gender paradox in suicide. *Suicide & Life-Threatening Behavior* 28, 1–23.
2. Suicide Prevention Australia (2008). *Position statement: Men and suicide: Future directions.* Retrieved: 12 October 2011 from www.suicidepreventionaust.org.
3. Australian Bureau of Statistics (2011). *Causes of Death 2009.* Cat. No. 3303.0. Canberra: ABS.

# Youth and young adult suicide: A study of life trajectory

Séguin M, Renaud J, Lesage A, Robert M, Turecki G (Canada)

*Journal of Psychiatry Research* 45, 863–870, 2011

*Objectives:* Explore the unique developmental challenges and early adversity faced by youth and young adult who died of suicide.

*Method:* Sixty-seven suicide victims (SG) were compared with 56 living control with no suicidal ideations in the last year, matched for age, gender, and geographical region. Mixed methods were used: consensus DSM-IV diagnoses were formulated based on Structured Clinical Interview for DSM-IV (SCID)-I and -II interviews complemented by medical charts. Life calendar method was conducted with closest third party informant. Life-history calendar served to measure life events and adversity throughout the life course and were analysed by attributing burden of adversity score per five-year segment, which was then cluster-analysed to define suicide victim profiles.

*Results:* During the last year, mood disorders, abuse and dependence disorders, and anxiety disorder were between 8 and 63 times more likely to be present in the suicide group. Between 0 and 4 years old, 50% of children in the SG were exposed to abuse, physical and/or sexual violence; 60% between 5 and 9 years old; and by the time they were 10–14 years old, 77% were exposed to these forms of violence. In the control group, the respective figures were 14%, 18% and 34%. In the suicide group, the trajectories leading to suicide are different as we observe 2 different subgroups, 1 with early-onset and 1 with later-onset of adversity. To a large extent, people in the suicide group were exposed to major adversity and they were more likely to present cumulative comorbid disorders.

## Comment

*Main findings:* This Canadian case-control study examined the possible link between the presence of violence and suicide deaths in youth and young adults. The study also investigated whether early adversity would impact differently on suicide victims compared to living controls. Results found differences in the life trajectories of the suicide group compared to living controls. Young people in the suicide group had more problems over their life course, which tended to start at an early age. The most important adverse events were difficulties in the relationship with parents, characterised by neglect, discord and violence. Furthermore, the lack of a protective adult relationship seemed to place young children at greater risk of suicide. It is possible that biological predispositions compound adverse life events and develop into mental health problems. These issues may accumulate into difficulties in the professional domain, with financial and legal difficulties by the time they are teens and young adults.

However, not all suicide victims followed the same developmental trajectory. The authors identified 2 trajectories of suicides on the basis of longitudinal patterns of adversities. Trajectory 1 was clearly characterised by severe developmental difficulties and a lack of adult protection, starting at a very early age, creating a spiral of events and mental health problems throughout the life cycle. However, Trajectory 2 may be characterised by a slower decline over time possibly due to a lesser harmful environment coupled with adaptive efforts. While experiencing family tension, discord and early learning difficulties, they had less behavioural difficulties in school in comparison to the Trajectory 1 group. Authors suggested that the absence of behavioural difficulties could have elicited less social stigmatisation and created more social connections.

*Implications:* This study is important as it among the first to analyse life trajectories of young people using comprehensive psychological autopsy methods. The difficulties identified during the life course of young persons enabled the researchers to suggest potential time points and pathways of intervention at early stages of childhood. As the authors indicate, people with a number of early adversities will not inevitably die by suicide. These children should be targeted and interventions should be planned for them and their families at a younger age, to reduce possible vulnerability. Consequently, clinicians (including social and other youth workers) should be trained to detect the presence of early adversities, especially abuse, neglect and physical and sexual violence among vulnerable families. Environmental interventions, including individual, family, school and community, should be used to alter risk factors and booster resilience.

# Predicting self- and other-directed violence among discharged psychiatric patients: The roles of anger and psychopathic traits

Swogger MT, Walsh Z, Homaifar BY, Caine ED, Conner KR (USA)

*Psychological Medicine.* Published online: 18 July 2011. doi: 10.1017/S0033291711001243, 2011

*Background:* We examined the extent to which trait anger and psychopathic traits predicted post-discharge self-directed violence (SDV) and other-directed violence (ODV) among psychiatric patients.

*Method:* Participants were 851 psychiatric patients sampled from in-patient hospitals for the MacArthur Violence Risk Assessment Study (MVRAS). Participants were administered baseline interviews at the hospital and 5 follow-up interviews in the community at approximately 10-week intervals. Psychopathy and trait anger were assessed with the Psychopathy Checklist: Screening Version (PSC:SV) and the Novaco Anger Scale (NAS) respectively. SDV was assessed during follow-ups with participants and ODV was assessed during interviews with participants and collateral informants. Psychopathy facets and anger were entered in logistic regression models to predict membership in 1 of 4 groups indicating violence status during follow-up: (1) SDV, (2) ODV, (3) co-occurring violence (COV), and (4) no violence.

*Results:* Anger predicted membership in all 3 violence groups relative to a non-violent reference group. In unadjusted models, all psychopathy facets predicted ODV and COV during follow-up. In adjusted models, interpersonal and antisocial traits of psychopathy predicted membership in the ODV group whereas only antisocial traits predicted membership in the COV group.

*Conclusions:* Although our results provide evidence for a broad role for trait anger in predicting SDV and ODV among discharged psychiatric patients, they suggest that unique patterns of psychopathic traits differentially predict violence toward self and others. The measurement of anger and facets of psychopathy during discharge planning for psychiatric patients may provide clinicians with information regarding risk for specific types of violence.

## Comment

*Main findings:* The authors of this paper suggest that behavioural factors and externalising psychopathology determine whether an individual chooses to engage in 'other-directed violence' (ODV) or 'self-directed violence' (SDV). This article focuses on 2 specific aspects of externalising behaviours that create risk of SDV, comparative to ODV: Psychopathology (a personality syndrome characterised by a diminished capacity for remorse, impulsive behaviour and superficial charm) and interpersonally violent behaviour such as anger. The study by Swogger and colleagues seeks to examine whether these broad psychopathological traits are related to both SDV and ODV, or whether SDV and ODV are predicted by unique behavioural factors.

Information for this study was drawn from interviews with patients in 3 acute inpatient departments ($n = 851$). Results showed that 29% of these persons had attempted to hurt themselves (i.e. SDV) at least once over a follow-up period of ten weeks and 28% committed ODV. Antisocial features of psychopathology and anger predicted ODV and co-occurring violence (i.e., COV, which refers to both SDV and ODV) relative to SDV alone. Anger (measured in terms of inclination towards anger reactions) was found to be a significant predictor SDV, as well as ODV and COV, even after adjusting for substance use and demographic factors. This suggests that trait levels of anger may increase the risk of both SDV and ODV. Individuals with a criminal behaviour and poor behavioural controls are also at risk of SDV and ODV. Among these persons, those who do not display superficial charm, pathological lying, and grandiosity may be more likely to engage in self-harm.

The main limitation of this study was that it represented a specific group of psychiatric patients (inclusion in the study necessitated a diagnosis of schizophrenia, schizo-affective disorder, dysthymia, mania, depression, brief reactive psychosis, alcohol or drug abuse or dependence, delusional disorder, or personality disorder). At the same time, a unique feature was its ability to assess anger in addition to psychopathology as a predictor of SDV.

*Implications:* Past studies suggest importance of biological factors in anger, suicide and aggressive behaviours, but have not measured the possible influences of personality features[1]. Further, past investigations have not usually considered the role of these factors in relation to a spectrum of violent behaviours – inclusive of suicidal behaviour and violence against others. This study finds that certain 'violent' psychiatric patients are particularly at risk of suicide, which indicates the need for better risk assessment and interventions designed to reduce aggressive behaviours. As identified by Swogger et al, violence is likely to be multifaceted and often inter-related with underlying personality traits.

## Endnotes

1. Giegling I, Hartmann AM, Möller HJ, Rujescu D (2006). Anger- and aggression-Related traits are associated with polymorphisms in the 5-HT-2A gene. *Journal of Affective Disorders* 96, 75–81.

# Familial clustering of suicide risk: A total population study of 11.4 million individuals

Tidemalm D, Runeson B, Waern M, Frisell T, Carlström E, Lichtenstein P, Långström N (Sweden)

*Psychological Medicine.* Published online: 1 June 2011. doi: 10.1017/S0033291711000833, 2011

*Background:* Research suggests that suicidal behaviour is aggregated in families. However, due to methodological limitations, including small sample sizes, the strength and pattern of this aggregation remains uncertain.

*Method:* We examined the familial clustering of completed suicide in a Swedish total population sample. We linked the Cause of Death and Multi-Generation Registers and compared suicide rates among relatives of all 83,951 suicide decedents from 1952–2003 with those among relatives of population controls.

*Results:* Patterns of familial aggregation of suicide among relatives to suicide decedents suggested genetic influences on suicide risk; the risk among full siblings (odds ratio 3.1, 95% confidence interval 2.8–3.5, 50% genetic similarity) was higher than that for maternal half-siblings (1.7, 1.1–2.7, 25% genetic similarity), despite similar environmental exposure. Further, monozygotic twins (100% genetic similarity) had a higher risk than dizygotic twins (50% genetic similarity) and cousins (12.5% genetic similarity) had higher suicide risk than controls. Shared (familial) environmental influences were also indicated; siblings to suicide decedents had a higher risk than offspring (both 50% genetically identical but siblings having a more shared environment, 3.1, 2.8–3.5 v. 2.0, 1.9–2.2), and maternal half-siblings had a higher risk than paternal half-siblings (both 50% genetically identical but the former with a more shared environment). Although comparisons of twins and half-siblings had overlapping confidence intervals, they were supported by sensitivity analyses, also including suicide attempts.

*Conclusions:* Familial clustering of suicide is primarily influenced by genetic and also shared environmental factors. The family history of suicide should be considered when assessing suicide risk in clinical settings or designing and administering preventive interventions.

## Comment

*Main findings:* This registry-based case-control study examined familial risks of completed suicide in the total population of Sweden using data from 1952–2003. The study design allowed researchers to assess relatives at varying distances from those who died by suicide. For each suicide case and sibling pair, 5 living control sibling pairs were selected and matched by gender and birth year. Results indicate strong evidence of familial suicide risk in relatives at varying genetic and environmental distance from each other, including half-siblings, grandchildren, cousins and spouses. For example, suicide risk for full siblings was significantly higher than for maternal half-siblings, regardless of similar environmental exposure. However, the fact that adopted children had higher risk than controls suggests that environmental factors also play an important role in suicidality. These findings suggest that suicide is influenced by both genetic and shared environmental factors. The authors suggest several underlying explanations for familial suicide risk, including a shared genetic component could that involve increased impulsive aggression, and a propensity to react with aggression or hostility when frustrated or provoked. Further, personality traits including neuroticism or neuro-developmental vulnerabilities involving impaired working memory or executive functioning (resulting in poor problem solving) could also be involved. However, environmental factors may increase or decrease a person's existing preposition for suicide, as may inadequate communication style or other negative affects, including those following the bereavement of a spouse or relative from suicide.

*Implications:* The authors of this study indicate the need for future epidemiological studies with adequate sample size and statistical power. Currently, various strategies have been proposed in research to gain more specific knowledge on how gene variants, development and environment are associated with suicidal behaviour[1,2]. These include refining the phenotype for suicidality and considering the different possible pathways through which these link to self-destructive behaviour. Consequently, endophenotypes (intermediate phenotypes between genes and a more overt phenotype or outcome), such as certain personality traits or altered neurocognitive function, should be the concern of future research. Further, the family history of suicide must be considered when assessing the suicide risk in clinical practice or when designing and administering preventive interventions.

## Endnotes

1. Mann JJ, Arango VA, Avenevoli S, Brent DA, Champagne FA, Clayton P et al. (2009). Candidate endophenotypes for genetic studies of suicidal behavior. *Biological Psychiatry* 65, 556–563.
2. Brezo J, Bureau A, Mérette C, Jomphe V, Barker ED, Vitaro F et al. (2010). Differences and similarities in the serotonergic diathesis for suicide attempts and mood disorders: A 22-year longitudinal gene-environment study. *Molecular Psychiatry* 15, 831–843.

# Now what should I do? Primary care physicians' responses to older adults expressing thoughts of suicide

Vannoy SD, Tai-Seale M, Duberstein P, Eaton LJ, Cook MA (USA)

*Journal of General Internal Medicine* 26, 1005–1011, 2011

*Background:* Many older adults who die by suicide have had recent contact with a primary care physician. As the risk-assessment and referral process for suicide is not readily comparable to procedures for other high-risk behaviors, it is important to identify areas in need of quality improvement (QI).

*Objective:* Identify patterns in physician-patient communication regarding suicide to inform QI interventions.

*Design:* Qualitative thematic analysis of video-taped clinical encounters in which suicide was discussed.

*Participants:* Adult primary care patients ($n = 385$) 65 years and older and their primary care physicians.

*Results:* Mental health was discussed in 22% of encounters ($n = 85$), with suicide content found in less than 2% ($n = 6$). Three patterns of conversation were characterised: (1) Arguing that 'Life's Not That Bad.' In this scenario, the physician strives to convince the patient that suicide is unwarranted, which results in mutual fatigue and discouragement. (2) 'Engaging in Chitchat.' Here the physician addresses psychosocial matters in a seemingly aimless manner with no clear therapeutic goal. This results in a superficial and misleading connection that buries meaningful risk assessment amidst small talk. (3) 'Identify, assess, and…?' This pattern is characterised by acknowledging distress, communicating concern, eliciting information, and making treatment suggestions, but lacks clearly articulated treatment planning or structured follow-up.

*Conclusions:* The physicians in this sample recognised and implicitly acknowledged suicide risk in their older patients, but all seemed unable to go beyond mere assessment. The absence of clearly articulated treatment plans may reflect a lack of a coherent framework for managing suicide risk, insufficient clinical skills, and availability of mental health specialty support required to address suicide risk effectively. To respond to suicide's numerous challenges to the primary care delivery system, QI strategies will require changes to physician education and may require enhancing practice support.

## Comment

*Main findings:* Similar to other Western countries, Australia has an aging population[1]. Considering the higher suicide risk in older adults; there will be increasing need to assess suicidality in elderly patients among primary care physicians. This innovative study focused on analysing physician–patient communications about suicide using videotaped visits. Suicide was discussed in 6 visits out of a total of 85 consultations in which mental health was addressed. The authors documented 3 main patterns of communication between doctors and patients: (1)

Argumentative: Life's Not That Bad; (2) Superficial: engaging in Chitchat; and (3) Insufficient: Identify, assess, and…? Results indicate that some primary care physicians were able to identify suicidality, but in general tended to 'manoeuvre around the topic' rather than directly addressing suididality. Further, the study findings suggest that a basic expression of concern for patient well-being was not likely to be helpful. In all cases, it appeared that physicians were concerned about their patient's well being at the time of the consultation (as evidenced by their giving substantial attention to psychosocial factors) but failed to make follow up appointments after the visit. The authors suggest that physicians who take greater time with their patients are more likely to discover suicide ideation and address it. However, they all seemed to be unable to go beyond mere assessment.

*Implications:* Primary care physicians play a crucial role in identifying and treating people with suicidal ideation. However, the authors of this study identified a lack of risk assessment and treatment planning when a patient discloses suicidality. This suggests the need for increased attention to these issues as well as to treatment planning and the provision of structured follow-ups in the primary health care setting. Adapting a core element of managing chronic illness in primary care, such as longitudinal monitoring and follow-up, along with timely referral to specialised care, may result in better patient engagement. The development of these approaches will require changes to physician education and enhancing practice support. Training of physicians has been proven to be effective in reducing suicides in the communities[1].

This study has important implications in Australian context. An Australian study found that many medical students and GPs rated themselves as least competent on skills-based suicide prevention capabilities[2]. They also identified that 80% of Australian Medical Schools provide some form of suicide prevention education, the quantity and quality is diverse. This suggests the education about suicide may increase a doctors perceived competency in risk assessment and treatment.

## Endnotes

1. Australian Bureau of Statistics (2010). *Population by Age and Sex, Australian States and Territories, June 2010.* Cat. No. 3201.0. Canberra: ABS.
2. Mann JJ, Apter A, Bertolote J, Beautrais A, Currier D, Haas A et al. (2005). Suicide prevention strategies: A systematic review. *JAMA* 294, 2064–2074.
3. Hawgood JL, Krysinska KE, Ide N, De Leo D (2008). Is suicide prevention properly taught in medical schools? *Medical Teacher* 30, 287–295.

# Recommended Readings

## Does Attention Deficit Hyperactivity Disorder increase the risk of suicide attempts?

Agosti V, Chen Y, Levin FR (USA)

*Journal of Affective Disorders* 133, 595–599, 2011

*Objective:* To determine if Attention Deficit Hyperactivity Disorder (ADHD) is a risk factor for suicide attempts.

*Methods:* Data were drawn from the National Comorbidity Replication Survey (NCS-R), a nationally representative sample of adults ($N = 8,098$).

*Results:* Of the 365 adults with current ADHD, 16% attempted suicide. After controlling for the presence of comorbid disorders, logistic regression analyses revealed that the ADHD was not a not a strong predictor of suicide attempts; having 1 or more comorbid disorders was associated with fourfold to twelvefold elevated risk.

*Limitations:* The small sample size of respondents with ADHD who attempted suicide significantly reduced the probability of determining which specific comorbid disorders were correlated with parasuicide.

*Conclusions:* Early treatment of ADHD and comorbidity may reduce the risk of suicide attempts and improve its prognosis.

## The social contagion effect of suicidal behavior in adolescents: Does it really exist?

Ali MM, Dwyer DS, Rizzo JA (USA)

*Journal of Mental Health Policy and Economics* 14, 3–12, 2011

*Background:* Suicide is the third leading cause of death among adolescents and a non-trivial percentage of adolescents report knowing someone who has attempted suicide. In light of this, a growing body of literature has explored whether suicidal behavior in 1 person may be imitated by others in their social networks.

*Aim:* We seek to determine the extent to which suicidal behavior in individuals is influenced by suicidal behaviors of their peer and family members.

*Methodology:* Using a nationally-representative sample of adolescents, we employ multivariate regression analysis with controls for known factors associated with suicidal behaviors to help isolate the effects of peer and family members on suicidal behaviors. Our methodology allows us to account for environmental confounders, simultaneity and to a limited extent, non-random peer selection. Our peer measures are drawn from the nomination of close friends by the individuals and suicidal behaviors among the peer group were constructed using the peers' own responses.

*Results and Discussion:* We find that a 10% increase in suicide attempts by family members were associated with a 2.13% and 1.23% increase in adolescent suicidal ideation and attempts, respectively. Our results also show that a 10% increase in peer suicidal ideation and attempts lead to a 0.7% and 0.3% increase in such behavior by the individuals. However, these positive associations between peer and individual suicide behavior become smaller and insignificant after adjustments were made for environmental confounders and peer selection.

*Limitations:* Although we are able to establish the overall importance of environmental confounding factors, we are unable to identify the specific components or characteristics of the surroundings that can explain suicidality. The complex relationships between peer selection and suicidality also limit the determination of causality.

*Conclusions and Implications:* An increase in suicidal behavior by family members is positively associated with suicidal behavior among adolescents and effective policies aimed at reducing suicidal rates should consider these impacts. However, attributing correlations in suicidal behaviors among peers to social network effects should be undertaken with caution, especially when environmental confounders are not adequately controlled for in the analysis.

*Future Research:* Recent studies have found evidence that family connectedness and parent-child relationships have a significant impact in deterring risky behaviors among adolescents. This motivates future work aimed at designing policies that would utilise these findings in order to effectively reduce suicidal behavior among adolescents.

## Mortality rates in patients with anorexia nervosa and other eating disorders: A meta-analysis of 36 studies

Arcelus J, Mitchell AJ, Wales J, Nielsen S (UK)
*Archives of General Psychiatry* 68, 724–731, 2011

*Background:* Brief depressive episodes (BDEs) cause psychosocial impairment and increased risk of suicide, worsening the outcome and long-term course of affective disorders. The aim of this naturalistic observational study was to assess the frequency of BDEs and very brief depressive episodes (VBDEs) and their impact on clinical outcome in a sample of patients with major depressive disorder (MDD) and bipolar disorder (BD).

*Method:* Seventy patients with a diagnosis of MDD or BD were followed up and monthly visited for a period of 12months, assessing the eventual occurrence of BDEs and/or VBDEs. Clinical and demographic variables of the total sample and of the groups divided according to the presence of BDEs or VBDEs were collected and compared by one-way ANOVAs. Hamilton Depression Rating Scale 21 items (HDRS), Young Mania Rating Scale (YMRS), Clinical Global Impression (severity of illness) (CGIs) and the Short Form Health Survey (SF-36-item 1) were administered at baseline and logistic regression was performed to evaluate whether baseline scores were predictive of the onset of BDEs or VBDEs.

*Results:* BDEs (88.6% of the total sample), VBDEs (44.3% of the total sample) and BDEs + VBDEs (40.0% of the total sample) were found to occur frequently across the sample. BDE patients showed more death thoughts during major depressive episodes ($\chi(2) = 4.14$, df = 1, $p = 0.04$, Phi = 0.24) compared to patients without BDEs. Indeed VBDE patients showed a higher rate of hospitalisation ($\chi(2) = 5.71$, df = 1, $p = 0.031$, phi = 0.29), a more frequent prescription of a combined treatment ($\chi(2) = 13.07$, df = 7, $p = 0.03$, phi = 0.43) and higher scores at SF-36 item 1 (F = 6.65, $p = 0.01$) compared to patients without VBDEs. Finally, higher SF-36 item 1 scores were found to be predictive of VBDEs (odds ratio = 2.81, $p = 0.03$).

*Discussion:* Major depressives, either unipolar or bipolar, with BDEs or VBDEs showed a worse outcome, represented by a more severe psychopathology and higher rates of hospitalisation. VBDEs were predicted by a negative subjective general health perception. Studies with larger samples and longer follow-up are warranted to confirm the results of the present study.

## Cluster hanging suicides in the young in South Australia

Austin AE, van den Heuvel C, Byard RW (Australia)
*Journal of Forensic Sciences.* Published online: 25 July 2011. doi: 10.1111/j.1556-4029.2011.01840.x, 2011

A retrospective review of hanging suicides in individuals aged ≤ 17 years was undertaken at Forensic Science South Australia, Australia, over 2 5-year periods: 1995–1999 and 2005–2009. Seven cases of hanging suicides were identified from 1995 to 1999, with a further 14 cases from 2005 to 2009, an increase of 100% ($p < 0.001$). Hanging accounted for 33.3% of all suicides in this age group (7/21) from 1995 to 1999, compared with 93.3% of the total number of suicides (14/15) in the second 5-year period. In contrast, Australian national data from 1998 and 2008 showed a 30% decrease in hanging suicides in the young, from 1 case/100,000 population in 1998 to 0.7 in 2008. Cluster suicides occur in the young and are often initiated by direct communication. As it is possible that Internet-based social sites may facilitate this phenomenon, investigations should include an evaluation of the victim's Internet access given the potential risk of similar actions by peers.

## Opposite effects of suicidality and lithium on gray matter volumes in bipolar depression

Benedetti F, Radaelli D, Poletti S, Locatelli C, Falini A, Colombo C, Smeraldi E (Italy)
*Journal of Affective Disorders.* Published online: 31 July 2011. doi:10.1016/j.jad.2011.07.006, 2011

*Background:* Mood disorders are associated with the highest increase of attempted and completed suicide. Suicidality in major depressive disorder and in schizophrenia has been associated with reduced gray matter volumes in orbitofrontal cortex. Lithium reduces the suicide risk of patients with bipolar disorder (BD) to the same levels of the general population, and can increase GM volumes. We studied the effect of a positive history of attempted suicide and ongoing lithium treatment on regional GM volumes of patients affected by bipolar depression.

*Methods:* With a correlational design, we studied 57 currently depressed inpatients with bipolar disorder: 19 with and 38 without a positive history of suicide attempts, 39 unmedicated and 18 with ongoing lithium treatment. Total and regional gray matter volumes were assessed using voxel-based morphometry.

*Results:* Total GM volume is inversely correlated with depression severity. A positive history of suicide attempts was associated with higher stress in early life. Suicide attempters showed reduced GM volumes in several brain areas including dorsolateral prefrontal cortex, orbitofrontal cortex, anterior cingulate, superior temporal cortex, parieto-occipital cortex, and basal ganglia. Long term lithium treatment was associated with increased GM volumes in the same areas where suicide was associated with decreased GM.

*Conclusions:* Reduced GM volumes in critical cortical areas of suicidal patients could be a biological correlate of an impaired ability to associate choices and outcomes and to plan goal-directed behaviors based on a lifetime historical perspective, which, coupled with mood-congruent depressive cognitive distortions, could lead to more hopelessness and suicide. Lithium could exert its specific therapeutic effect on suicide by acting in the same areas.

## Suicidal behavior and firearm access: Results from the second injury control and risk survey

Betz ME, Barber C, Miller M (USA)
*Suicide and Life-Threatening Behavior* 41, 384–391, 2011

The association between home firearms and the likelihood and nature of suicidal thoughts and plans was examined using the Second Injury Control and Risk Survey, a 2001–2003 representative telephone survey of U.S. households. Of 9,483 respondents, 7.4% reported past-year suicidal thoughts, 21.3% with a plan. Similar proportions of those with and without a home firearm reported suicidal thoughts, plans, and attempts. Among respondents with suicidal plans, the odds of reporting a plan involving a firearm were over 7 times greater among those with firearms at home, compared with those without firearms at home. The results suggest people with home firearms may not be more likely to be suicidal, but when suicidal they may be more likely to plan suicide by firearm.

## Suicide and traumatic brain injury among individuals seeking veterans health administration services

Brenner LA, Ignacio RV, Blow FC (USA)

*The Journal of Head Trauma Rehabilitation* 26, 257–264, 2011

*Objective:* To examine associations between history of traumatic brain injury (TBI) diagnosis and death by suicide among individuals receiving care within the Veterans Health Administration (VHA).

*Method:* Individuals who received care between fiscal years 2001 to 2006 were included in analyses. Cox proportional hazards survival models for time to suicide, with time-dependent covariates, were utilised. Covariance sandwich estimators were used to adjust for the clustered nature of the data, with patients nested within VHA facilities. Analyses included all patients with a history of TBI ($n = 49626$) plus a 5% random sample of patients without TBI ($n = 389053$). Of those with a history of TBI, 105 died by suicide. Models were adjusted for demographic and psychiatric covariates.

*Results:* Veterans with a history of TBI were 1.55 (95% confidence interval [CI], 1.24–1.92) times more likely to die by suicide than those without a history of TBI. Analyses by TBI severity were also conducted, and they suggested that in comparison to those without an injury history, those with (1) concussion/cranial fracture were 1.98 times more likely (95% CI, 1.39–2.82) to die by suicide and (2) cerebral contusion/traumatic intracranial hemorrhage were 1.34 times more likely (95% CI, 1.09–1.64) to die by suicide. This increased risk was not explained by the presence of psychiatric disorders or demographic factors.

*Conclusions:* Among VHA users, those with a diagnosis of TBI were at greater risk for suicide than those without this diagnosis. Further research is indicated to identify evidence-based means of assessment and treatment for those with TBI and suicidal behavior.

## Influence of social and material individual and area deprivation on suicide mortality among 2.7 million Canadians: A prospective study

Burrows S, Auger N, Gamache P, St-Laurent D, Hamel D (Canada)

*BMC Public Health* 11, 577, 2011

*Background:* Few studies have investigated how area-level deprivation influences the relationship between individual disadvantage and suicide mortality. The aim of this study was to examine individual measures of material and social disadvantage in relation to suicide mortality in Canada and to determine whether these relationships were modified by area deprivation.

*Methods:* Using the 1991–2001 Canadian Census Mortality Follow-up Study cohort ($N = 2,685,400$), measures of individual social (civil status, family structure, living alone) and material (education, income, employment) disadvantage were entered into Cox proportional hazard models to calculate hazard ratios (HR) and 95% confidence intervals (CI) for male and female suicide mortality. Two indices of area deprivation were computed — one capturing social, and the other material, dimensions — and models were run separately for high versus low deprivation.

*Results:* After accounting for individual and area characteristics, individual social and material disadvantage were associated with higher suicide mortality, especially for individuals not employed, not married, with low education and low income. Associations between social and material area deprivation and suicide mortality largely disappeared upon adjustment for individual-level disadvantage. In stratified analyses, suicide risk was greater for low income females in socially deprived areas and males living alone in materially deprived areas, and there was no evidence of other modifying effects of area deprivation.

*Conclusions:* Individual disadvantage was associated with suicide mortality, particularly for males. With some exceptions, there was little evidence that area deprivation modified the influence of individual disadvantage on suicide risk. Prevention strategies should primarily focus on individuals who are unemployed or out of the labour force, and have low education or income. Individuals with low income or who are living alone in deprived areas should also be targeted.

# Young people's risk of suicide attempts after contact with a psychiatric department — A nested case-control design using Danish register data

Christiansen E, Larsen KJ (Denmark)

*The Journal of Child Psychology and Psychiatry.* Published online: 12 May 2011. doi: 10.1111/j.1469-7610.2011.02405.x., 2011

*Background:* There seems to be an increased risk of children and adolescents committing or attempting suicide after contact with a psychiatric department. Children and adolescents living in families with low socio-economic status (SES) might have an especially increased suicide attempt risk.

*Methods:* A complete extraction of Danish register data for every individual born in the period 1983–1989 was made. Of these 403,431 individuals, 3,465 had attempted suicide. In order to control for confounder effects from gender, age and calendar-time, a nested case-control study was designed. A total population of 72,765 individuals was used to analyse the risk of suicide attempts after contact with a psychiatric department. The case-control data were analysed using conditional logistic regression.

*Results:* This study shows that a child/adolescent's risk of suicide attempt peaks immediately after discharge from last contact with a psychiatric department. The risk of suicide attempt is highest for children and adolescents suffering from personality disorders, depression and substance use disorders. Children and adolescents with previous contact with a psychiatric department and parental income in the lowest third have a significantly higher risk of suicide attempt. Suicide attempters were more likely to have been given several different diagnoses and several different psychopharmacological drugs prior to their attempted suicide.

*Conclusions:* The findings in this study highlight the need for psychopathology assessment in every case of attempted suicide. This study also shows that well-known risk factors such as contact with a psychiatric department do not affect all individuals in the same way. Individuals from families with low SES had the highest risk. This suggests that the presence of factors influencing both vulnerability and resiliency, e.g., family level of SES, needs to be included in the assessment.

## Preference of lethal methods is not the only cause for higher suicide rates in males

Cibis A, Mergl R, Bramesfeld A, Althaus D, Niklewski G, Schmidtke A, Hegerl U (Germany)

*Journal of Affective Disorders.* Published online: 19 September 2011. doi:10.1016/j.jad.2011.08.032, 2011

*Background:* In most countries worldwide suicide rates are higher for males whereas attempted suicide rates are higher for females. The aim is to investigate if the choice of more lethal methods by males explains gender differences in suicide rates.

*Methods:* Data on completed and attempted suicides were collected ($n = 3235$, Nuremberg and Wuerzburg, years 2000–2004). The research question was analysed by comparing the method-specific case fatality (= completed suicides/completed+attempted suicides) for males and females.

*Results:* Among the events captured, men chose high-risk methods like hanging significantly more often than women ($\phi = -0.27$; $p < 0.001$). However, except for drowning, case fatalities were higher for males than for females within each method. This was most apparent in 'hanging' (men 83.5%, women 55.3%; $\phi = -0.28$; $p < 0.001$) and 'poisoning by drugs' (men 7.2%, women 3.4%; $\phi = -0.09$; $p < 0.001$).

*Limitations:* The sample size ($n = 3235$) was not enough for comparing method and gender specific case fatalities with a fine-meshed stratification regarding age.

*Conclusions:* Higher suicide rates in males not only result from the choice of more lethal methods. Other factors have to be considered.

# Sexual orientation and mortality among US men aged 17 to 59 years: Results from the National Health and Nutrition Examination Survey III

Cochran SD, Mays VM (USA)

*American Journal of Public Health* 101, 1133–1138, 2011

We investigated associations between minority sexual orientation and mortality among US men. We used data from a retrospective cohort of 5574 men aged 17 to 59 years, first interviewed in the National Health and Nutrition Examination Survey III (NHANES III; 1988–1994) and then followed for mortality status up to 18 years later. We classified men into 3 groups: those reporting (1) any same-sex sexual partners (men who have sex with men [MSM]; $n = 85$), (2) only female sexual partners ($n = 5292$), and (3) no sexual partners ($n = 197$). Groups were then compared for all-cause mortality, HIV-related mortality, suicide-related mortality, and non-HIV-related mortality. Compared with heterosexual men, MSM evidenced greater all-cause mortality. Approximately 13% of MSM died from HIV-related causes compared with 0.1% of men reporting only female partners. However, mortality risk from non-HIV-related causes, including suicide, was not elevated among MSM. In the United States, the HIV epidemic continues to be the major contributing factor for premature death rates among MSM. Cohorts such as the NHANES III offer a unique opportunity to track the effects of the HIV epidemic on this population.

# Stressful life events and suicidal behavior in adults with alcohol use disorders: Role of event severity, timing, and type

Conner KR, Houston RJ, Swogger MT, Conwell Y, You S, He H, Gamble SA, Watts A, Duberstein PR (USA)

*Drug and Alcohol Dependence.* Published online: 10 August 2011. doi:10.1016/j.drugalcdep.2011.07. 013, 2011

*Background:* Stressful life events (SLEs) play a key role in suicidal behavior among adults with alcohol use disorders (AUD), yet there are meager data on the severity of SLEs preceding suicidal behavior or the timing of such events.

*Method:* Patients in residential substance use treatment who made a recent suicide attempt (cases, $n = 101$) and non-suicidal controls matched for site ($n = 101$) were recruited. SLEs that occurred within 30 days of the attempt and on the day of the attempt in cases were compared to SLEs that occurred in the corresponding periods in controls. SLEs were categorised by type (interpersonal, non-interpersonal) and severity (major, minor) and were dated to assess timing. Degree of planning of suicide attempts was also assessed.

*Results:* Major interpersonal SLEs conferred risk for a suicide attempt, odds ratio (95% CI) = 5.50 (1.73, 17.53), $p = 0.005$. Cases were also more likely to experience an SLE on the day of the attempt than on the corresponding day in controls, OR (95% CI) = 6.05 (1.31, 28.02), $p = 0.021$. However, cases that made an attempt on the day of a SLE did not make lower planned suicide attempts compared to other cases, suggesting that suicide attempts that are immediately preceded by SLEs cannot be assumed to be unplanned.

*Conclusions:* Results suggest the central importance of major interpersonal SLEs in risk among adults with AUD, a novel finding, and documents that SLEs may lead to suicide attempts within a short window of time (i.e., same day), a daunting challenge to prevention efforts.

# Suicide in the United States Air Force: Risk factors communicated before and at death

Cox DW, Ghahramanlou-Holloway M, Greene FN, Bakalar JL, Schendel CL, Nademin ME, Jobes DA, Englert DR, Kindt M (USA)

*Journal of Affective Disorders* 133, 398–405, 2011

*Background:* Over the last decade, suicide rates in the U.S. military have steadily increased, resulting in a call for suicide-related research with military populations. The present project aimed to describe and evaluate the communications (i.e., verbally and in suicide notes) of 13 suicide risk factors in the suicide death investigation files of 98 active duty U.S. Air Force (USAF) members.

*Methods:* Two-hundred thirty-seven suicide death investigation files were coded. Ninety-eight decedents left suicide notes and were included in the current analyses. Descriptive statistics were computed to evaluate the types of risk factors most commonly communicated prior to and at the time of death as well as the medium for their communication. Specifically, verbal and note communications were compared to evaluate which medium decedents most often used to communicate risk factors. Also, the frequency that interpersonal compared to intrapsychic risk factors were communicated was evaluated.

*Results:* Hopelessness (35.7% of cases) and perceived burdensomeness (31.6% of cases) were the risk factors most often communicated in suicide notes but not verbally. Thwarted belongingness (29.6% of cases) was the risk factor most often communicated verbally and in the suicide note. Further, evaluated risk factors were more frequently communicated in suicide notes than verbally. Finally, interpersonal risk factors were more often communicated than intrapsychic risk factors.

*Limitations:* The validity of the data relies on interviews of decedents' acquaintances and various medical/military records.

*Conclusions:* Our findings support emphasising certain risk factors over others in USAF suicide prevention efforts. Further, interpersonal risk factors appeared to be more salient than intrapsychic risk factors in the minds of decedents.

# Suicidal behavior is associated with reduced corpus callosum area

Cyprien F, Courtet P, Malafosse A, Maller J, Meslin C, Bonafé A, Le Bars E, Menjot de Champfleur N, Ritchie K, Artero S (France)

*Biological Psychiatry* 70, 320–326, 2011

*Background:* Corpus callosum (CC) size has been associated with cognitive and emotional deficits in a range of neuropsychiatric and mood disorders. As such deficits are also found in suicidal behavior, we investigated specifically the association between CC atrophy and suicidal behavior.

*Methods:* We studied 435 right-handed individuals without dementia from a cohort of community-dwelling persons aged 65 years and over (the European Strategic Program on Research in Information Technology study). They were divided in 3 groups: suicide attempters ($n = 21$), affective control subjects (AC) ($n = 180$) without history of suicide attempt but with a history of depression, and healthy control subjects (HC) ($n = 234$). T1-weighted magnetic resonance images were traced to measure the midsagittal areas of the anterior, mid, and posterior CC. Multivariate analysis of covariance was used to compare CC areas in the 3 groups.

*Results:* Multivariate analyses adjusted for age, gender, childhood trauma, head trauma, and total brain volume showed that the area of the posterior third of CC was significantly smaller in suicide attempters than in AC ($p = .020$) and HC ($p = .010$) individuals. No significant differences were found between AC and HC. No differences were found for the anterior and mid thirds of the CC.

*Conclusions:* Our findings emphasise a reduced size of the posterior third of the CC in subjects with a history of suicide, suggesting a diminished interhemispheric connectivity and a possible role of CC in the pathophysiology of suicidal behavior. Further studies are needed to strengthen these results and clarify the underlying cellular changes leading to these morphometric differences.

# Media awards for responsible reporting of suicide: Experiences from Australia, Belgium and Denmark

Dare AJ, Andriessen KA, Nordentoft M, Meier M, Huisman A, Pirkis JE (Australia)

*International Journal of Mental Health Systems* 5, 15, 2011

*Background:* Media awards to encourage responsible reporting of suicide have been introduced in several countries, including Australia, Belgium and Denmark.

*Aims:* This study aimed to examine the experiences of Australian, Belgian and Danish award recipients in preparing stories on suicide, and consider the impacts of the awards for these recipients and for media professionals more broadly.

*Method:* We conducted semi-structured telephone interviews with the majority (14 out of 15) of past recipients of the awards in the 3 countries of interest.

*Results:* Media awards appear to show promise as a method of reinforcing national and international media guidelines on reporting suicide. The recipients of awards were proud to have had their achievements recognised in this way, and had developed a heightened awareness of the issues inherent in reporting suicide. Although relatively few had prepared subsequent stories on suicide, a number had been given opportunities to provide advice to other media professionals about how best to approach this sensitive topic. Recipients viewed the awards as an important means by which good quality reporting can be rewarded, and a springboard for raising community awareness about suicide.

*Conclusion:* The experience from Australia, Belgium and Denmark suggests that media awards which recognise responsible reporting of suicide are extremely worthwhile.

## Toxicology and characteristics of fatal oxycodone toxicity cases in New South Wales, Australia 1999–2008

Darke S, Duflou J, Torok M (Australia)
*Journal of Forensic Sciences* 56, 690–693, 2011

All cases of fatal oxycodone toxicity presenting to the New South Wales Department of Forensic Medicine over the period January 1, 1999, to December 31, 2008, were retrieved. A total of 70 cases were identified. The mean age was 48.9 years, 58.6% were men, 21.4% were suicides, and in 30% oxycodone had not been prescribed to the decedent. Injecting drug users constituted 27.1% of cases, and oxycodone tablets were injected immediately prior to death by 21.4%. The mean blood oxycodone concentration was 0.40mg/L (range 0.06–53.00mg/L). In all cases, psychoactive substances other than oxycodone were also detected, most frequently hypnosedatives (68.6%), other opioids (54.3%), antidepressants (41.4%), and alcohol (32.9%). Preexisting systemic disease was common: cardiovascular (64.2%), pulmonary (49.3%), hepatic (66.7%), and renal (43.9%).

## Prevalence and correlates of lifetime deliberate self-harm and suicidal ideation in naturalistic outpatients: The Leiden Routine Outcome Monitoring study

de Klerk S, van Noorden MS, van Giezen AE, Spinhoven P, den Hollander-Gijsman ME, Giltay EJ, Speckens AEM, Zitman FG (The Netherlands)
*Journal of Affective Disorders* 133, 257–264, 2011

*Background:* Deliberate self-harm and suicidal ideation (DSHI) are common phenomena in general and mental health populations. Identifying factors associated with DSHI may contribute to the early identification, prevention and treatment of DSHI. Aims of the study are to determine the prevalence and correlates of lifetime DSHI in a naturalistic sample of psychiatric outpatients with mood, anxiety or somatoform (MAS) disorders.

*Methods:* Of 3798 consecutive patients from January 2004 to December 2006, 2844 (74.9%) patients were analysed (mean age = 37.5, *SD* = 12.0; age range: 18–65; 62.7% women). Lifetime DSHI was assessed with routine outcome monitoring (ROM), including demographic parameters, DSM-IV diagnosis, depressive symptoms, symptoms of anxiety, general psychopathology and personality traits.

*Results:* Of the 2,844 subjects, 55% reported lifetime DSHI. In multivariable logistic regression analysis, the most important factors associated with lifetime DSHI were being unmarried, low education, high number of psychiatric diagnoses, lower anxiety scores, higher depression scores and the personality trait of emotional dysregulation.

*Limitations:* Deliberate self-harm may have been under-reported in self-report questionnaires; The assessment of personality traits may have been influenced by state psychopathology; traumatic events were not assessed.

*Conclusions:* The findings suggest that DSHI is common among psychiatric outpatients with MAS disorders and that current symptoms and underlying personality vulnerabilities were independently involved in DSHI. Whether symptoms of somatic anxiety are protective should be confirmed in subsequent studies. These findings may help clinicians in identifying patients at risk for deliberate self-harm and suicide.


## Risk factors for self-harm in children and adolescents admitted to a mental health inpatient unit

de Kloet L, Starling J, Hainsworth C, Berntsen E, Chapman L, Hancock K (Australia)
*Australian and New Zealand Journal of Psychiatry* 45, 749–755, 2011

*Objective:* The aim of this study was to identify risk factors for self-harm for children and adolescents in a mental health inpatient unit.

*Methods:* A retrospective file audit of patient files over 3 years (2006–2009) was conducted to determine risk factors associated with self-harm in children and adolescents admitted to a mental health unit. A checklist of potential factors was based on risk factors found in a review of the literature including demographic information, diagnosis, home situation, environmental stressors, childhood trauma and previous mental health care. The study compared those who self-harmed with a control group who did not self-harm.

*Results:* There were 150 patients who self-harmed (mean age 14 years) and 56 patients who did not self-harm with a mean age of 13 years. Several factors were identified that increased the likelihood of self-harm, including a diagnosis of depression, female gender, increasing age, being Australian-born, living with a step parent, not having received previous mental health care, having a history of trauma, and having other stressors including problems within the family.

*Conclusions:* While increasing age, female gender, a history of trauma and a diagnosis of depression are well known as risk factors for self-harm, this study confirms that family factors, in particular living with a step parent, significantly add to the risk. Child and adolescent services should be aware of the increased risk of self-harm in young people with mental health problems who live in blended families. Treatment approaches need to involve parents as well as the child or young person.

## Exposure to trauma and Posttraumatic Stress Disorder symptoms in older veterans attending primary care: Comorbid conditions and self-rated health status

Durai UNB, Chopra MP, Coakley E, Llorente MD, Kirchner JE, Cook JM, Levkoff SE (USA)

*Journal of the American Geriatrics Society* 59, 1087–1092, 2011

*Objectives:* Assess the prevalence of posttraumatic stress disorder (PTSD) symptomatology and its association with health characteristics in a geriatric primary care population.

*Design:* Cross-sectional screening assessments during a multisite trial for the treatment of depression, anxiety, and at-risk drinking.

*Setting:* Department of Veterans Affairs (VA)-based primary care clinics across the United States.

*Participants:* Seventeen thousand two hundred five veterans aged 65 and older.

*Measurements:* Sociodemographic information, the General Health Questionnaire (GHQ-12), questions about death wishes and suicidal ideation, quantity and frequency of alcohol use, smoking, exposure to traumatic events, and PTSD symptom clusters.

*Results:* Twelve percent (2,041/17,205) of participants screened endorsed PTSD symptoms. Veterans with PTSD symptoms from some (partial PTSD) or each (PTSD all clusters) of the symptom clusters were significantly more likely to report poor general health, currently smoke, be divorced, report little or no social support, and have a higher prevalence of mental distress, death wishes, and suicidal ideation than those with no trauma history or those with trauma but no symptoms. Group differences were most pronounced for mental distress and least for at-risk drinking. Presence of PTSD all clusters was associated with poorer outcomes on all of the above-mentioned health characteristics than partial PTSD.

*Conclusions:* PTSD symptoms are common in a substantial minority of older veterans in primary care, and careful inquiry about these symptoms is important for comprehensive assessment in geriatric populations.

## Prevalence of suicidal behaviours in two Australian general population surveys: Methodological considerations when comparing across studies

Fairweather-Schmidt AK, Anstey KJ (Australia)

*Social Psychiatry and Psychiatric Epidemiology.* Published online: 29 March 2011. doi: 10.1007/s00127-011-0369-5, 2011

*Purpose:* To investigate whether methodological differences between 2 Australian general population surveys have the capacity to affect the apparent prevalence rates of suicidal ideation and suicide attempts.

*Methods:* 609 Wave 1 of the Personality and Total Health (PATH) Through Life Project participants, and 83 participants derived from the 1997 National Survey of Mental Health and Wellbeing (NSMHWB) met the criteria for inclusion (suicidal ideation/suicide attempt). Analysis involved Chi-square and binary logistic regression.

*Results:* Twelve-month prevalence rates for suicidal ideation and suicide attempt were 8.2%, (95% CI = 7.6–8.8) and 0.8% (95% CI = 0.6–1.0) for PATH ($N$ = 7,485), and contrast with 2.9% (95% CI = 2.6–3.2) and 0.3% (95% CI = 0.2–0.5) for NSMHWB ($N$ = 10,641) samples, respectively. While notable discrepancies are apparent between the prevalence statistics, both sets of statistics are within the bounds of other Australian and international studies. Parallel rate disparities for suicidal ideation are found across age-by-gender groups. Aside from differences in the basic prevalence rates, surveys have analogous age-by-gender profiles for suicidal ideation.

*Conclusions:* While it is possible that samples are representative of the populations from which they are derived, 12-month prevalence rate discrepancies between PATH and NSMHWB surveys are likely to originate from demographic and survey methodology differences. Where investigations employ different methodologies, especially in relation to modes of survey administration and the assessment items utilised, a cautious approach should be taken when comparing findings.

## Suicide survivor support groups: Comings and goings, part II

Feigelman B, Feigelman W (USA)
*Illness, Crisis and Loss* 19, 165–185, 2011

This two-part report examines important aspects of survivor of suicide support groups: some of the motivating factors attracting survivors to join these groups and why many withdraw as time after a loss passes. In this second part we analyse the support group departures issue, drawing primarily upon participant observation data collected over a 7-year period from more than 300 suicide survivors observed at monthly group meetings and from follow-up interviews with 24 respondents who withdrew from groups. Findings suggest that support group affiliation is a time-limited activity for most of those bereaved by suicide. This very preliminary data suggests that most survivors feel that 2 things were especially indispensable to them in their efforts to advance after a suicide loss: 1) affiliation to a support group (or to several groups); and 2) the help received from friendships established with other survivors along their healing journeys.

## Strategies for quantifying the relationship between medications and suicidal behaviour: What has been learned?

Gibbons RD, Mann JJ (USA)

*Drug Safety* 34, 375–395, 2011

In recent years there has been considerable concern that certain classes of drugs, for example antidepressants, may increase the risk of suicide. In this current opinion article, we examine the literature on methodological and statistical approaches to the design and analysis of suicidal event studies. Experimental, ecological and observational studies of the relationship between drugs and suicidal events (thoughts, attempts and completion) are discussed. Areas considered include analysis of spontaneous reporting system data, ecological trends in national and/or small area (e.g. county) suicide rates, meta-analyses of randomised clinical trials, and large-scale medical claims data. New statistical and experimental strategies for investigating possible associations between drugs and suicide are highlighted, and we suggest directions for future statistical/methodological research. To put this into context, we then review the most recent literature on the relationship between drugs (antidepressants, antiepileptics, varenicline, montelukast and antipsychotics) and suicidal events.

Overall, there appears to be little evidence that drugs increase the risk of suicide and related behaviour. Numerous lines of evidence in adults clearly demonstrate that inadequate treatment of depression (pharmacotherapy and/or psychotherapy) is associated with increased risk of suicidal behaviour. In children, the results are less clear and further study is required to better delineate which children benefit from treatment and who may be at increased risk as a consequence of treatment. From a statistical and methodological perspective, the field of pharmacoepidemiology is a fertile area for statistical research, both in theory and in application. In general, methods have been adopted from other areas such as general epidemiology, despite the singular nature of many of the problems that are unique to drug safety in general, in particular the study of rare events. Finally, there is considerable debate concerning the communication of risk. For suicide, regulatory action has been taken largely on the basis of evidence suggesting increased risk of suicidal thoughts. However, suicidal thoughts are quite common, particularly among patients with depression, and may have little relationship to suicidal behaviour and/or completion.

## Changes in statistical methods affected the validity of official suicide rates

Gjertsen F, Johansson LA (Norway)

*Journal of Clinical Epidemiology* 64, 1102–1108, 2011

*Objective:* This study investigates whether changes in registration and coding practices influenced official suicide rates in Norway from 1988 to 2002.

*Study Design and Setting:* A Poisson regression model was used to evaluate rates of suicide and potentially competing underlying causes of death. Setting in Norway 1988–2002.

*Results:* From 1988 to 1994, suicide mortality decreased significantly, by 23.7%. Simultaneously, rates of causes of death potentially masking suicide decreased or remained fairly stable. From 1994 to 2002, however, there were no significant changes in suicide rates but accidental poisoning, which may mask suicide, increased significantly by 32.4%. Also, 'ill-defined causes' of death increased by 16.7%, indicating poorer data quality.

*Conclusion:* This study suggests that the decreasing suicide rate in 1988–94 reflects a real change. However, the general quality of mortality statistics has deteriorated since the late 1990s, making it difficult to assess developments since 1994. Such variations in the reliability of official suicide statistics complicate international comparisons. However, shifts in the death rate because of 'ill-defined' causes could serve as a warning that data quality is not consistent over time.

## Screening for suicidality in the emergency department: When must researchers act to protect subjects' interests?

Gold A, Appelbaum PS, Stanley B (USA)
*Archives of Suicide Research* 15, 140–150, 2011

The emergency department (ED) is a key site in preventing suicide. Yet there has been very little research on ED screening and interventions targeting the suicidal patient. Conducting research on interventions for preventing suicidal behavior in the ED population may evoke the dilemma of how to fulfill ethical obligations to protect research subjects when doing so can impair the validity of the study. In this paper we present a case study of a research protocol on the utility of routine screening with a brief intervention for suicidal ideation that raised issues regarding researchers' obligation to disclose information about subjects' suicidality to ED staff. After exploring the imperfect relationship between suicidal ideation and completed suicide (i.e., many people with ideation never attempt or commit suicide), we present an analysis of the causal relationship between these phenomena. This leads us to suggest that it should not be mandatory for researchers to disclose to ED staff when a subject reveals suicide ideation in a screening questionnaire-although other preventive measures may be called for. In general, the extent of the duty placed on researchers to intervene on behalf of their subjects should be proportional to the likelihood and magnitude of risk presented to subjects by the underlying condition, and should be balanced against the importance of the research question.

## Group therapy for adolescents with repeated self harm: Randomised controlled trial with economic evaluation

Green JM, Wood AJ, Kerfoot MJ, Trainor G, Roberts C, Rothwell J, Woodham A, Ayodeji E, Barrett B, Byford S, Harrington R (UK)

*British Medical Journal* 342, d682, 2011

*Objective:* To examine the effectiveness and cost-effectiveness of group therapy for self harm in young people.

*Design:* Two arm, single (assessor) blinded parallel randomised allocation trial of a group therapy intervention in addition to routine care, compared with routine care alone. Randomisation was by minimisation controlling for baseline frequency of self harm, presence of conduct disorder, depressive disorder, and severity of psychosocial stress.

*Participants:* Adolescents aged 12–17 years with at least 2 past episodes of self harm within the previous 12 months.

*Exclusion Criteria were:* not speaking English, low weight anorexia nervosa, acute psychosis, substantial learning difficulties (defined by need for specialist school), current containment in secure care.

*Setting:* Eight child and adolescent mental health services in the northwest UK. Interventions Manual based developmental group therapy programme specifically designed for adolescents who harm themselves, with an acute phase over 6 weekly sessions followed by a booster phase of weekly groups as long as needed. Details of routine care were gathered from participating centres.

*Main Outcome Measures:* Primary outcome was frequency of subsequent repeated episodes of self harm. Secondary outcomes were severity of subsequent self harm, mood disorder, suicidal ideation, and global functioning. Total costs of health, social care, education, and criminal justice sector services, plus family related costs and productivity losses, were recorded.

*Results:* 183 adolescents were allocated to each arm (total $n = 366$). Loss to follow-up was low ($< 4\%$). On all outcomes the trial cohort as a whole showed significant improvement from baseline to follow-up. On the primary outcome of frequency of self harm, proportional odds ratio of group therapy versus routine care adjusting for relevant baseline variables was 0.99 (95% confidence interval 0.68 to 1.44, $P = 0.95$) at 6 months and 0.88 (0.59 to 1.33, $P = 0.52$) at 1 year. For severity of subsequent self harm the equivalent odds ratios were 0.81 (0.54 to 1.20, $P = 0.29$) at 6 months and 0.94 (0.63 to 1.40, $P = 0.75$) at 1 year. Total 1 year costs were higher in the group therapy arm (21 pound 781) than for routine care (15 pound 372) but the difference was not significant (95% CI -1416 to 10782, $P = 0.132$).

*Conclusions:* The addition of this targeted group therapy programme did not improve self harm outcomes for adolescents who repeatedly self harmed, nor was there evidence of cost effectiveness. The outcomes to end point for the cohort as a whole were better than current clinical expectations.

# Does stigma predict a belief in dealing with depression alone?

Griffiths KM, Crisp DA, Jorm AF, Christensen H (Australia)
*Journal of Affective Disorders* 132, 413–417, 2011

*Background:* Community surveys indicate that many people with depressive disorders do not obtain professional help and that a preference for self-reliance is an important factor in this treatment gap. The current study sought to investigate whether stigmatising attitudes predict a belief in the helpfulness of dealing with depression without external assistance.

*Methods:* Data were collected as part of a national household survey of 2000 Australian adults aged 18 years and above. Participants were presented with either a vignette depicting depression ($n = 1001$) or a vignette depicting depression with suicidal ideation ($n = 999$) and asked if it would be helpful or harmful to deal alone with the problem. Logistic regression analyses were conducted to determine if belief in dealing with depression alone was predicted by personal stigma, perceived stigma or sociodemographic characteristics.

*Results:* Higher levels of personal stigma independently predicted a belief in the helpfulness of dealing alone with both depression and depression with suicidal ideation. By contrast, lower levels of perceived stigma were associated with a belief in the helpfulness of dealing alone with depression without suicidal ideation.

*Conclusions:* Personal stigma is associated with a belief in the helpfulness of self-reliance in coping with depression. Public health programs should consider the possibility that a belief in self-reliance is partly attributable to stigma. The findings also point to the potential importance of providing evidence-based self-help programs for those who believe in self-care.

# Aggression, impulsivity, and suicide behavior: A review of the literature

Gvion Y, Apter A (Israel)
*Archives of Suicide Research* 15, 93–112, 2011

This article reviews the literature on the association between impulsivity aggression and suicide. The key words impulsivity, aggression, and suicide were entered into the pubmed, psychlit, and proqest databases. Significant articles were scrutinised for relevant information. Impulsivity and aggression are highly correlated with suicidal behavior across psychiatric samples, nosological borders, and non-psychiatric populations. Impulsivity and aggression are related but the nature of this relationship remains unclear. The literature is confusing and contradictory. This is probably due to the difficulty in defining and separating out these concepts and the fact that there is much overlap between them. Future research should aim at clarifying and refining these concepts as well as their link to all the different forms of suicidal behavior.

# Internet suicide searches and the incidence of suicide in young people in Japan

Hagihara A, Miyazaki S, Abe T (Japan)

*European Archives of Psychiatry and Clinical Neuroscience.* Published online: 20 April 2011. doi: 10.1007/s00406-011-0212-8, 2011

Although several case reports have suggested a relationship between accessing Internet suicide sites and the incidence of suicide, the influence of the Internet on the incidence of suicide is not known. Thus, we examined the association between Internet suicide-related searches and the incidence of suicide in 20- and 30-year-old individuals in Japan. The Box-Jenkins transfer function model was applied to monthly time series data from January 2004 to May 2010 (77 months). The terms 'hydrogen sulfide,' 'hydrogen sulfide suicide,' and 'suicide hydrogen sulfide suicide' at (t-11) were related to the incidence of suicide among people aged in their 20 s ($P = 0.005$, 0.005, and 0.006, respectively) and people aged in their 30 s ($P = 0.013$, 0.011, and 0.012, respectively). 'BBS on suicide' at (t-5) and 'suicide by jumping' at (t-6) were related to the incidence of suicide in people aged 30–39 ($P = 0.006$ and 0.001, respectively). Internet searches for specific suicide-related terms are related to the incidence of suicide among 20- and 30-year-old individuals in Japan. Routine interrogation by a clinician about visiting Internet suicide websites and stricter regulation of these websites may reduce the incidence of suicide among young people.

# Media reporting and suicide: A time-series study of suicide from Clifton Suspension Bridge, UK, 1974–2007

Hamilton S, Metcalfe C, Gunnell D (UK)

*Journal of Public Health (Oxford).* Published online: 12 July 2011. doi: 10.1093/pubmed/fdr043, 2011

*Background:* Media reports of suicide may provoke further 'copy-cat' suicides. Trends in reporting quality and impact of reporting on suicides from a particular 'hot-spot' have not been investigated previously.

*Methods:* Inquest files and death certificates were used to identify suicides from Clifton Suspension Bridge, Bristol, UK, 1974–2007. Copies of local newspaper and television reports within 3 days of death or inquest were obtained. Parametric survival models were used to examine the impact of media reports on subsequent suicides.

*Results:* Over 34 years, there were 206 suicides and 427 media reports of suicide from the bridge. The number of reports per suicide has declined markedly from 2.8 per suicide in the 1970s to 0.7 per suicide in the 2000s ($P < 0.001$). While some aspects of reporting improved, others deteriorated or remained poorly reported. There has been an increase in sensational reporting (use of images was 5% in the 1970s and 16% in the 2000s) and in information about the suicide method. There was no evidence that media reports provoked further suicides.

*Conclusions:* Media reporting of suicide from Clifton Suspension Bridge declined over the study period; however, most aspects of the quality of reporting remained poor. There was no evidence of media reports provoking further suicides.

## Deliberate self-harm in rural and urban regions: A comparative study of prevalence and patient characteristics

Harriss L, Hawton K (UK)
*Social Science & Medicine* 73, 274–281, 2011

In countries like the UK, people living in urban regions are more likely to suffer poor physical and mental health than rural populations, and to have increased rates of psychiatric disorder. Urban/rural differences in suicidal behaviour have most frequently focussed on variations in the occurrence of suicide. We have investigated rates of deliberate self-harm (DSH) in urban and rural districts of Oxfordshire, England, and compared characteristics of DSH patients resident in these 2 areas. Information was collected on 6833 DSH episodes by 4,054 persons aged 15 years and over presenting to the local general hospital between 2001 and 2005. We found that urban DSH rates were substantially higher than rural rates amongst both males and females aged between 15 and 64 years. This relationship was sustained even when socio-economic deprivation and social fragmentation were taken into account. There was little difference between urban and rural rates for patients aged 65 years and over. Urban DSH patients were more likely to be younger, non-white in ethnic origin, unemployed, living alone, to have a criminal record, to have previously engaged in DSH, and to report problems with housing. Rural DSH patients were more likely to suffer from physical illness, and to have higher suicide intent scores. Results of studies such as this can help identify where resources for preventive initiatives should be primarily directed and also what types of individuals may be at most risk in different areas. However, since variation by area will in part be due to differences at the individual level, further research utilising multi-level modelling techniques would be useful.

## Impact of different pack sizes of paracetamol in the United Kingdom and Ireland on intentional overdoses: A comparative study

Hawton K, Bergen H, Simkin S, Arensman E, Corcoran P, Cooper J, Waters K, Gunnell D, Kapur N (UK)
*BMC Public Health* 11, 460, 2011

*Background:* In order to reduce fatal self-poisoning legislation was introduced in the UK in 1998 to restrict pack sizes of paracetamol sold in pharmacies (maximum 32 tablets) and non-pharmacy outlets (maximum 16 tablets), and in Ireland in 2001, but with smaller maximum pack sizes (24 and 12 tablets). Our aim was to determine whether this resulted in smaller overdoses of paracetamol in Ireland compared with the UK.

*Methods:* We used data on general hospital presentations for non-fatal self-harm for 2002–2007 from the Multicentre Study of Self-harm in England (6 hospitals), and from the National Registry of Deliberate Self-harm in Ireland. We compared sizes of overdoses of paracetamol in the 2 settings.

*Results:* There were clear peaks in numbers of non-fatal overdoses, associated with maximum pack sizes of paracetamol in pharmacy and non-pharmacy outlets in both England and Ireland. Significantly more pack equivalents (based on maximum non-pharmacy pack sizes) were used in overdoses in Ireland (mean 2.63, 95% CI 2.57–2.69) compared with England (2.07, 95% CI 2.03–2.10). The overall size of overdoses did not differ significantly between England (median 22, interquartile range (IQR) 15–32) and Ireland (median 24, IQR 12–36).

*Conclusions:* The difference in paracetamol pack size legislation between England and Ireland does not appear to have resulted in a major difference in sizes of overdoses. This is because more pack equivalents are taken in overdoses in Ireland, possibly reflecting differing enforcement of sales advice. Differences in access to clinical services may also be relevant.

# Concordance of self- and proxy-reported suicide ideation in depressed adults 50 years of age or older

Heisel MJ, Conwell Y, Pisani AR, Duberstein PR (Canada)
*Canadian Journal of Psychiatry* 56, 219–226, 2011

*Objective:* To assess whether social supports (proxies) can detect the presence of suicide ideation in a clinical sample of depressed adults 50 years of age or older, and to additionally assess the potential impact of depression symptom severity on patient-proxy concordance in reports of patient suicide ideation.

*Method:* Cross-sectional data were collected regarding Axis I diagnoses, severity of depressive symptoms, and suicide ideation in a clinical sample of 109 patients 50 years of age and older. Patients were administered study measures by trained interviewers. Patients' social supports completed proxy measures of these same variables. We assessed concordance in self- and proxy-reported suicide ideation, employing global suicide ideation items derived from depression scales and more fine-grained suicide ideation items drawn from multi-item suicide ideation measures. We investigated patient-proxy concordance regarding the presence of patient suicide ideation.

*Results:* Patients who endorsed suicide ideation and were concordantly seen by their social supports to be suicidal reported significantly greater depressive symptom severity than patients concordantly reported to be nonsuicidal. Patients' social supports reported significantly less depressive symptom severity in patients who endorsed suicide ideation yet who did not appear to be suicidal to them.

*Conclusions:* Our findings suggest that family and friends can broadly ascertain the presence of suicide ideation in depressed middle-aged and older adults, yet in doing so may largely be responding to their broad perceptions of depressive symptom severity in patients and not specifically to the presence of suicidal thoughts.

## Mental health screening and follow-up care in public high schools

Husky MM, Sheridan M, McGuire L, Olfson M (USA)
*Journal of the American Academy of Child and Adolescent Psychiatry* 50, 881–891, 2011

*Objective:* Despite increased interest in screening adolescents for mental health problems and suicide risk, little is known regarding the extent to which youth are identified and connected with appropriate services.

*Method:* Between 2005 and 2009, a total of 4,509 ninth-grade students were offered screening. We reviewed the records of the 2,488 students who were screened. Students identified as being at risk were provided with a referral. Data were collected on screening results, mental health referrals, and completion of recommended treatment over approximately 90 days.

*Results:* Among students screened, 19.6% were identified as being at risk, 73.6% of whom were not currently receiving any treatment. Students referred for school services tended to be less severely ill than those referred for community services, with lower rates of suicidal ideation, prior suicide attempts, and self-injury. Among at-risk students not currently in treatment, 76.3% of students referred received at least 1 mental health visit during the follow-up period. Overall, 74.0% of students were referred to school and 57.3% to community services. A great majority of school referrals (80.2%) successfully accessed services, although a smaller proportion of community services referrals successfully accessed treatment (41.9%).

*Conclusions:* Systematic voluntary school-based mental health screening and referral offers a feasible means of identifying and connecting high-risk adolescents to school- and community-based mental health services, although linkages to community-based services may require considerable coordination.

## The effects of celebrity suicide on copycat suicide attempt: A multi-center observational study

Jeong J, Shin SD, Kim H, Hong YC, Hwang SS, Lee EJ (Korea)
*Social Psychiatry & Psychiatric Epidemiology*. Published online: 8 June 2011. doi: 10.1007/s00127-011-0403-7, 2011

*Background:* The effect of celebrity suicides on copycat suicide attempts is not well known. Our objective was to determine the association between celebrity suicide and copycat suicide attempts.

*Methods:* We conducted a retrospective multi-center observational time series analysis. Celebrity suicides were selected by an operational definition via 3 nationwide television news internet sites from January 2005 to December 2008. The reference week was defined as the week preceding date of suicide notification to the public. Then 2 pre-event weeks and 4 post-event weeks were analysed for suicide attempts. We derived a prediction model for suicide attempt visits for each ED for these 7 observational weeks using a General Additive Model with data from the National Emergency Department Information System (NEDIS) database. We calculated the mean excess visit (EV = observed visit — expected visit) and mean excess visit ratio (EVR = EV/expected visit). We tested the mean EV and EVR between reference weeks versus the observational weeks using independent t test and repeated measures ANOVA.

*Results:* Five celebrity suicides occurred during the study period. Total number of ED visits was 5,453,441 in the 85 EDs over the 4-year period, and suicide attempt or self-injury occurred in 27,605. The mean excess visit for each observational interval per ED was less than 0.1 during pre-event periods but increased to 0.695 in the second post-event week. EVs were significantly higher in the first to the third post-event weeks ($p = 0.02$, $p < 0.01$, $p = 0.03$, respectively) compared to reference week. The mean EVRs were significantly higher (= 0.215) in the second post-week intervals compared with the reference week ($p = 0.03$). Mean EVs and mean EVRs showed significant increase in the post event period compared with the observational period ($p = 0.001$ in EV, $p = 0.021$ in EVR).

*Conclusion:* From a prediction model using a 4-year nationwide ED database, ED visits for suicide attempts or self injury increased following the announcements of celebrity suicides.

## Changes in mental health services and suicide mortality in Norway: An ecological study

Johannessen HA, Dieserud G, Claussen B, Zahl PH (Norway)

*BMC Health Services Research* 11, 68, 2011

*Background:* Mental disorders are strongly associated with excess suicide risk, and successful treatment might prevent suicide. Since 1990, and particularly after 1998, there has been a substantial increase in mental health service resources in Norway. This study aimed to investigate whether these changes have had an impact on suicide mortality.

*Methods:* We used Poisson regression analyses to assess the effect of changes in 5 mental health services variables on suicide mortality in 5 Norwegian health regions during the period 1990–2006. These variables included: number of man-labour years by all personnel, number of discharges, number of outpatient consultations, number of inpatient days, and number of hospital beds. Adjustments were made for sales of alcohol, sales of antidepressants, education, and unemployment.

*Results:* In the period 1990–2006, we observed a total of 9,480 suicides and the total suicide rate declined by 26%. None of the mental health services variables were significantly associated with female or male suicide mortality in the adjusted analyses ($p > 0.05$). Sales of antidepressants (adjusted Incidence Rate Ratio = 0.98; 95% CI = 0.97–1.00) and sales of alcohol (adjusted IRR = 1.41; 95% CI = 1.18–1.72) were significantly associated with female suicide mortality; education (adjusted IRR = 0.86; 95% CI = 0.79–0.94) and unemployment (adjusted IRR = 0.91; 95% CI = 0.85–0.97) were significantly associated with male suicide mortality.

*Conclusions:* The adjusted analyses in the present study indicate that increased resources in Norwegian mental health services in the period 1990–2006 were statistically unrelated to suicide mortality.

## Explaining gender differences in non-fatal suicidal behaviour among adolescents: A population-based study

Kaess M, Parzer P, Haffner J, Steen R, Roos J, Klett M, Brunner R, Resch F (Germany)
*BMC Public Health* 11, 597, 2011

*Background:* While suicide is the second leading cause of death among young people in most industrial countries, non-fatal suicidal behaviour is also a very important public health concern among adolescents. The aim of this study was to investigate gender differences in prevalence and emotional and behavioural correlates of suicidal behaviour in a representative school-based sample of adolescents.

*Methods:* A cross-sectional design was used to assess suicidal behaviour and various areas of emotional and behavioural problems by using a self-report booklet including the Youth Self-Report. One hundred sixteen schools in a region of Southern Germany agreed to participate. A representative sample of 5,512 ninth-grade students was studied. Mean age was 14.8 years ($SD$ 0.73); 49.8% were female.

*Results:* Serious suicidal thoughts were reported by 19.8% of the female students and 10.8% of the females had ever attempted suicide. In the male group, 9.3% had a history of suicidal thoughts and 4.9% had previously attempted suicide. Internalising emotional and behavioural problems were shown to be higher in the female group (difference of the group means 4.41) while externalising emotional and behavioural problems slightly predominated in the male students (difference of the group means -0.65). However, the total rate of emotional and behavioural problems was significantly higher in the adolescent female group (difference of the group means 4.98). Using logistic regression models with suicidal thoughts or attempted suicide as dependent variables, the pseudo-$R^2$ of gender alone was only 2.7% or 2.3%, while it was 30% or 23.2% for emotional and behavioural problems measured by the YSR syndrome scales. By adding gender to the emotional and behavioural problems only an additional 0.3% of information could be explained.

*Conclusions:* The findings suggest that gender differences in non-fatal suicidal behaviour among adolescents can to a large extent be explained by the gender differences in emotional and behavioural problems during this age.

## Panic as an independent risk factor for suicide attempt in depressive illness: Findings from the National Epidemiological Survey on Alcohol and Related Conditions (NESARC)

Katz C, Yaseen ZS, Mojtabai R, Cohen LJ, Galynker II (USA)
*Journal of Clinical Psychiatry.* Published online: 22 March 2011. doi:10.4088/JCP.10m06186blu., 2011

*Context:* The relationship between comorbid panic and suicide in depressed persons remains unclear.

*Objective:* To examine the relationship of panic attacks and panic symptoms to suicidality in individuals with a major mood disorder meeting DSM-IV criteria for past-year major depressive episodes in a large epidemiologic study.

*Method:* In data on 2,679 community-dwelling participants of the National Epidemiologic Survey on Alcohol and Related Conditions (2001–2002) with major depressive episodes, the associations of panic attacks and panic symptoms with lifetime suicidal ideation and suicide attempts were assessed. The adjusted odds ratios (AORs) of suicidal ideation, suicide attempt, and suicide attempt among ideators for subjects with panic attacks were the primary outcome measures.

*Results:* Past-year panic attacks were associated with increased risk of lifetime suicidal ideations (AOR = 1.17; 95% CI, 1.02–1.35) and suicide attempts (AOR = 2.10; 95% CI, 1.77–2.50) and significantly increased risk of suicide attempts among those reporting suicidal ideations (AOR = 1.79; 95% CI, 1.49–2.15). Some panic symptoms, most notably catastrophic cognitions (fear of dying and fear of 'losing control' or 'going insane'), were more strongly and specifically associated with suicide attempt (AORs = 2.13–2.95), while others were more related to suicidal ideation.

*Conclusions:* Panic attacks appear to be an independent risk factor for suicide attempt among depressed individuals with and without suicidal ideation. Further, panic attacks, particularly those characterised by prominent catastrophic cognitions, may mediate the transition from suicidal ideations to suicide attempts in subjects with depressive episodes. Assessment of these symptoms may improve prediction of suicide attempts in clinical settings.

# Hyperlinked suicide assessing the prominence and accessibility of suicide websites

Kemp CG, Collings SC (USA)
*Crisis*, 32, 143–151, 2011

*Background:* The relationship between the Internet and suicide is a topic of growing concern among suicide researchers and the public, though to date few have actually attempted to investigate the accessibility and prominence of suicide-related information online, and there have been no comprehensive studies of site networking structure.

*Aims:* To assess the visibility of various types of online information to suicide-risk individuals, and to assess the prominence and accessibility of 'pro-suicide,' suicide prevention, and support sites by measuring their networking structure.

*Methods:* Employing empirically derived search terms, we used the web-based Virtual Observatory for the Study of Online Networks (VOSON) to conduct hyperlink network analysis (HNA) of suicide-related websites.

*Results:* Pro-suicide sites are rare and marginal, while sites dedicated to information about suicide as well as sites dedicated to prevention policy and advocacy are readily accessible.

*Conclusions:* The networking structure of suicide-related Internet content has not been described previously. Our analysis shows that HNA is a useful method for gaining an indepth understanding of network traffic in relation to suicide-content websites. This information will be useful for strengthening the web presence of support and suicide prevention sites, and for monitoring changes over time.

# Ecstasy use and suicidal behavior among adolescents: Findings from a national survey

Kim J, Fan B, Liu X, Kerner N, Wu P (USA)

*Suicide and Life-Threatening Behavior* 41, 435–444, 2011

The relationship between ecstasy use and suicidal behavior among adolescents in the United States was examined. Data from the adolescent subsample (ages 12–17, $N = 19,301$) of the 2000 National Household Survey on Drug Abuse were used in the analyses. Information on adolescent substance use, suicidal behaviors, and related sociodemographic, family, and individual factors was obtained in the survey. The rate of past year suicide attempt among adolescents with lifetime ecstasy use was almost double that of adolescents who had used other drugs only, and 9 times that of adolescents with no history of illicit drug use. In multinomial logistic regression analyses controlling for related factors, the effect of ecstasy use remained significant. Adolescent ecstasy users may require enhanced suicide prevention and intervention efforts.

# High and low suicidality in Europe: A fine-grained comparison of France and Spain within the ESEMeD surveys

Kovess-Masféty V, Boyd A, Haro JM, Bruffaerts R, Villagut G, Lépine JP, Gasquet I, Alonso J (France)

*Journal of Affective Disorders* 133, 247–256, 2011

*Background:* Suicidality risk-factors between countries with similar economic and religious background have been rarely compared, especially within genders.

*Methods:* Lifetime prevalence of suicide ideation, plans, and attempts in the ESEMeD surveys were stratified on 4 separate groups: French women, Spanish women, French men, and Spanish men. Outcome odds-ratios (OR) were modelled within each group using logistic regression including demographic characteristics, lifetime mood/anxiety disorders, parental bonding, marital status, and health service-use.

*Results:* Lifetime prevalence of suicide attempts was 3.4% in France (1.1% men, 5.4% women) and 1.5% in Spain (1.2% men, 1.7% women), with a significantly greater gender difference in France ($p = 0.001$). Regarding risk-factors, French women reported suicide attempt more commonly with authoritarian mothers (OR = 1.51; 95%CI = 1.04–2.18), unlike Spanish women (OR = 0.77; 95%CI = 0.51–1.15) ($p < 0.001$). Spanish men showed more than eight-times higher odds of suicide attempt with overprotecting mothers than French men ($p = 0.03$). General practitioner-(GP)-use was significantly protective of suicide attempt among Spanish women (OR = 0.08; 95%CI = 0.02–0.35) with no effect in French women (OR = 1.03; 95%CI = 0.54–2.00) ($p = 0.01$). No significant differences in the effect of marital status, any lifetime antidepressant use, mental disorders, or religiosity on suicide attempt were observed between France and Spain within gender-stratum.

*Limitations:* Parental bonding is retrospective and potentially influenced by mental state. Response rate was considerably lower in France than in Spain.

*Conclusions:* Suicidality risk-factors play different roles across genders between France and Spain. Parental bonding dimensions may be interpreted differently according to country, underlining cultural importance. As recommended by WHO, mental health decisions must involve GPs in conjunction with psychiatrists or psychologists.

# Risk factors for suicide within a year of discharge from psychiatric hospital: A systematic meta-analysis

Large M, Sharma S, Cannon E, Ryan C, Nielssen O (Australia)
*Australian and New Zealand Journal of Psychiatry* 45, 619–628, 2011

*Background:* The increased risk of suicide in the period after discharge from a psychiatric hospital is a well-recognised and serious problem.

*Objective:* The aim of this study was to establish the risk factors for suicide in the year after discharge from psychiatric hospitals and their usefulness in categorising patients as high or low risk for suicide in the year following discharge.

*Method:* A systematic meta-analysis of controlled studies of suicide within a year of discharge from psychiatric hospitals.

*Results:* There was a moderately strong association between both a history of self-harm (OR = 3.15) and depressive symptoms (OR = 2.70) and post-discharge suicide. Factors weakly associated with post-discharge suicide were reports of suicidal ideas (OR = 2.47), an unplanned discharge (OR = 2.44), recent social difficulty (OR = 2.23), a diagnosis of major depression (OR = 1.91) and male sex (OR = 1.58). Patients who had less contact with services after discharge were significantly less likely to commit suicide (OR = 0.69). High risk patients were more likely to commit suicide than other discharged patients, but the strength of this association was not much greater than the association with some individual risk factors (OR = 3.94, sensitivity = 0.40, specificity = 0.87).

*Conclusions:* No factor, or combination of factors, was strongly associated with suicide in the year after discharge. About 3% of patients categorised as being at high risk can be expected to commit suicide in the year after discharge. However, about 60% of the patients who commit suicide are likely to be categorised as low risk. Risk categorisation is of no value in attempts to decrease the numbers of patients who will commit suicide after discharge.

## The economic and potential years of life lost from suicide in Taiwan, 1997–2007

Law CK, Yip PS, Chen YY (Taiwan)

*Crisis* 32, 152–159, 2011

*Background:* Taiwan has experienced a marked increase in the suicide rate in the last decade. However, the socioeconomic burden and impact to the community has not been adequately assessed.

*Aims:* This study aimed to estimate the social and economic burden of premature mortality from suicide in Taiwan in 1997–2007.

*Methods:* The suicide rate, potential years of life lost (PYLL), and present value of lifetime earnings (PVLE) by sex and age groups in 1997–2007 were calculated. The contribution of each suicide method to PYLL for each age group was also assessed.

*Results:* Using the PYLL calculations, suicide had become the third leading cause of death in Taiwan in 2007, compared to its ninth position in terms of absolute numbers. Furthermore, the PYLL was associated with an estimated NTD (New Taiwan Dollars) 32.5 billion of lost earnings in 2007. The increase in PYLL and PVLE from suicide was highest in middle-aged men (aged 25–59 years). Charcoal burning suicide accounted for most of the increase in PYLL in the middle-aged group in the past decade.

*Conclusions:* The loss of life in middle-aged males contributes disproportionately to the social and economic burden of suicide in Taiwan. Suicide intervention effort should target this high-risk population.

## Antidepressants and risks of suicide and suicide attempts: A 27-year observational study

Leon AC, Solomon DA, Li C, Fiedorowicz JG, Coryell WH, Endicott J, Keller MB (USA)

*Journal of Clinical Psychiatry* 72, 580–586, 2011

*Objective:* The 2007 revision of the black box warning for suicidality with antidepressants states that patients of all ages who initiate antidepressants should be monitored for clinical worsening or suicidality. The objective of this study was to examine the association of antidepressants with suicide attempts and with suicide deaths.

*Method:* A longitudinal, observational study of mood disorders with prospective assessments for up to 27 years was conducted at 5 US academic medical centers. The study sample included 757 participants who enrolled from 1979 to 1981 during an episode of mania, depression, or schizoaffective disorder, each based on Research Diagnostic Criteria. Unlike randomised controlled clinical trials of antidepressants, the analyses included participants with psychiatric and other medical comorbidity and those receiving acute or maintenance therapy, polypharmacy, or no psychopharmacologic treatment at all. Over follow-up, these participants had 6,716 time periods that were classified as either exposed to an antidepressant or not exposed. Propensity score-adjusted mixed-effects survival analyses were used to examine risk of suicide attempt or suicide, the primary outcome.

*Results:* The propensity model showed that antidepressant therapy was significantly more likely when participants' symptom severity was greater (odds ratio [OR] = 1.16; 95% CI, 1.12–1.21; z = 8.22; $P$ .001) or when it was worsening (OR = 1.69; 95% CI, 1.50–1.89; z = 9.02; $P <$ .001). Quintile-stratified, propensity-adjusted safety analyses using mixed-effects grouped-time survival models indicate that the risk of suicide attempts or suicides was reduced by 20% among participants taking antidepressants (hazard ratio, 0.80; 95% CI, 0.68–0.95; z = -2.54; $P =$ .011).

*Conclusions:* This longitudinal study of a broadly generalisable cohort found that, although those with more severe affective syndromes were more likely to initiate treatment, antidepressants were associated with a significant reduction in the risk of suicidal behavior. Nonetheless, we believe that clinicians must closely monitor patients when an antidepressant is initiated.

## Are consumers of Internet health information 'cyberchondriacs'? Characteristics of 24,965 users of a depression screening site

Leykin Y, Muñoz RF, Contreras O (USA)

*Depression and Anxiety.* Published online: 16 June 2011. doi: 10.1002/da.20848, 2011

*Background:* The number of individuals looking for health information on the Internet continues to expand. The purpose of this study was to understand the prevalence of major depression among English-speaking individuals worldwide looking for information on depression online.

*Methods:* An automated online Mood Screener website was created and advertised via Google AdWords, for 1 year. Participants ($N =$ 24,965) completed a depression screening measure and received feedback based on their results. Participants were then invited to participate in a longitudinal mood screening study.

*Results:* Of the 24,965 who completed the screening, 66.6% screened positive for current major depression, 44.4% indicated current suicidality, and 7.8% reported a recent (past 2 weeks) suicide attempt. Of those consenting to participate in the longitudinal study ($n =$ 1,327 from 86 countries), 77.4% screened positive for past depression, 64.6% reported past suicidality, and 17.5% past suicide attempt. Yet, only 25% of those screening positive for current depression, and only 37.2% of those reporting a recent suicide attempt are in treatment.

*Conclusions:* Many of the consumers of Internet health information may genuinely need treatment and are not 'cyberchondriacs'. Online screening, treatment, and prevention efforts may have the potential to serve many currently untreated clinically depressed and suicidal individuals.

## The effect of social adjustment and attachment style on suicidal behaviour

Lizardi D, Grunebaum MF, Burke A, Stanley B, Mann JJ, Harkavy-Friedman J, Oquendo M (USA)

*Acta Psychiatrica Scandinavica* 124, 295–300, 2011

*Objective:* Prior studies examining the relationship between social adjustment and suicidal ideation or behaviour have not examined attachment. This study examines the effect of attachment on the association between current social adjustment and suicide attempt risk.

*Method:* Attachment, social adjustment, and history of suicide attempt were assessed in patients participating in research on major depressive disorder ($N$ = 524). Suicide attempters and non-attempters were compared with attachment style and social adjustment using hierarchical logistic regression models. The two factor scoring method of the Adult Attachment Scale (secure vs. avoidant) was utilised as each measures unique aspects of attachment.

*Results:* Anxious attachment (OR = 1.33; 95%CI = 1.016–1.728; $P$ = 0.038) but not overall social adjustment ($P$ = 0.14) was associated with a history of a past suicide attempt when both attachment and social adjustment were assessed in the same model. Among subtypes of social adjustment, work adjustment was associated with past history of suicide attempt (OR = 1.25; 95%CI = 1.019–1.540; $P$ = 0.033). As impairment in work adjustment increased by 1 unit, the likelihood of reporting a suicide attempt increased by approximately 25%. There was no interaction between anxious attachment and work adjustment ($P$ = 0.81).

*Conclusion:* Anxious attachment and work adjustment warrant further study as potential treatment targets in depressed suicidal patients.

## Psychological characteristics, stressful life events and deliberate self-harm: Findings from the Child & Adolescent Self-harm in Europe (CASE) Study

Madge N, Hawton K, McMahon EM, Corcoran P, De Leo D, de Wilde EJ, Fekete S, van Heeringen K, Ystgaard M, Arensman E (UK)

*European Child and Adolescent Psychiatry.* Published online: 17 August 2011. doi: 10.1007/s00787-011-0210-4, 2011

There is evidence to suggest that both psychological characteristics and stressful life events are contributory factors in deliberate self-harm among young people. These links, and the possibility of a dose-response relationship between self-harm and both psychological health and life events, were investigated in the context of a seven-country school-based study. Over 30,000, mainly 15 and 16 year olds, completed anonymous questionnaires at secondary schools in Belgium, England, Hungary, Ireland, the Netherlands, Norway and Australia. Pupils were asked to report on thoughts and episodes of self-harm, complete scales on depression and anxiety symptoms, impulsivity and self-esteem and indicate stressful events in their lives. Level and frequency of self-harm was judged according to whether they had thought about harming themselves or reported single or multiple self-harm episodes. Multinomial logistic regression assessed the extent to which psychological characteristics and stressful life events distinguished between adolescents with different self-harm histories. Increased severity of self-harm history was associated with greater depression, anxiety and impulsivity and lower self-esteem and an increased prevalence of all ten life event categories. Female gender, higher impulsivity and experiencing the suicide or self-harm of others, physical or sexual abuse and worries about sexual orientation independently differentiated single-episode self-harmers from adolescents with self-harm thoughts only. Female gender, higher depression, lower self-esteem, experiencing the suicide or self-harm of others, and trouble with the police independently distinguished multiple-from single-episode self-harmers. The findings reinforce the importance of psychological characteristics and stressful life events in adolescent self-harm but nonetheless suggest that some factors are more likely than others to be implicated.

# Mortality in alcohol use disorder in the Lundby Community Cohort- A 50 year follow-up

Mattisson C, Bogren M, Ojehagen A, Nordström G, Horstmann V (Sweden)
*Drug and Alcohol Dependence* 118, 141–147, 2011

*Aims:* To describe the mortality and causes of death among subjects with alcohol use disorder in comparison with those without alcohol disorder and to study whether mental disorders increase mortality in alcoholics.

*Design and Setting:* Data were analysed from the database of the Lundby Study, comprising 3563 subjects followed from 1947 to 1997.

*Method:* A community-based sample was investigated in 1947 with follow-ups in 1957, 1972 and 1997. Best-estimate consensus diagnoses of mental disorders, including alcohol use disorder, were assessed. In the total cohort, 427 cases of alcohol use disorders were identified. Differences in mortality between subjects with alcohol use disorders and non-alcoholics were studied using Cox regression models and causes of death were compared between alcoholic subjects and other participants. Risk factors for mortality among the 348 individuals with alcohol use disorders and known age-of-onset were analysed by means of Cox regression analyses.

*Results:* The hazard ratio for mortality was higher for alcoholics compared to other subjects in the cohort. A substantial proportion of the causes of death among the alcoholics was suicide $N = 27$ (6.3%) (26 males, 1 female). In the multivariate models of risk factors in alcohol use disorders, anxiety disorders, psychotic disorders, alcohol induced psychotic disorders and dementia were risk factors for premature death.

*Conclusion:* The mortality risk for subjects with alcohol use disorder was increased, females were especially vulnerable. The risk for suicide was high among males with alcohol problems. Anxiety disorders and severity of alcohol use disorder turned out as risk factors for premature death.

## The economic analysis of prevention in mental health programs

Mihalopoulos C, Vos T, Pirkis J, Carter R (Australia)
*Annual Review of Clinical Psychology* 7, 169–201, 2011

This article introduces the role economics can play in deciding whether programs designed to prevent mental disorders, which carry large disease and economic burdens, are a worthwhile use of limited healthcare resources. Fortunately, preventive interventions for mental disorders exist; however, which interventions should be financed is a common issue facing decision makers, and economic evaluation can provide answers. Unfortunately, existing economic evaluations of preventive interventions have limited applicability to local healthcare contexts. An approach to priority setting largely based on economic techniques-Assessing Cost-Effectiveness (ACE)-has been developed and used in Australia to answer questions regarding the economic credentials of competing interventions. Eleven preventive interventions for mental disorders and suicide, mostly psychological in nature, have been evaluated using this approach, with many meeting the criteria of good value for money. Interventions targeting the prevention of suicide, adult and childhood depression, childhood anxiety, and early psychosis have particular merit.

## Globalisation and suicide: An empirical investigation in 35 countries over the period 1980–2006

Milner A, McClure R, Sun J, De Leo D (Australia)
*Health & Place* 17, 996–1003, 2011

*Background:* Globalisation is mediated through a variety of flows including persons, information and ideas, capital, and goods. The process is increasingly recognised as a potential mediator of changes in attitudes and habits around the globe.

*Aim:* This research investigated the relationship between globalisation and suicide rates in 35 countries over the period 1980–2006.

*Methods:* The association between a globalisation 'index' and suicide rates was tested using a fixed-effects regression model. The model also tested the influence of eleven other socio-economic variables on male and female suicide rates.

*Results:* Overall, high levels of the globalisation index were associated with higher male and female suicide rates; however, the significance of this association dropped when assessed alongside other social and economic variables.

*Conclusions:* While the nature of these findings should be regarded as exploratory, this paper highlights the need for researchers to consider the influence of world-changing phenomena like globalisation on suicide, which might deeply upset the traditional structure of societies with mixed types of impact.

# The role of suicide risk in the decision for psychiatric hospitalisation after a suicide attempt

Miret M, Nuevo R, Morant C, Sainz-Cortón E, Jiménez-Arriero MA, López-Ibor JJ, Reneses B, Saiz-Ruiz J, Baca-Garcia E, Ayuso-Mateos JL (Spain)

*Crisis* 32, 65–73, 2011

*Background:* Suicide prevention can be improved by knowing which variables physicians take into account when considering hospitalisation or discharge of patients who have attempted suicide.

*Aims:* To test whether suicide risk is an adequate explanatory variable for predicting admission to a psychiatric unit after a suicide attempt.

*Methods:* Analyses of 840 clinical records of patients who had attempted suicide (66.3% women) at 4 public general hospitals in Madrid (Spain).

*Results:* 180 (21.4%) patients were admitted to psychiatric units. Logistic regression analyses showed that explanatory variables predicting admission were: male gender; previous psychiatric hospitalisation; psychiatric disorder; not having a substance-related disorder; use of a lethal method; delay until discovery of more than 1 hour; previous attempts; suicidal ideation; high suicidal planning; and lack of verbalisation of adequate criticism of the attempt.

*Conclusions:* Suicide risk appears to be an adequate explanatory variable for predicting the decision to admit a patient to a psychiatric ward after a suicide attempt, although the introduction of other variables improves the model. These results provide additional information regarding factors involved in everyday medical practice in emergency settings.

## Childhood physical abuse and suicide-related behavior: A systematic review

Mironova P, Rhodes AE, Bethell JM, Tonmyr L, Boyle MH, Wekerle C, Goodman D, Leslie B (Canada)

*Vulnerable Children and Youth Studies* 6, 1–7, 2011

Childhood physical abuse is associated with suicide-related behavior. We investigate how shared environment with perpetrator(s) identified as a family member or parent/parental figure or an adult at home contribute to this association. This systematic review of school- and population-based studies in children and youth reports on 5 relevant studies. The association was statistically significant in each study, and when examined the association was independent of childhood sexual abuse and other factors. Childhood physical abuse may translate into suicide-related behavior through mechanisms unique from childhood sexual abuse. Future research is needed to strengthen causal inferences to inform the prevention of suicide-related behavior.

## Measurement of total serum cholesterol in the evaluation of suicidal risk

Olié E, Picot MC, Guillaume S, Abbar M, Courtet P (France)

*Journal of Affective Disorders* 133, 234–238, 2011

*Background:* Many studies have demonstrated an association between suicidal behavior and low levels of total serum cholesterol. To our knowledge, this association has mainly been reported in men. This case-control study was undertaken to assess the association between serum cholesterol level and suicide attempts in both genders.

*Methods:* A total of 3207 subjects was included, divided into 3 groups: 510 patients with a history of suicidal attempts, 275 patients with no history of suicidal attempts, and 2422 controls. Mean and quartile total cholesterol levels were compared between the 3 groups according to gender. ROC curves were drawn to determine the biologically relevant threshold.

*Results:* After adjustment for age, cholesterol level was significantly lower ($p < 0.01$) in suicide attempters than in non-attempters and controls for both genders. Male non-suicide attempters had similar cholesterol levels to controls ($p = 0.7$), but the levels in female non-attempters were significantly higher ($p = 0.004$). The proportion of suicide attempters in the lowest cholesterol level quartile (51.3% of men, 40.1% of women) was significantly higher than that in the highest quartile (8.1% of men, 12.4% of women). For triglyceride level, no difference was found between the 3 groups, suggesting that this association was not due to malnutrition linked to depression.

*Limitations:* The effect of acute or chronic administration of medications on serum cholesterol levels was not controlled. Psychiatric history in surgical controls was not recorded.

*Conclusions:* Total serum cholesterol levels measured at admission may be a useful biological marker of suicidal risk.

# Treatment of suicide attempters with bipolar disorder: A randomised clinical trial comparing lithium and valproate in the prevention of suicidal behavior

Oquendo MA, Galfalvy HC, Currier D, Grunebaum MF, Sher L, Sullivan GM, Burke AK, Harkavy-Friedman J, Sublette ME, Parsey RV, Mann JJ (USA)

*American Journal of Psychiatry.* Published online: 18 July 2011. doi: 10.1176/appi.ajp.2011.11010163, 2011

*Objective:* Bipolar disorder is associated with high risk for suicidal acts. Observational studies suggest a protective effect of lithium against suicidal behavior. However, testing this effect in randomised clinical trials is logistically and ethically challenging. The authors tested the hypothesis that lithium offers bipolar patients with a history of suicide attempt greater protection against suicidal behavior compared to valproate.

*Method:* Patients with bipolar disorder and past suicide attempts ($N = 98$) were randomly assigned to treatment with lithium or valproate, plus adjunctive medications as indicated, in a double-blind 2.5-year trial. An intent-to-treat analysis was performed using the log-rank test for survival data. Two models were fitted: time to suicide attempt and time to suicide event (attempt or hospitalisation or change in medication in response to suicide plans).

*Results:* There were 45 suicide events in 35 participants, including 18 suicide attempts made by 14 participants, 6 from the lithium group and 8 from the valproate group. There were no suicides. Intent-to-treat analysis using the log-rank test showed no differences between treatment groups in time to suicide attempt or to suicide event. Post hoc power calculations revealed that the modest sample size, reflective of challenges in recruitment, only permits detection of a relative risk of 5 or greater.

*Conclusions:* Despite the high frequency of suicide events during the study, this randomised controlled trial detected no difference between lithium and valproate in time to suicide attempt or suicide event in a sample of suicide attempters with bipolar disorder. However, smaller clinically significant differences between the 2 drugs were not ruled out.

# First episode of self-harm in older age: A report from the 10-year prospective Manchester self-harm project

Oude Voshaar RC, Cooper J, Murphy E, Steeg S, Kapur N, Purandare NB (UK)

*Journal of Clinical Psychiatry* 72, 737–743, 2011

*Objective:* Self-harm is closely related to completed suicide, especially in older age. As empirical research of self-harm in older age is scarce, with no studies confined to first-ever episodes in older age, we examined the clinical characteristics and the risk of repetition in first-ever self-harm in older age.

*Method:* The Manchester Self-Harm (MaSH) project, a prospective cohort study, gathered data from September 1, 1997, through August 31, 2007, for individuals presenting with self-harm at emergency departments of 3 large hospitals in North West England. The characteristics of older patients (aged ≥ 55 years) who presented with a first-ever episode of self-harm are described and compared to those of middle-aged patients (35–54 years) presenting with a first-ever episode of self-harm. Following each episode, the MaSH form, a standard assessment form developed for the MaSH project, was completed by a clinician. Potential risk factors for repetition were examined by Cox regression analyses.

*Results:* A total of 374 older patients and 1,937 middle-aged patients presented with a first-ever episode of self-harm. The circumstances at the time of self-harm suggested higher suicidal intent in older age. In comparison with middle-aged patients, the rate of repetition in older-aged patients was lower (15.4% versus 11.8%, respectively; hazard ratio for older age = 0.65; 95% CI, 0.45–0.93; $P$ = .019), although repetition was more often fatal among the older group (3.3% versus 13.6%, respectively; $P$ = .009). The most important predictor of repetition in older age, ie, physical health problems, had no predictive value in middle-aged patients, whereas psychiatric characteristics had little impact on the risk of repetition in old age.

*Conclusions:* High suicidal intent and different predictors of repetition in first-ever self-harm in older age highlight the need for age-specific interventions beyond the scope of psychiatric care alone.

# Farm-link: Improving the mental health and well-being of people who live and work on NSW farms

Perceval M, Fuller J, Holley A-M (Australia)

*International Journal of Mental Health* 40, 88–110, 2011

The Farm-Link Program is funded by the Australian Government through the Department of Health and Ageing under the National Suicide Prevention Strategy and is coordinated by the University of Newcastle's Centre for Rural and Remote Mental Health in collaboration with New South Wales (NSW) Health's Rural Area Mental Health Services and the NSW Farmers' Association. It was operational across NSW from July 2007 to December 2009 and is funded to continue in the New England region until June 2011. A major aim of the program was to improve access to and responsiveness of mental health services to the needs of people who live and work on farms. Frontline agricultural workers, who have a lot of contact with farmers and their families, received Mental Health First Aid training provided by Farm-Link staff. Across NSW, 220 participants received this training during 2008, and an additional 133 participants received training in the New England region throughout 2009–10. This training is still being delivered by Farm-Link in the New England region. Farmers' mental health networks were developed and expanded to engage both agricultural and mental health agencies, so that pathways to mental health care could be defined, described, and utilised. These networks were developed in selected sites across 3 rural area health services. By establishing the conditions for successful cross-agency networks to flourish in rural NSW, Farm-Link developed a credible reputation in target communities. An external evaluation, including comparative service network analysis, indicated that Farm-Link successfully identified and established mental health service development interventions in target communities. The evaluation identified a requirement for substantial change within a short-time frame as an inhibiting factor in Farm-Link 2007–09. Farm-Link's ongoing work indicates further time and continuity of service in rural communities has a positive impact on the depth of knowledge built and project aims being delivered. In addition, although documentation of referrals for farmers to various mental health service providers and general practitioners has occurred, more adequate systems need to be developed for the future.

## Clinical and genetic correlates of suicidal ideation during antidepressant treatment in a depressed outpatient sample

Perroud N, Bondolfi G, Uher R, Gex-Fabry M, Aubry J-M, Bertschy G, Malafosse A, Kosel M (Switzerland)

*Pharmacogenomics* 12, 365–377, 2011

*Aims:* This study investigated clinical and genetic predictors of increasing suicidal ideation during antidepressant treatment.

*Materials & Methods:* A total of 131 depressed outpatients were allocated to 4 antidepressants (paroxetine, venlafaxine, clomipramine or nefazodone) in a sequential step procedure until remission. Suicidality was assessed using the 10th item of the Montgomery-Asberg Depression Rating Scale (MADRS). A total of 11 candidate genes involved in different mechanisms of antidepressant action were selected for association with increasing suicidality.

*Results:* Increasing suicidality correlated with depression severity and higher antidepressant blood levels. Risk of increasing suicidal ideation was higher in subjects taking antidepressants other than paroxetine (odds ratio: 1.11). The strongest genetic predictor was found to be rs1360780 within the FKBP5 gene ($p = 2.9 \times 10(-5)$), followed by 2677G>T in the ABCB1 gene. The rs130058 SNP within the 5-HTR1B gene demonstrated a differential association with increasing suicidal ideation depending on antidepressant type.

*Conclusion:* Increasing suicidal ideation might be an adverse effect of antidepressants. The involvement of FKBP5 indicates that dysregulation of the hypothalamic-pituitary-adrenal axis is involved in treatment increasing suicidal ideation.

## Temperaments mediate suicide risk and psychopathology among patients with bipolar disorders

Pompili M, Rihmer Z, Akiskal H, Amore M, Gonda X, Innamorati M, Lester D, Perugi G, Serafini G, Telesforo L, Tatarelli R, Girardi P (Italy)

*Comprehensive Psychiatry.* Published online: 8 June 2011. doi:10.1016/j.comppsych.2011.04.004, 2011

*Background:* Several studies have demonstrated that bipolar II (BD-II) disorder represents a quite common, distinct form of major mood disorders that should be separated from bipolar I (BD-I) disorder. The aims of this cross-sectional study were to assess temperament and clinical differences between patients with BD-I and BD-II disorders and to assess whether temperament traits are good predictors of hopelessness in patients with bipolar disorder, a variable highly associated with suicidal behavior and ideation.

*Method:* Participants were 216 consecutive inpatients (97 men and 119 women) with a Diagnostic and Statistical Manual of Mental Disorders, Fourth Edition, Text Revision (DSM-IV-TR), BD who were admitted to the Sant'Andrea Hospital's psychiatric ward in Rome (Italy). Patients completed the Temperament Evaluation of Memphis, Pisa, Paris, and San Diego-Autoquestionnaire, the Beck Hopelessness Scale (BHS), the Mini International Neuropsychiatric Interview (MINI), and the Gotland Scale of Male Depression.

*Results:* Patients with BD-II had higher scores on the BHS ($9.78 \pm 5.37$ vs $6.87 \pm 4.69$; $t(143.59) = -3.94$; $P < .001$) than patients with BD-I. Hopelessness was associated with the individual pattern of temperament traits (ie, the relative balance of hyperthymic vs cyclothymic-irritable-anxious-dysthmic). Furthermore, patients with higher hopelessness (compared with those with lower levels of hopelessness) reported more frequently moderate to severe depression (87.1% vs 38.9%; $P < .001$) and higher MINI suicidal risk.

*Conclusion:* Temperaments are important predictors both of suicide risk and psychopathology and may be used in clinical practice for better delivery of appropriate care to patients with bipolar disorders.

# The Werther effect reconsidered in light of psychological vulnerabilities: Results of a pilot study

Pouliot L, Mishara BL, Labelle R (Canada)

*Journal of Affective Disorders* 134, 488–496, 2011

*Background:* Findings from 3 decades of epidemiological studies suggest that media diffusion of stories about suicide is related to increases in suicidal behaviours in the population exposed to the media reports. However, we still know little about the psychological processes and personal vulnerabilities that prompt some people to engage in suicidal behaviours after exposure to media presentations of suicides. This cross-sectional study explored the possible impact of exposure to film suicide in normal young people.

*Methods:* Undergraduates from a university (mean age 23 years) completed a questionnaire on exposure to suicide portrayal in fictional films, in which assessment of negative emotional and cognitive reactions resulting from exposure, as well as emotional reactivity, dissociation, thought suppression, and suicidal tendencies were made.

*Results:* Of the 101 participants, 70% reported being distressed by the portrayal of a suicide in a fictional film. Among those, 33% stated they felt distressed about the portrayal for several days to several weeks. The majority of the affected participants (71%) indicated having been mentally preoccupied for some time by the portrayal and experienced intrusive memories (68%). Emotional reactivity and dissociation tendencies were significant predictors of the negative reactions to the suicide film they viewed. Participants who reported that the idea had crossed their mind to imitate the suicidal protagonist in the film were 3.45 times more likely to be suicidal and tended to present higher dissociation and thought suppression propensities compared to those who did not report these thoughts.

*Limitations:* The results showing possible influences of suicide portrayal in fictional film on suicide related cognitions were based on a survey methodology.

*Conclusion:* Results suggest that fictional suicide portrayals in the media may have a deleterious impact on viewers, and such impacts do not appear to be limited to people having a clinical profile of mental disorders, as previously assumed by researchers in the field.

# The protective effect of marriage for survival: A review and update

Rendall MS, Weden MM, Favreault MM, Waldron H (USA)

*Demography* 48, 481–506, 2011

The theory that marriage has protective effects for survival has itself lived for more than 100 years since Durkheim's groundbreaking study of suicide (Durkheim 1951 [1897]). Investigations of differences in this protective effect by gender, by age, and in contrast to different unmarried statuses, however, have yielded inconsistent conclusions. These investigations typically either use data in which marital status and other covariates are observed in cross-sectional surveys up to 10 years before mortality exposure, or use data from panel surveys with much smaller sample sizes. Their conclusions are usually not based on formal statistical tests of contrasts between men and women or between never-married, divorced/separated, and widowed statuses. Using large-scale pooled panel survey data linked to death registrations and earnings histories for U.S. men and women aged 25 and older, and with appropriate contrast tests, we find a consistent survival advantage for married over unmarried men and women, and an additional survival 'premium' for married men. We find little evidence of mortality differences between never-married, divorced/separated, and widowed statuses.

## Mortality of eating disorders: A follow-up study of treatment in a specialist unit 1974–2000

Rosling AM, Sparén P, Norring C, von Knorring AL (Sweden)
*International Journal of Eating Disorders* 44, 304–310, 2011

*Objective:* To study excess mortality, causes of death, and co-morbidity in patients with eating disorder (ED), treated in a Swedish specialist facility.

*Method:* A retrospective cohort study of 201 patients with ED followed from 1974 to year 2001 in the Swedish Causes of Death Register (SCODR). Standardised mortality ratio (SMR) was calculated with respect to the Swedish population, by gender, age, and calendar time.

*Results:* In the complete follow-up of 201 patients, 23 had died. At a mean follow-up of 14.3 years the overall SMR was 10. Patients with body mass index (BMI) over 11.5 had an average SMR of about 7 and for those with BMI lower than 11.5 had SMR above 30. Six patients died from AN/starvation, 9 due to suicide, and 8 from other causes.

*Discussion:* SMR in anorexia nervosa (AN) is high but not in bulimia nervosa. A risk stratification of AN, based on BMI is suggested.

## Impact of employment status and work-related factors on risk of completed suicide: A case-control psychological autopsy study

Schneider B, Grebner K, Schnabel A, Hampel H, Georgi K, Seidler A (Germany)
*Psychiatry Research.* Published online: 3 September 2011. doi:10.1016/j.psychres.2011.07.037, 2011

The objective of this study was to determine the impact of work-related factors on risk for completed suicide. Psychiatric disorders and socio-demographic factors including work-related factors were assessed by a semi-structured interview using the psychological autopsy method in 163 completed suicide cases and by personal interview in 396 living population-based control persons. Unemployment (in particular more than 6 months), (early) retirement, or homemaker status were associated with highly significantly increased suicide risk, independently of categorised psychiatric diagnosis. In addition, adverse psychosocial working conditions, such as monotonous work, increased responsibility and pronounced mental strain due to contact with work clients significantly increased suicide risk as well, again independently of categorised psychiatric diagnosis. These findings demonstrate that negative consequences of unemployment, homemaker status with no outside occupation, or (early) retirement, as well as adverse psychosocial working conditions present relevant risk factors contributing to suicidal behavior, independently of diagnosed psychiatric disorders. Employment and a positive modification of working conditions may possibly be preventive to important adverse mental health outcomes, including suicidality.

## Childhood adversity and suicidal ideation in a clinical military sample: Military unit cohesion and intimate relationships as protective factors

Skopp NA, Luxton DD, Bush N, Sirotin A (USA)
*Journal of Social and Clinical Psychology* 30, 361–377, 2011

Suicide risk and protective factors among 5,187 active duty service members who presented for services at a military outpatient behavioral health clinic were examined. Results indicated that childhood adversity was a significant predictor of suicidal ideation even after controlling for legal, work, financial, and relationship problems, and psychiatric disorders (alcohol abuse, depression, and posttraumatic stress disorder). Childhood adversity was significantly higher among service members who reported prior suicide attempts as compared with service members who did not report prior suicide attempts. The presence of an intimate partner was inversely associated with suicidal ideation. Military unit support moderated the relation between childhood adversity and suicidal ideation, such that this association was positive at lower, but not higher, levels of unit support.

## Problem presentation and responses on an online forum for young people who self-harm

Smithson J, Sharkey S, Hewis E, Jones R, Emmens T, Ford T, Owens C (UK)
*Discourse Studies* 13, 487–501, 2011

In this article we investigate the nature of problem presentation and responses on an online forum for young people who self-harm. Previous studies have raised concerns about the peer encouragement of self-harming behaviours in online forums, and this analysis considers the nature of peer interaction on a specific forum, 'SharpTalk'. This was a research forum which explored the potential of online communities to foster engagement and shared learning between NHS professionals and young people who self-harm. This analysis draws on conversation analysis methods to study problem presentation and responses, and nature of advice given. Analysis highlighted both the tendency to offer advice where it was not asked for, and the mundane 'safe' nature of advice. This awareness of how young people interact and provide support online is important for those setting up online interventions to support young people who self-harm.

## An empirical investigation into the relationship between changes in the business cycle and the incidence of suicide

Snipes M, Cunha TM, Hemley DD (USA)

*International Journal of Social Economics* 38, 477–491, 2011

*Purpose:* The purpose of this paper is to explore the relationship between changes in the business cycle (as indicated by the incidence and duration of unemployment) and the incidence of suicide.

*Design/Methodology/Approach:* A theoretical utility model with savings and consumption is used, while time series micro-level suicide data and probit analysis is used to empirically test the implications of the model.

*Findings:* With declining economic activity and the corresponding increase in unemployment the propensity to commit suicide rises among men for numerable reasons. The authors hypothesise that there is a negative impact with respect to the decline in economic activity and as the intensity increases with respect to the declining business cycle, female's suicides will tend to accelerate.

*Research Limitations/Implications:* One of the primary limitations of this study is the amount of control variables to which the authors had access. There are many factors that would influence an individual when determining whether or not to take their own life. Religious convictions, the presence of children, income, educational attainment, occupational attainment, pre-unemployment income, and how long one had been married or divorced (or unmarried) are all variables that could influence the likelihood of a suicide. The center of disease control (CDC) public use files, however, do not include these variables; thus, the authors were unable to control for their impact.

*Practical Implications:* The authors believe that these findings merit greater public awareness and increases in various forms of public and private support for recently unemployed individuals, being particularly attentive to the effect of higher than normal rates and durations of unemployment and the differences based on gender. These findings also establish another sound rationale for public policies to encourage the increase of personal savings during times of employment to make weathering periods of unemployment easier.

*Social Implications:* In times of increased incidence and duration of unemployment, the tendency of legislators and other public policy makers presumably would be to establish programs targeted to address the population with the highest rates of unemployment-related suicide — white males. It can be argued, however, that since the increased incidence and duration of unemployment have a greater effect on increasing the rate of suicide in women, public policies and programs targeting the specific needs and issues of those unemployed women with an increased risk of suicide would be more cost-effective, preventing or reducing those incremental suicides and mitigating their negative economic, social, and familial impacts.

*Originality/Value:* Previous studies used descriptive statistics, contingency tables, and the traditional statistical regression techniques in their empirical analysis; this study deviates from the norm by the use of probit analysis. Using the probit technique allowed the authors to focus their analysis on the probabilities of suicide with regard not just to the business cycle itself but also to the intensity of the business cycle.

## Age variation in the prevalence of DSM-IV disorders in cases of suicide of middle-aged and older persons in Sydney

Snowdon J, Draper B, Wyder M (Australia)
*Suicide and Life-Threatening Behavior* 41, 465–470, 2011

Data concerning 127 persons aged 35 years or above who died by suicide (as determined in consecutive cases by a Sydney coroner) were analysed. Psychological autopsy (PA) interviews were conducted in 52 cases, and details were compared with the 75 cases where data were available only from coroner's files (CF). Most characteristics of the 2 groups were similar, although more CF suicide victims were of Asian background and unable to speak English fluently. Consensus diagnoses were reached following detailed discussion about PA and CF cases. Logistic regression showed no significant difference between age-groups in the proportion diagnosed with major depression, which contrasts with the results of an earlier U.S. study.

## Post-suicide intervention programs: A systematic review

Szumilas M, Kutcher S (Canada)
*The Canadian Journal of Public Health* 102, 18–29, 2011

*Objective:* The purposes of this study were: (1) to determine the effectiveness of suicide postvention programs on suicide attempts and suicide as well as grief symptoms, mental distress, and mental health broadly defined; and (2) to investigate their cost-effectiveness.

*Methods:* Computerised database searches (PubMed, PsycINFO, Cinahl, Cochrane Database, Crisis and Suicide & Life-Threatening Behavior) were performed in September 2009 to obtain evaluations of suicide postvention programs and in February 2010 (Centre for Research and Dissemination Database, Cochrane Database of Systematic Reviews, PubMed, PsycINFO, and Cinahl) to obtain cost-effectiveness analyses of bereavement programs. Hand searches of relevant articles and reviews were also conducted. Publications were included in the analysis if they described an evaluation/cost-effectiveness analysis of a suicide postvention program, provided data, and were published in English-language peer-reviewed journals. There was no restriction on publication date. Studies were excluded if they were narrative systematic reviews or dissertations or if they described a postvention program but provided no evaluation. Because very few cost-effectiveness analyses were identified, articles describing 'costs' of bereavement programs were also included. Studies were evaluated for quality using Centres for Evidence-Based Medicine Levels of Evidence, and for program effectiveness using Office of Justice Programs 'What Works Repository' Analytic Framework.

*Results:* Of the 49 studies of suicide postvention programs retrieved, 16 met inclusion criteria for evaluation of study quality and evidence of effectiveness. Three target populations for postvention programs were identified: school-based, family-focused, and community-based. No protective effect of any postvention program could be determined for number of suicide deaths or suicide attempts from the available studies. Few positive effects of school-based postvention programs were found. One study reported negative effects of a suicide postvention. Gatekeeper training for proactive postvention was effective in increasing knowledge pertaining to crisis intervention among school personnel. Outreach at the scene of suicide was found to be helpful in encouraging survivors to attend a support group at a crisis centre and seek help in dealing with their loss. Contact with a counseling postvention for familial survivors (spouses, parents, children) of suicide generally helped reduce psychological distress in the short term. There was no statistical analysis of community-based suicide postvention programs; however media guidelines for reporting of suicide and suicide attempts have been adopted by mental health organisations in numerous countries. No analyses of cost-effectiveness of suicide postvention programs were found.

*Conclusion:* Recommendations to provide guidance to policy-makers, administrators and clinicians are presented and directions for future research are outlined.

# Association between non-suicidal self-injuries and suicide attempts in Chinese adolescents and college students: A cross-section study

Tang J, Yu Y, Wu Y, Du Y, Ma Y, Zhu H, Zhang P, Liu Z (China)
*PLoS ONE* 6, e17977, 2011

*Purpose:* This study examined the association between non-suicidal self-injury (NSSI) and suicide attempts among Chinese adolescents and college students.

*Methods:* A total sample of 2013 Chinese students were randomly selected from 5 schools in Wuhan, China, including 1101 boys and 912 girls with the age ranging between 10 and 24 years. NSSI, suicidal ideation, suicide attempts and depressive symptoms were measured by self-rated questionnaires. Self-reported suicide attempts were regressed on suicidal ideation and NSSI, controlling for participants' depressive symptoms, and demographic characteristics.

*Results:* The self-reported prevalence rates of NSSI, suicidal ideation, suicide attempts were 15.5%, 8.8%, and 3.5%, respectively. Logistic regression analyses indicated that NSSI was significantly associated with self-reported suicide attempts. Analyses examining the conditional association of NSSI and suicidal ideation with self-reported suicide attempts revealed that NSSI was significantly associated with greater risk of suicide attempts in those not reporting suicidal ideation than those reporting suicidal ideation in the past year.

*Conclusions:* These findings highlight the importance of NSSI as a potentially independent risk factor for suicide attempts among Chinese/Han adolescents and college students.

# Suicide epidemics: The impact of newly emerging methods on overall suicide rates- A time trends study

Thomas K, Chang SS, Gunnell D (UK)
*BMC Public Health* 11, 314, 2011

*Background:* The impact of newly emerging, popular suicide methods on overall rates of suicide has not previously been investigated systematically. Understanding these effects may have important implications for public health surveillance. We examine the emergence of 3 novel methods of suicide by gassing in the 20th and 21st centuries and determine the impact of emerging methods on overall suicide rates.

*Methods:* We studied the epidemic rises in domestic coal gas (1919–1935, England and Wales), motor vehicle exhaust gas (1975–1992, England and Wales) and barbecue charcoal gas (1999–2006, Taiwan) suicide using Poisson and joinpoint regression models. Joinpoint regression uses contiguous linear segments and join points (points at which trends change) to describe trends in incidence.

*Results:* Epidemic increases in the use of new methods of suicide were generally associated with rises in overall suicide rates of between 23% and 71%. The recent epidemic of barbecue charcoal suicides in Taiwan was associated with the largest rise in overall rates (40–50% annual rise), whereas the smallest rise was seen for car exhaust gassing in England and Wales (7% annual rise). Joinpoint analyses were only feasible for car exhaust and charcoal burning suicides; these suggested an impact of the emergence of car exhaust suicides on overall suicide rates in both sexes in England and Wales. However there was no statistical evidence of a change in the already increasing overall suicide trends when charcoal burning suicides emerged in Taiwan, possibly due to the concurrent economic recession.

*Conclusions:* Rapid rises in the use of new sources of gas for suicide were generally associated with increases in overall suicide rates. Suicide prevention strategies should include strengthening local and national surveillance for early detection of novel suicide methods and implementation of effective media guidelines and other appropriate interventions to limit the spread of new methods.

# Effects of combat deployment on risky and self-destructive behavior among active duty military personnel

Thomsen CJ, Stander VA, McWhorter SK, Rabenhorst MM, Milner JS (USA)
*Journal of Psychiatric Research* 45, 1321–1331, 2011

Although research has documented negative effects of combat deployment on mental health, few studies have examined whether deployment increases risky or self-destructive behavior. The present study addressed this issue. In addition, we examined whether deployment effects on risky behavior varied depending on history of pre-deployment risky behavior, and assessed whether psychiatric conditions mediated effects of deployment on risky behavior. In an anonymous survey, active duty members of the U.S. Marine Corps and U.S. Navy ($N = 2116$) described their deployment experiences and their participation in risky recreational activities, unprotected sex, illegal drug use, self-injurious behavior, and suicide attempts during 3 time frames (civilian, military pre-deployment, and military post-deployment). Respondents also reported whether they had problems with depression, anxiety, or PTSD during the same 3 time frames. Results revealed that risky behavior was much more common in civilian than in military life, with personnel who had not deployed, compared to those who had deployed, reporting more risky behavior and more psychiatric problems as civilians. For the current time period, in contrast, personnel who had deployed (versus never deployed) were significantly more likely to report both risky behavior and psychiatric problems. Importantly, deployment was associated with increases in risky behavior only for personnel with a pre-deployment history of engaging in risky behavior. Although psychiatric conditions were associated with higher levels of risky behavior, psychiatric problems did not mediate associations between deployment and risky behavior. Implications for understanding effects of combat deployment on active duty personnel and directions for future research are discussed.

# Characteristics and predictors of long-term institutionalisation in patients with schizophrenia

Uggerby P, Nielsen RE, Correll CU, Nielsen J (Denmark)
*Schizophrenia Research* 131, 120–126, 2011

*Background:* Patients with schizophrenia requiring long-term institutionalisation represent those with the worst outcome, leading to personal costs for patients and relatives and constituting a large economical burden for society.

*Aim:* To identify characteristics and predictors of outcome of institutionalised patients with schizophrenia.

*Method:* One-year follow-up cohort study, utilising the Danish national registers, of all institutionalised and non-institutionalised patients with schizophrenia in Denmark with an ICD-10 lifetime diagnosis of schizophrenia (F20.0–F20.9) since 1969 and alive at the index date of January 1st 2006 (total number 22,395).

*Results:* Compared with non-institutionalised patients, institutionalised patients ($n = 2188$; 9.8%) had earlier onset of schizophrenia and lower scholastic achievements, were more often diagnosed with a hebephrenic subtype (odds ratio (OR), 2.34; 95% confidence interval (CI), 1.95–2.80; $p < 0.001$), received higher dosages of antipsychotics, more antipsychotic polypharmacy and more concomitant medications, and had more substance misuse and early retirement pension. In a logistic regression model adjusted for sex and age, institutionalised patients with schizophrenia had an increased risk of type II diabetes (AOR, 1.22; CI, 1.01–1.42; $p < 0.001$), but the mean age of onset of type II diabetes did not differ. The mean patient age was higher in the institutionalised group (62.7 vs. 58.7 years; $p = 0.027$), which was mainly driven by absence of death from suicide in the institutionalised group. Multivariate predictors of institutionalisation included hebephrenic subtype, a diagnosis of epilepsy, early retirement pension, male sex, a greater proportion of prior hospitalisation, and substance misuse.

*Conclusions:* Institutionalised patients with schizophrenia had a more complex and worse outcome of the disorder, except for less suicide, illustrated by lower scholastic achievement, receiving higher dosages of antipsychotic medications, more concomitant medications and more prior bed-days.

# Rate of readmission and mortality risks of schizophrenia patients who were discharged against medical advice

Valevski A, Zalsman G, Tsafrir S, Lipschitz-Elhawi R, Weizman A, Shohat T (Israel)

*European Psychiatry.* Published online: 25 June 2011. doi:10.1016/j.eurpsy.2011.04.009, 2011

*Purpose:* To compare the readmission and the mortality rates of schizophrenia patients who were discharged against medical advice (AMA) and patients who were discharged by physician recommendation.

*Methods:* The records (1984–2005) of all consecutive admissions ($n = 12,937$) of schizophrenia patients ($n = 8,052$) were reviewed. Out of this group, 673 (8.3%) refused to remain in the hospital and signed a hospital form for discharge AMA. Their records were analysed for rates of re-hospitalisation and mortality at study closure. The records of AMA patients were compared to those of patients with regular discharge ($n = 1345$).

*Results:* AMA patients were younger at admission ($P < 0.001$), comprised more males ($P < 0.01$), more were single ($P < 0.0001$), and had a shorter duration of illness than the controls ($P < 0.05$). A total of 49.9% of AMA events occurred within the first 2 weeks of hospitalisation. The readmission rate was significantly higher for AMA patients than for the controls ($P < 0.001$). The mortality rate as a result of suicide ($P < 0.0001$) and accidents ($P < 0.05$) was higher for AMA patients compared to controls.

*Conclusion:* The schizophrenia patients discharged AMA have a higher readmission rate and a higher mortality rate due to suicide and accidents compared to non-AMA discharged patients. Patients with AMA discharge warrant special community surveillance to improve outcome.

# Disability weights for suicidal thoughts and non-fatal suicide attempts

van Spijker BA, van Straten A, Kerkhof AJ, Hoeymans N, Smit F (The Netherlands)

*Journal of Affective Disorders* 134, 341–347, 2011

*Background:* Although there are disability weights available for a wide range of health states, these do not include suicidality. This makes it difficult to evaluate the severity of suicidality in comparison with other health states. The aim of this study therefore is to estimate disability weights for suicidal thoughts and for mental distress involved in non-fatal suicide attempts.

*Methods:* A Dutch expert panel of sixteen medical practitioners who were knowledgeable about suicidality estimated disability weights (DWs) for twelve health states by interpolating them on a calibrated Visual Analogue Scale. The DWs for ten of these health states had been estimated in previous studies and were used to determine the external consistency of the panel. The other 2 concerned health states for suicidal thoughts and non-fatal suicide attempts. The resulting DWs could vary between 0 (best imaginable health state) and 1 (worst imaginable health state).

*Results:* Both internal (Cronbach's $\alpha = 0.98$) and external consistency of the panel were satisfactory. The DWs for suicidal thoughts and non-fatal suicide attempts were estimated to be 0.36 and 0.46 respectively.

*Limitations:* The panel was relatively small, which resulted in broad confidence intervals.

*Conclusions:* Suicidal thoughts are considered to be as disabling as alcohol dependence and severe asthma. The mental distress involved in non-fatal suicide attempts is thought to be comparable in disability to heroin dependence and initial stage Parkinson's. These results demonstrate the severity of suicidality.

## Patient perceptions of the potential lethality associated with deliberate self-poisoning

Vlad IA, Fatovich DM, Fenner SG, Daly FF, Soderstrom JH-M, Burrows SA (Australia)

*EMA — Emergency Medicine Australasia.* Published online: 15 June 2011. doi: 10.1111/j.1742-6723. 2011.01434.x, 2011

*Introduction:* Little is known about patient perceptions of the lethality of their overdose. Our aim was to compare patient perceptions with the risk assessment of clinical toxicologists.

*Methods:* A prospective observational study of overdose patients presenting to a tertiary hospital. Eligible patients were surveyed once they were medically fit for psychiatric evaluation. Descriptive data were collected, including the Pierce Suicide Intent Scale (SIS). In response to 'how dangerous did you think this overdose was when you took the tablets?' patients marked a 10cm VAS, with 0 = would be harmless, 10 = certain to cause death. A panel of clinical toxicologists independently made a risk assessment on a 10cm VAS, with 0 = non-toxic ingestion and 10 = uniform lethality even with full medical intervention.

*Results:* Of 202 patients enrolled, 118 (58.4%, 95% CI 51–65) were female; median age 33 years (interquartile range [IQR] 24–42). One hundred and three (51%, 95% CI 44–58) stated it was their intention to kill themselves and 44 (21.8%, 95% CI 16–28) wrote a suicide note. They most commonly used their own prescription medications (141, 69.8%, 95% CI 63–76). The median patient visual analog scale (VAS) was 5.8 (IQR 2.3–8.3) and median toxicology VAS was 1.4 (IQR 0.6–2.8); this difference was statistically significant ($P < 0.0001$). The correlation between the patient visual analog scale (VAS) and Pierce SIS (median 8.5/25 [IQR 4–12]) was strong (r= 0.73, $P < 0.0001$).

*Conclusions:* Patient perceptions of the lethality of their overdose are correlated with their suicidal intent as measured on the Pierce SIS, with a significant mismatch between patient perceptions and the toxicological risk assessment.

# Suicide in Ireland: The influence of alcohol and unemployment

Walsh B, Walsh D (Ireland)

*The Economic and Social Review* 42, 27–47, 2011

We model the behaviour of the Irish suicide rate over the period 1968–2009 using the unemployment rate and the level of alcohol consumption as the principal explanatory variables. We find that alcohol consumption is a significant influence on the suicide rate among younger males. Its influence on the female suicide rate is not well-established, although there is some evidence that it plays a role in the 15–24 age group. The unemployment rate is also a significant influence on the male suicide rate in the younger age groups but evidence of its influence on the female suicide rate is lacking. The behaviour of suicide rates among males aged 55 and over and females aged 25 and over is unaccounted for by our model. The findings suggest that higher alcohol consumption played a significant role in the very rapid increase in suicide mortality among young Irish males between the late 1980s and the end of the century. In the early twenty first century a combination of falling alcohol consumption and low unemployment led to a marked reduction in suicide rates. The recent rise in suicide rates may be attributed to the sharp rise in unemployment, especially among males, but it has been moderated by the continuing fall in alcohol consumption. Finally, we discuss some policy implications of our findings.

# Integrating medical examiner and police report data

Ward BW, Shields RT, Cramer BR (USA)

*Crisis* 32, 160–168, 2011

*Background:* Recently, suicide in the United States has begun to be viewed as a preventable public health issue. This has led to the creation of a National Violent Death Reporting System that collects and integrates data on the social circumstances surrounding suicides.

*Aims:* The study examines data on social circumstances surrounding suicides as collected by the medical examiner report (ME) and police report (PR) and subsequently integrated into the state of Maryland's violent death reporting system.

*Methods:* Reported data on social circumstances surrounding suicides occurring in the years 2003–2006 in Maryland ($n = 1,476$) were analysed by examining their prevalence in the ME and PR, strength of association, and integration.

*Results:* With the exception of 3 circumstances, there was variation among reported circumstances in the ME and PR. Furthermore, there was only a moderately strong relationship between the ME and PR for most circumstances, while a significant increase occurred in the prevalence of these circumstances when ME and PR were integrated.

*Conclusions:* The integration of ME and PR has the potential to increase our knowledge of the circumstances surrounding suicide and to better inform prevention efforts. However, before this potential can be reached, there are still issues that must be considered.

## Predictors of suicide relative to other deaths in patients with suicide attempts and suicide ideation: A 30-year prospective study

Wenzel A, Berchick ER, Tenhave T, Halberstadt S, Brown GK, Beck AT (USA)

*Journal of Affective Disorders* 132, 375–382, 2011

*Background:* Although there is a large literature that prospectively examines predictors of suicide, low base rates of suicide and imprecision of measurement hinder definitive conclusions from being drawn.

*Method:* This study examined predictors of suicide relative to other types of death in a sample of 297 patients who had been hospitalised for suicide ideation or a suicide attempt between 1970 and 1975 and who were confirmed dead in 2005. Many predictors were measured using well-validated assessment instruments.

*Results:* Fifty-five patients had died by suicide. Univariate predictors of an increased risk for eventual suicide included younger age, completion of at least a high school degree, a diagnosis of a psychotic disorder, taking active precautions against discovery during the attempt, and a non-zero score on the suicide item of the Beck Depression Inventory, whereas African American ethnicity was associated with a decreased risk of eventual suicide. Variables that remained significant in a multivariate analysis included younger age, African American ethnicity, and taking active precautions against discovery during the attempt. Risk factors did not vary as a function of whether eventual suicide occurred less than or more than 5 years after the initial evaluation or by attempter v. ideator status.

*Limitations:* Despite the attempt to maximise statistical power by following a high-risk sample for 30 years, the number of deaths by suicide was still relatively low.

*Conclusions:* Taking active precautions against discovery of a suicide attempt has the potential to be an important predictor of eventual suicide and should be assessed by clinicians. Future prospective studies should assess predictors at multiple time points to gain a richer clinical picture of the circumstances surrounding deaths by suicide.

## Predictors of psychiatric boarding in the pediatric emergency department: Implications for emergency care

Wharff EA, Ginnis KB, Ross AM, Blood EA (USA)

*Pediatric Emergency Care* 27, 483–489, 2011

*Objectives:* Patients who present to the emergency department (ED) and require psychiatric hospitalisation may wait in the ED or be admitted to a medical service because there are no available inpatient psychiatric beds. These patients are psychiatric 'boarders.' This study describes the extent of the boarder problem in a large, urban pediatric ED, compares characteristics of psychiatrically hospitalised patients with boarders, and compares predictors of boarding in 2 ED patient cohorts.

*Methods:* A retrospective cohort study was conducted in 2007/2008. The main outcome measure was placement into a psychiatric facility or boarding. Predictors of boarding in the present analysis were compared with predictors from a similar study conducted in the same ED in 1999/2000.

*Results:* Of 461 ED patient encounters requiring psychiatric admission, 157 (34.1%) boarded. Mean and median boarding duration for the sample were 22.7(SD, 8.08) and 21.18 hours, respectively. Univariate generalised estimating equations demonstrated increased boarding odds for patients carrying Diagnostic and Statistical Manual of Mental Disorders, Fourth Edition diagnoses of autism, mental retardation, and/or developmental delay ($P = 0.01$), presenting during the weekend ($P = 0.03$) or presenting during months without school vacation ($P = 0.02$). Suicidal ideation (SI) significantly predicted boarding status, with increased likelihood of boarding for severe SI ($P = 0.02$). Age, race, insurance status, and homicidal ideation did not significantly predict boarding in the 2007/2008 patient cohort, although they did in the earlier study. Systemic factors and SI predicted boarding status in both cohorts.

*Conclusions:* Suicidal patients continue to board. Limits within the system, including timing of ED presentation and a dearth of specialised services, still exist, elevating the risk of boarding for some populations. Implications for pediatric ED psychiatric care delivery are discussed.

## Birthday blues: Examining the association between birthday and suicide in a national sample

Williams A, While D, Windfuhr K, Bickley H, Hunt IM, Shaw J, Appleby L, Kapur N (UK)

*Crisis* 32, 134–142, 2011

*Background:* Socioculturally meaningful events have been shown to influence the timing of suicide, but the influence of psychiatric disorder on these associations has seldom been studied.

*Aims:* To investigate the association between birthday and increased risk of suicide in the general population and in a national sample of psychiatric patients.

*Methods:* Data on general population suicides and suicide by individuals in recent care of mental health services were examined for day of death in relation to one's birthday using Poisson regression analysis.

*Results:* An increased risk of suicide was observed on day of one's birthday itself for males in both the general population (IRR = 1.39, 95% CI = 1.18–1.64, $p <$ .01) and the clinical population (IRR = 1.48, 95% CI = 1.07–2.07, $p =$ .03), especially for those aged 35 years and older. In the clinical population, risk was restricted to male patients aged 35–54 and risk extended to the 3 days prior to one's birthday.

*Conclusions:* Birthdays are periods of increased risk for men aged 35 and older in the general population and in those receiving mental health care. Raising healthcare professionals' awareness of patient groups at greater risk at this personally significant time may benefit care planning and could facilitate suicide prevention in these individuals.

## Prospective cohort study of suicide attempters aged 70 and above: One-year outcomes

Wiktorsson S, Marlow T, Runeson B, Skoog I, Waern M (Sweden)
*Journal of Affective Disorders* 134, 333–340, 2011

*Background:* Most elderly persons who attempt suicide suffer from depression. This study aimed to investigate one-year outcomes in suicide attempters aged 70+, and to identify predictors of these outcomes.

*Methods:* 101 persons (mean age 80) who were hospitalised after a suicide attempt were interviewed at baseline and followed for 1 year by record linkage. Face-to-face interviews were carried out with 71% of those who were alive after 1 year (60 out of 85). Outcome measures included major/minor depression, Montgomery-Asberg Depression Rating Scale (MADRS) score, repeat non-fatal/fatal suicidal behavior and all-cause mortality.

*Results:* One half (52%) of all those who were interviewed scored <10 on the MADRS at follow-up. Among those with major depression at baseline, two-thirds (26 out of 39) no longer fulfilled criteria for this disorder. Factors associated with non-remission of major depression (MADRS >/=10) included higher baseline depression and anxiety scores, higher suicide intent and lower Sense of Coherence. There were 2 suicides and 6 non-fatal repeat attempts. The relative risk of death (any cause) was 2.53 (95% CI=1.45–4.10, $p < 0.001$).

*Limitations:* This is a naturalistic study; participants received non-uniform treatment as usual. The proportion with repeat suicidal behavior was lower than anticipated and the study was thus underpowered with regard to this outcome.

*Conclusions:* Half of the surviving attempters were free from depressive symptoms at one-year follow-up and there were relatively few repeat attempts. However, all cause mortality remained high in this elderly cohort.

# The relation between nicotine dependence and suicide attempts in the general population

Yaworski D, Robinson J, Sareen J, Bolton JM (Canada)

*Canadian Journal of Psychiatry* 56, 161–170, 2011

*Objective:* There has been much debate as to whether nicotine is a risk factor for suicidal behaviour. This study sought to examine the relation between nicotine dependence and suicide attempts in a population-based sample of adults.

*Method:* Our study used the National Epidemiologic Survey on Alcohol and Related Conditions Wave 2 (NESARC; 2004–2005), a large ($n = 34,653$) nationally representative survey of community-dwelling American adults. Multiple logistic regression analyses examined the relation between suicide attempts and Diagnostic and Statistical Manual of Mental Disorders, Fourth Edition, nicotine dependence, compared with nonusers of nicotine. Associations between suicide attempts and other measures of nicotine use (nicotine cessation, age of first use, frequency, and amount of use) were also examined.

*Results:* Lifetime (AOR 1.78; 95% CI 1.48 to 2.15) and past-year nicotine dependence (AOR 1.77; 95% CI 1.02 to 3.06) were independently associated with lifetime and past-year suicide attempts, respectively, even after adjusting for sociodemographic factors, other mental disorders, and physical disease. Nicotine dependence cessation was associated with a decreased likelihood of suicide attempt compared with people currently dependent on nicotine (AOR 0.15; 95% CI 0.05 to 0.43). Greater amount of daily cigarette use was associated with suicide attempts in the model that adjusted for sociodemographic factors and other mental disorders (AOR 1.53; 95% CI 1.05 to 2.24).

*Conclusions:* Nicotine dependence is associated with suicide attempts, independently of comorbid mental disorders and physical disease. The association attenuates when a person ceases using nicotine, suggesting a state, rather than trait, effect. These findings provide evidence for additional concern regarding the deleterious health effects of tobacco.

# Citation List

# FATAL SUICIDAL BEHAVIOUR

## Epidemiology

Abrams RC, Leon AC, Tardiff K, Marzuk PM, Santos RD (2011). Suicidal overdoses of psychotropic drugs by elderly in New York City: Comparison with younger adults. *Psychiatry Research* 188, 459–461.

Adhikary P, Keen S, van Teijlingen E (2011). Health issues among Nepalese migrant workers in the Middle East. *Health Science Journal* 5, 169–175.

Agoramoorthy G, Hsu MJ (2011). Suicide in Taiwan's society. *Drustvena Istrazivanja* 20, 137–149.

Ahoniemi E, Pohjolainen T, Kautiainen H (2011). Survival after spinal cord injury in Finland. *Journal of Rehabilitation Medicine* 43, 481–485.

Ala A, Vahdati SS, Moosavi L, Sadeghi H (2011). Studying the relationship between age, gender and other demographic factors with the type of agent used for self-poisoning at a poisoning referral center in North West Iran. *Journal of Academic Emergency Medicine* 10, 100–102.

Alvarez P, Urretavizcaya M, Benlloch L, Vallejo J, Menchon JM (2011). Early- and late-onset depression in the older: No differences found within the melancholic subtype. *International Journal of Geriatric Psychiatry* 26, 615–621.

Anestis MD, Bender TW, Selby EA, Ribeiro JD, Joiner TE (2011). Sex and emotion in the acquired capability for suicide. *Archives of Suicide Research* 15, 172–182.

Austin AE, van den Heuvel C, Byard RW (2011). Causes of community suicides among indigenous South Australians. *Journal of Forensic and Legal Medicine* 18, 299–301.

Baker TD, Baker SP, Haack SA (2011). Trauma in the Russian Federation: Then and now. *Journal of Trauma-Injury Infection and Critical Care* 70, 991–995.

Bakke HK, Wisborg T (2011). Rural high north: A high rate of fatal injury and prehospital death. *World Journal of Surgery* 35, 1615–1620.

Basham C, Denneson LM, Millet L, Shen X, Duckart J, Dobscha SK (2011). Characteristics and VA health care utilization of U.S. veterans who completed suicide in Oregon between 2000 and 2005. *Suicide and Life-Threatening Behavior* 41, 287–296.

Bashir MSM, Khade A, Bhagat S, Irfanuddin M (2011). Gender differences in the pattern of organophosphorus poisoning in a tribal distict of Andhra Pradesh. *Indian Journal of Forensic Medicine and Toxicology* 5, 54–57.

Betz ME, Krzyzaniak SM, Hedegaard H, Lowenstein SR (2011). Completed suicides in Colorado: differences between Hispanics and Non-Hispanic Whites. *Suicide and Life-Threatening Behavior* 41, 445–452.

Betz ME, Valley MA, Lowenstein SR, Hedegaard H, Thomas D, Stallones L, Honigman B (2011). Elevated suicide rates at high altitude: Sociodemographic and health issues may be to blame. *Suicide and Life-Threatening Behavior.* Published online: 29 August 2011. doi: 10.1111/j.1943-278X.2011.00054.x

Black SA, Gallaway MS, Bell MR, Ritchie EC (2011). Prevalence and risk factors associated with suicides of army soldiers 2001–2009. *Military Psychology* 23, 433–451.

Blair G (2011). Japan's suicide rate is expected to rise after triple disasters in March. *BMJ: British Medical Journal* 343, d5839.

Bloem B, Xu L, Morava E, Faludi G, Palkovits M, Roubos EW, Kozicz T (2011). Sex-specific differences in the dynamics of cocaine- and amphetamine-regulated transcript and nesfatin-1 expressions in the midbrain of depressed suicide victims vs. Controls. *Neuropharmacology.* Published online: 22 July 2011. doi:10.1016/j.neuropharm.2011. 07.023

Brüne M, Schöbel A, Karau R, Faustmann PM, Dermietzel R, Juckel G, Petrasch-Parwez E (2011). Neuroanatomical correlates of suicide in psychosis: The possible role of von economo neurons. *PLoS ONE* 6, e20936.

Bryan CJ (2011). Suicide among service members. *Psychiatric Times* 28, 34–39.

Bulayeva KB, Lencz T, Glatt S, Takumi T, Gurgenova FR, Bulayev OA (2011). Genome-wide linkage scan of major depressive disorder in two Dagestan genetic isolates. *Central European Journal of Medicine* 6, 616–624.

Burlingame J, Horiuchi B, Ohana P, Onaka A, Sauvage LM (2011). The contribution of heart disease to pregnancy-related mortality according to the pregnancy mortality surveillance system. *Journal of Perinatology*. Published online: 9 June 2011. doi: 10.1038/jp.2011.74

Callanan VJ, Davis MS (2011). Gender and suicide method: Do women avoid facial disfiguration? *Sex Roles*. Published online: 27 August 2011. doi: 10.1007/s11199-011-0043-0

Centers for Disease Control and Prevention (CDC) (2011). Chemical suicides in automobiles — Six States, 2006–2010. *Morbidity & Mortality Weekly Report* 9, 1189–1192.

Centers for Disease Control and Prevention (CDC) (2011). Progress toward interruption of wild violence-related firearm deaths among residents of metropolitan areas and cities — United States, 2006–2007. *Morbidity & Mortality Weekly Report* 60, 573–578.

Chen SC, Hwu HG, Hsiung PC (2011). Clinical manifestations of aggressive acts by schizophrenic inpatients: A prospective study. *Perspectives in Psychiatric Care* 47, 110–116.

Chen VC, Stewart R, Lee CT (2011). Weekly lottery sales volume and suicide numbers: A time series analysis on national data from Taiwan. *Social Psychiatry & Psychiatric Epidemiology*. Published online: 17 June 2011. doi: 10.1007/s00127-011-0410-8

Chen YY, Yip PS (2011). Suicide sex ratios after the inception of charcoal-burning suicide in Taiwan and Hong Kong. *Journal of Clinical Psychiatry* 72, 566–567.

Chia BH, Chia A, Ng WY, Tai BC (2011). Suicide methods in Singapore (2000–2004): Types and associations. *Suicide and Life-Threatening Behavior*. Published online: 14 September 2011. doi: 10.1111/j.1943-278X.2011.00055.x

Chien WC, Lin JD, Lai CH, Chung CH, Hung YC (2011). Trends in poisoning hospitalization and mortality in Taiwan, 1999–2008: A retrospective analysis. *BMC Public Health* 11, 703.

Chowdhury FR, Rahman AU, Mohammed FR, Chowdhury A, Ahasan HA, Bakar MA (2011). Acute poisoning in southern part of Bangladesh- The case load is decreasing. *Bangladesh Medical Research Council Bulletin* 37, 61–65.

Christodoulou C, Douzenis A, Papadopoulos FC, Papadopoulou A, Bouras G, Gournellis R, Lykouras L (2011). Suicide and seasonality. *Acta Psychiatrica Scandinavica*. Published online: 13 August 2011. doi: 10.1111/j.1600-0447.2011.01750.x

Classen TJ, Dunn RA (2011). Suicide, social integration and fertility rates. *Applied Economics Letters* 18, 1011–1014.

Congdon P (2011). The spatial pattern of suicide in the US in relation to deprivation, fragmentation and rurality. *Urban Studies* 48, 2101–2122.

Coyne-Beasley T, Lees AC (2010). Fatal and nonfatal firearm injuries in North Carolina. *North Carolina Medical Journal* 71, 565–568.

Crosby AE, Ortega L, Stevens MR, Centers for Disease Control and Prevention (CDC) (2011). Suicides- United States, 1999–2007. *Morbidity & Mortality Weekly Report: Surveillance Summaries* 60, 56–59.

Cryer C, Fingerhut L, Segui-Gomez M, on behalf of the ICE Injury Indicators Working Group (2011). Injury mortality indicators: Recommendations from the International Collaborative Effort on Injury Statistics. *Injury Prevention*. Published online: 14 June 2011. doi:10.1136/injuryprev-2011-040037

Curtis C, Curtis B (2011). The origins of a New Zealand suicidal cohort: 1970–2007. *Health Sociology Review* 20, 219–228.

Dennehy EB, Marangell LB, Allen MH, Chessick C, Wisniewski SR, Thase ME (2011). Suicide and suicide attempts in the Systematic Treatment Enhancement Program for Bipolar Disorder (STEP-BD). *Journal of Affective Disorders* 133, 423–427.

Diaz-Granados N, McDermott S, Wang F, Posada-Villa J, Saavedra J, Rondon MB, DesMeules M, Dorado L, Torres Y, Stewart DE (2011). Monitoring gender equity in mental health in a low-, middle-, and high-income country in the Americas. *Psychiatric Services* 62, 516–524.

Doble N, Supriya MV (2011). Student life balance: Myth or reality? *International Journal of Educational Management* 25, 237–251.

Felthous AR (2011). Suicide behind bars: Trends, inconsistencies, and practical implications. *Journal of Forensic Sciences.* Published online: 9 August 2011. doi: 10.1111/j.1556-4029.2011.01858.x

Franciskovic T, Stevanovic A, Blazic D, Petric D, Sukovic Z, Tovilovic Z, Moro IN (2011). Croatian war veterans in print media in 1996 and in 2006. *Psychiatria Danubina* 23, 171–177.

Gagne P, Moamai J, Bourget D (2011). Psychopathology and suicide among Quebec Physicians: A nested case control study. *Depression Research and Treatment.* Published online: 28 July 2011. doi: 10.1155/2011/936327

Gil-Pisa I, Munarriz-Cuezva E, Ramos-Miguel A, Urigüen L, Meana JJ, García-Sevilla JA (2011). Regulation of munc18-1 and syntaxin-1A interactive partners in schizophrenia prefrontal cortex: Down-regulation of munc18-1a isoform and 75 kDa SNARE complex after antipsychotic treatment. *International Journal of Neuropsychopharmacology.* Published online: 14 June 2011. doi: 10.1017 /S1461145711000861

Gotsens M, Mari-Dell'Olmo M, Martinez-Beneito MA, Perez K, Pasarin MI, Daponte A, Puigpinos-Riera R, Rodriguez-Sanz M, Audicana C, Nolasco A, Gandarillas A, Serral G, Dominguez-Berjon F, Martos C, Borrell C (2011). Socio-economic inequalities in mortality due to injuries in small areas of ten cities in Spain (MEDEA Project). *Accident Analysis and Prevention* 43, 1802–1810.

Guaiana G (2011). Antidepressant prescribing and suicides in Emilia-Romagna region (Italy) from 1999 to 2008: An ecological study. *Clinical Practice and Epidemology in Mental Health* 7, 120–122.

Gulland A (2011). One in 10 suicides is among people with a physical illness. *BMJ: British Medical Journal* 343, d5464.

Güth U, Myrick ME, Reisch T, Bosshard G, Schmid SM (2011). Suicide in breast cancer patients: An individual-centered approach provides insight beyond epidemiology. *Acta Oncologica* 50, 1037–1044.

Haines J, Williams CL, Lester D (2011). The characteristics of those who do and do not leave suicide notes: Is the method of residuals valid? *Omega: Journal of Death and Dying* 63, 79–94.

Hampson NB (2011). Commentary on: Schmitt MW, Williams TL, Woodard KR, Harruff RC. Trends in suicide by carbon monoxide inhalation in King County, Washington: 1996–2009. *Journal of Forensic Sciences* 56, 1076.

Han PP, Holbrook TL, Sise MJ, Sack DI, Sise CB, Hoyt DB, Coimbra R, Potenza B, Anderson JP (2011). Postinjury depression is a serious complication in adolescents after major trauma: Injury severity and injury-event factors predict depression and long-term quality of life deficits. *Journal of Trauma-Injury Infection and Critical Care* 70, 923–930.

Harlow W, Happell B, Brown G (2011). The wait on the nurses' shoulders. *Australian Nursing Journal* 19, 48.

Hill C, Cook L (2011). Narrative verdicts and their impact on mortality statistics in England and Wales. *Health Statistics Quarterly Spring*, 81–100.

Hjelmeland H (2011). Doing qualitative research on suicide in a developing country: Practical and ethical challenges. *Crisis* 32, 64.

Hooghe M, Vanhoutte B (2011). An ecological study of community-level correlates of suicide mortality rates in the Flemish REGION of Belgium, 1996–2005. *Suicide and Life-Threatening Behavior* 41, 453–464.

Humber N, Piper M, Appleby L, Shaw J (2011). Characteristics of and trends in subgroups of prisoner suicides in England and Wales. *Psychological Medicine* 41, 2275–2285.

Hummingbird LM (2011). The public health crisis of Native American youth suicide. *NASN School Nurse* 26, 110–114.

Jansson C, Alderling M, Hogstedt C, Gustavsson P (2011). Mortality among Swedish chimney sweeps (1952–2006): An extended cohort study. *Occupational and Environmental Medicine*. Published online: 24 June 2011. doi: 10.1136/oem.2010.064246

Kaess M, Hille M, Parzer P, Maser-Gluth C, Resch F, Brunner R (2010). Alterations in the neuroendocrinological stress response to acute psychosocial stress in adolescents engaging in non-suicidal self-injury. *Psychoneuroendocrinology*. Published online: 15 June 2011. doi:10.1016/j.psyneuen.2011.05.009

Kalucy M, Rodway C, Finn J, Pearson A, Flynn S, Swinson N, Roscoe A, Cruz DD, Appleby L, Shaw J (2011). Comparison of British national newspaper coverage of homicide committed by perpetrators with and without mental illness. *Australia and New Zealand Journal of Psychiatry* 45, 539–548.

Karayal ON, Anway SD, Batzar E, Vanderburg DG (2011). Assessments of suicidality in double-blind, placebo-controlled trials of ziprasidone. *Journal of Clinical Psychiatry* 72, 367–375.

Karch D (2011). Sex differences in suicide incident characteristics and circumstances among older adults: surveillance data from the National Violent Death Reporting System-17 US States, 2007–2009. *International Journal of Environmental Research and Public Health* 8, 3479–3495.

Kerr WC, Subbaraman M, Ye Y (2011). Per capita alcohol consumption and suicide mortality in a panel of US states from 1950 to 2002. *Drug and Alcohol Review* 30, 473–480.

Kim YK (2011). Suicide and suicidal behavior. *Progress in Neuro-psychopharmacology and Biological Psychiatry* 35, 795.

Kinyanda E, Wamala D, Musisi S, Hjelmeland H (2011). Suicide in urban Kampala, Uganda: A preliminary exploration. *African Health Sciences* 11, 219–227.

Kohlboeck G, Quadflieg N, Fichter MM (2011). Acting out and self-harm in children, adolescents and young adults and mental illness 18 years later: The longitudinal upper Bavarian community study. *European Journal of Psychiatry* 25, 32–40.

Koulapur VV, Yoganarsimha K, Gouda H, Mugadlimath AB, Vijay Kumar GA (2011). Analysis of fatal burns cases — A 5 year study at Sri B M Patil Medical College, Bijapur, Karnataka. *Medico-Legal Update* 11, 114–116.

Krakowiak A, Kotwica M, Sliwkiewicz K, Piekarska-Wijatkowska A (2011). Epidemiology of acute poisonings during 2003–2007 in toxicology unit, department of occupational medicine and toxicology, Nofer Institute of Occupational Medicine, Łód , Poland. *International Journal of Occupational Medicine and Environmental Health* 24, 199–207.

Kristiansen MG, Lochen ML, Gutteberg TJ, Mortensen L, Eriksen BO, Florholmen J (2011). Total and cause-specific mortality rates in a prospective study of community-acquired hepatitis C virus infection in northern Norway. *Journal of Viral Hepatitis* 18, 237–244.

Lane R (2011). 'The events of October': Murder-suicide on a small campus. *Michigan Historical Review* 37, 160–163.

Lederer D (2011). Suicide in Nazi Germany. *German History* 29, 532–533.

Lee EAD (2011). Complex contribution of combat-related post-traumatic stress disorder to veteran suicide: Facing an increasing challenge. *Perspectives in Psychiatric Care*. Published online: 20 June 2011. doi: 10.1111/j.1744-6163.2011.00312.x

Lester D (2011). Suicide and the partition of India: A need for further investigation. *Suicidology Online* 1, 2–4.

Lester D (2010). Suicide in mass murderers and serial killers. *Suicidology Online* 1, 19–27.

Lester D, Gunn III JF (2011). National anthems and suicide rates. *Psychological Reports* 108, 43–44.

Lester D, Saito Y, Park BCB (2011). Suicide among foreign residents of Japan. *Psychological Reports* 108, 139–140.

Lopes D, Barbarro A, Reche B (2011). Comparative study of suicide in domiciliary palliative care unit in Madrid, Spain. *Journal of Palliative Care* 26, 247.

Ma S (2011). China struggles to rebuild mental health programs. *CMAJ: Canadian Medical Association Journal* 183, E89–90.

Madhavan SR, Reddy S, Panuganti PK, Joshi R, Mallidi J, Raju K, Raju KR, Iyengar S, Reddy KS, Patel A, Neal B, Calambur N, Tandri H (2011). Epidemiology of sudden cardiac death in rural South India — Insights from the Andhra Pradesh rural health initiative. *Indian Pacing and Electrophysiology Journal* 11, 93–102.

Maqsood M, Muhammad KCh, Khokhar JI, Mughal MI (2011). Fatal compressive trauma to neck. *Medical Forum Monthly* 22, 51–57.

Martin SL, Proescholdbell S, Norwood T, Kupper LL (2010). Suicide and homicide in North Carolina: Initial findings from the North Carolina Violent Death Reporting System, 2004–2007. *North Carolina Medical Journal* 71, 519–525.

McNamara RK (2011). Long-chain omega-3 fatty acid deficiency in mood disorders: Rationale for treatment and prevention. *Current Drug Discovery Technologies*. Published online: 15 August 2011. E-publication.

Meerten M, Bland J, Gross SR, Garelick AI (2011). Doctors' experience of a bespoke physician consultation service: Cross-sectional investigation. *Psychiatrist* 35, 206–212.

Merrall EL, Bird SM, Hutchinson SJ (2011). Mortality of those who attended drug services in Scotland 1996–2006: Record-linkage study. *International Journal of Drug Policy*. Published online: 30 June 2011. doi:10.1016/j.drugpo.2011.05.010

Miziara ID (2011). Suicidal hanging in Franco da Rocha, Brazil — A six-year prospective and retrospective study. *Indian Journal of Forensic Medicine and Toxicology* 5, 14–17.

Modrek S, Ahern J (2011). Longitudinal relation of community-level income inequality and mortality in Costa Rica. *Health Place*. Published online: 27 July 2011. doi:10.1016/j.healthplace.2011.07.006

Morgan BW, Geller RJ, Kazzi ZN (2011). Intentional ethylene glycol poisoning increase after media coverage of antifreeze murders. *Western Journal of Emergency Medicine* 12, 296–299.

Motohashi Y (2011). Suicide in Japan. *The Lancet*. Published online: 27 July 2011. doi: 10.1016/j.healthplace.2011.07.006

Muramatsu RS, Goebert D (2011). Psychiatric services: Experience, perceptions, and needs of nursing facility multidisciplinary leaders. *Journal of the American Geriatrics Society* 59, 120–125.

Narayan KA, Nithin MD (2011). Correlation & pattern of ligature marks in cases of deaths due to hanging. *Indian Journal of Forensic Medicine and Toxicology* 5, 42–45.

Neuner T, Hübner-Liebermann B, Hausner H, Hajak G, Wittmann M (2011). Small numbers, big results: Weiden — A suicide stronghold? *Psychiatrische Praxis* 38, 253–255.

Newman LK, Procter NG, Dudley M (2011). Suicide and self-harm in immigration detention. *Medical Journal of Australia* 195, 310–311.

Nikolic S, Zivkovi V, Babic D, Jukovi F, Atanasijevi T, Popovi V (2011). Hyoid-laryngeal fractures in hanging: Where was the knot in the noose? *Medicine, Science and the Law* 51, 21–25.

Norström T, Stickley A, Shibuya K (2011). The importance of alcoholic beverage type for suicide in Japan: A time-series analysis, 1963–2007. *Drug and Alcohol Review*. Published online: 31 March 2011. doi: 10.1111/j.1465-3362.2011.00300.x

Nyamathi A, Leake B, Albarran C, Zhang S, Hall E, Farabee D, Marlow E, Marfisee M, Khalilifard F, Faucette M (2011). Correlates of depressive symptoms among homeless men on parole. *Issues in Mental Health Nursing* 32, 501–511.

Ogata K, Ishikawa T, Michiue T, Nishi Y, Maeda H (2011). Posttraumatic symptoms in Japanese bereaved family members with special regard to suicide and homicide cases. *Death Studies* 35, 525–535.

Okoye CN, Okoye MI (2011). Forensic epidemiology of childhood deaths in Nebraska, USA. *Journal of Forensic and Legal Medicine*. Published online: 27 August 2011. doi:10.1016/j.jflm.2011.07.013

Othman N (2011). Suicide by self-burning in Iraqi Kurdistan: Description and risk factors. *Archives of Suicide Research* 15, 238–249.

Paggiaro P, Bacci E (2011). Montelukast in asthma: A review of its efficacy and place in therapy. *Therapeutic Advances in Chronic Disease* 2, 47–58.

Patil B, Raghavendra KM, Uzair S, Deepak (2011). A study on pattern of injuries in railway deaths. *Indian Journal of Forensic Medicine and Toxicology* 5, 20–22.

Patil B, Garampalli S, Uzair HS, Kuppast N, Raghavendra KM (2011). Suicidal trends in children and adolescents. *Indian Journal of Forensic Medicine and Toxicology* 5, 23–26.

Pestian J, Nasrallah H, Matykiewicz P, Bennett A, Leenaars A (2010). Suicide note classification using natural language processing: A content analysis. *Biomedical Informatics Insights* 2010, 19–28.

Piatkov I, Jones T, Van Vuuren RJ (2011). Suicide cases and venlafaxine. *Acta Neuropsychiatrica* 23, 156–160.

Pinto LW, Assis SG, Minayo MCS, Oliveira TP, Silva CMFP (2011). Completed suicide in elderly population in Brazilian cities, 1996–2007. *American Journal of Epidemiology* 173, S55.

Poeschla B, Combs H, Livingstone S, Romm S, Klein MB (2011). Self-immolation: Socioeconomic, cultural and psychiatric patterns. *Burns* 37, 1049–1057.

Prajapati P, Sheikh MI, Brahmbhatt J, Choksi C (2011). A study of violent asphyxial deaths at Surat, Gujarat. *Indian Journal of Forensic Medicine and Toxicology* 5, 66–70.

Radecki RP, Sittig DF (2011). Application of electronic health records to the Joint Commission's 2011 National Patient Safety Goals. *JAMA: Journal of the American Medical Association* 306, 92–93.

Redaniel MT, Lebanan-Dalida MA, Gunnell D (2011). Suicide in the Philippines: Time trend analysis (1974–2005) and literature review. *BMC Public Health* 11, 536.

Reedy SJ, Schwartz MD, Morgan BW (2011). Suicide fads: Frequency and characteristics of hydrogen sulfide suicides in the United States. *Western Journal of Emergency Medicine* 12, 300–304.

Rezaeian M (2011). An analysis of WHO data on lethal violence: Relevance of the new western millennium. *Asia-Pacific Journal of Public Health* 23, 163–170.

Richardson T (2011). Correlates of substance use disorder in bipolar disorder: A systematic review and meta-analysis. *Mental Health and Substance Use: Dual Diagnosis* 4, 239–255.

Rihmer Z, Erdos P, Ormos M, Fountoulakis KN, Vazquez G, Pompili M, Gonda X (2011). Association between affective temperaments and season of birth in a general student population. *Journal of Affective Disorders* 132, 64–70.

Riihimäki M, Thomsen H, Brandt A, Sundquist J, Hemminki K (2011). Death causes in breast cancer patients. *Annals of Oncology*. Published online: 17 May 2011. doi: 10.1093/annonc/mdr160

Roma P, Spacca PD, Pompili PD, Lester D, Tatarelli R, Girardi P, Ferracuti S (2011). The epidemiology of homicide-suicide in Italy: A newspaper study from 1985 to 2008. *Forensic Science International*. Published online: 18 July 2011. doi:10.1016/j.forsciint.2011.06.022

Sani G, Tondo L, Koukopoulos A, Reginaldi D, Kotzalidis GD, Koukopoulos AE, Manfredi G, Mazzarini L, Pacchiarotti I, Simonetti A, Ambrosi E, Angeletti G, Girardi P, Tatarelli R (2011). Suicide in a large population of former psychiatric inpatients. *Psychiatry and Clinical Neurosciences* 65, 286–295.

Schumock T, Lee TA, Joo MJ, Valuck RJ, Stayner LT, Gibbons RD (2011). Association between leukotriene-modifying agents and suicide: What is the evidence? *Drug Safety* 34, 533–544.

Schwartz AJ (2011). Rate, relative risk, and method of suicide by students at 4-year colleges and universities in the United States, 2004–2005 through 2008–2009. *Suicide and Life-Threatening Behavior* 41, 353–371.

Shah A (2011). A replication of the relationship between elderly suicides rates and elderly dependency ratios: A cross-national study. *Journal of Injury and Violence Research* 2, 19–24.

Shah A (2011). Elderly suicide rates: A replication of cross-national comparisons and association with sex and elderly age-bands using five year suicide data. *Journal of Injury and Violence Research* 3, 80–84.

Shah A (2011). Further evidence for epidemiological transition hypothesis for elderly suicides. *Journal of Injury and Violence Research* 3, 29–34.

Shah A (2011). The relationship between elderly suicide rates and different components of education: A cross-national study. *Journal of Injury and Violence Research*. Published online: 16 April 2011. doi: 10.5249/jivr.v4i2.75.

Shah A (2011). The relationship between the use of mental health act and general population suicide rates in England and Wales. *Journal of Injury and Violence Research*. Published online: 16 April 2011. doi: 10.5249/jivr.v4i1.66

Shah A, Buckley L (2011). The current status of methods used by the elderly for suicides in England and Wales. *Journal of Injury and Violence Research* 3, 68–73.

Shelton RC, Hal Manier D, Lewis DA (2009). Protein kinases A and C in post-mortem prefrontal cortex from persons with major depression and normal controls. *The International Journal of Neuropsychopharmacology* 12, 1223–1232.

Sher L (2011). Towards a model of suicidal behavior among physicians. *Revista Brasileira de Psiquiatria* 33, 111–112.

Slater GY (2011). The Missing Piece: A sociological autopsy of firearm suicide in the United States. *Suicide and Life-Threatening Behavior*. Published online: 27 July 2011. doi: 10.1111/ j.1943-278X.2011.00038.x

Smith G (2011). Birth month is not related to suicide among major league baseball players. *Perceptual and Motor Skills* 112, 55–60.

Stark K, Joubert G, Struwig M, Pretorius M, van der Merwe N, Botha H, Kotze J, Krynauw D (2011). Suicide cases investigated at the state mortuary in Bloemfontein, 2003–2007. *South African Family Practice* 52, 332–335.

Stevovi LI, Jašovi -Gaši M, Vukovi O, Pekovi M, Terzi N (2011). Gender differences in relation to suicides committed in the capital of Montenegro (Podgorica) in the period 2000–2006. *Psychiatria Danubina* 23, 45–52.

Strukcinskiene B, Andersson R, Janson S (2011). Suicide mortality trends in young people aged 15 to 19 years in Lithuania. *Acta Paediatrica*. Published online: 1 June 2011. doi: 10.1111/j.1651-2227.2011.02347.x

Stuckler D, Meissner C, Fishback P, Basu S, McKee M (2011). Banking crises and mortality during the Great Depression: Evidence from US urban populations, 1929–1937. *Journal of Epidemiology and Community Health*. Published online: 24 March 2011. doi:10.1136/jech.2010.121376

Sueki H (2011). Does the volume of Internet searches using suicide-related search terms influence the suicide death rate: Data from 2004 to 2009 in Japan. *Psychiatry and Clinical Neurosciences* 65, 392–394.

Sun J, Guo X, Ma J, Zhang J, Jia C, Xu A (2011). Seasonality of suicide in Shandong China, 1991–2009: Associations with gender, age, area and methods of suicide. *Journal of Affective Disorders*. Published online: 27 August 2011. doi:10.1016/j.jad.2011.08.008

Swinson N, Flynn SM, While D, Roscoe A, Kapur N, Appleby L, Shaw J (2011). Trends in rates of mental illness in homicide perpetrators. *British Journal of Psychiatry* 198, 485–489.

Toft M, Lilleeng B, Ramm-Pettersen J, Skogseid IM, Gundersen V, Gerdts R, Pedersen L, Skjelland M, Roste GK, Dietrichs E (2011). Long-term efficacy and mortality in Parkinson's disease patients treated with subthalamic stimulation. *Movement Disorders*. Published online: 8 June 2011. doi: 10.1002/mds.23817

Tseng MC, Cheng IC (2011). Response to Sher regarding Tseng et al's 'Standardized Mortality Ratio of Inpatient Suicide in a General Hospital'. *Journal of the Formosan Medical Association* 110, 665.

Tseng MC, Cheng IC, Hu FC (2011). Standardized mortality ratio of inpatient suicide in a general hospital. *Journal of the Formosan Medical Association* 110, 267–269.

Varley J, Pilcher D, Butt W, Cameron P (2011). Self harm is an independent predictor of mortality in trauma and burns patients admitted to ICU. *Injury*. Published online: 28 June 2011. doi: 10.1016/j.injury.2011.06.005

Vento AE, Schifano F, Corkery JM, Pompili M, Innamorati M, Girardi P, Ghodse H (2011). Suicide verdicts as opposed to accidental deaths in substance-related fatalities (UK, 2001–2007). *Progress in Neuro-Psychopharmacology and Biological Psychiatry* 35, 1279–1283.

Vijayamahantesh SN, Vijayanath V (2011). Patterns of suicidal deaths in Gulbarga region of Karnataka. *Indian Journal of Forensic Medicine and Toxicology* 5, 94–98.

Viner RM, Coffey C, Mathers C, Bloem P, Costello A, Santelli J, Patton GC (2011). 50-year mortality trends in children and young people: A study of 50 low-income, middle-income, and high-income countries. *The Lancet* 377, 1162–1174.

Vyssoki B, Willeit M, Blüml V, Hofer P, Erfurth A, Psota G, Lesch OM, Kapusta ND (2011). Inpatient treatment of major depression in Austria between 1989 and 2009: Impact of downsizing of psychiatric hospitals on admissions, suicide rates and outpatient psychiatric services. *Journal of Affective Disorders* 133, 93–96.

Wasnik RN (2011). Trends of unnatural deaths in Nagpur, India. *Medico-Legal Update* 11, 121–124.

Westling S, Ahren B, Traskman-Bendz L, Brundin L (2011). Increased IL-1 reactivity upon a glucose challenge in patients with deliberate self-harm. *Acta Psychiatrica Scandinavica* 124, 301–306.

Yerpude PN, Jogdand KS (2011). A hospital based study of burn patients in an apex institute of Maharashtra. *Indian Journal of Forensic Medicine and Toxicology* 5, 85–87.

Yin S, Heard KJ (2011). Complex suicide: Self-incineration and acetaminophen overdose. *Injury*. Published online: 4 July 2011. doi:10.1016/j.injury.2011.06.025

Zamparutti G, Schifano F, Corkery JM, Oyefeso A, Ghodse AH (2011). Deaths of opiate/opioid misusers involving dihydrocodeine, UK, 1997–2007. *British Journal of Clinical Pharmacology* 72, 330–337.

Zariwala RC, Mehta TJ, Bhise RS (2011). A retrospective study of 5 years of organ phosphorous poisoning in Ahmedabad. *Indian Journal of Forensic Medicine and Toxicology* 5, 100–101.

Zhang J, Gao Q, Jia C (2011). Seasonality of Chinese rural young suicide and its correlates. *Journal of Affective Disorders* 134, 356–364.

Zhang J, Li Z (2011). Suicide means used by Chinese rural youths: A comparison between those with and without mental disorders. *Journal of Nevous and Mental Disorders* 199, 410–415.

# Risk and protective factors

Anonymous (2011). Health of lesbian, gay, bisexual, and transgender populations. *The Lancet* 377, 1211.

Albert PR, Le Francois B, Millar AM (2011). Transcriptional dysregulation of 5-HT1A autoreceptors in mental illness. *Molecular Brain* 4, 21.

Aldaz P, Moreno-Iribas C, Egues N, Irisarri F, Floristan Y, Sola-Boneta J, Martinez-Artola V, Sagredo M, Castilla J (2011). Mortality by causes in HIV-infected adults: Comparison with the general population. *BMC Public Health* 11, 300.

Alonzo DM, Harkavy-Friedman JM, Stanley B, Burke A, Mann JJ, Oquendo MA (2011). Predictors of treatment utilization in major depression. *Archives of Suicide Research* 15, 160–171.

Andreescu C, Reynolds CF (2011). Late-life depression: Evidence-based treatment and promising new directions for research and clinical practice. *Psychiatric Clinics of North America* 34, 335–355.

Arya A, Kumar T (2011). Depression: A review. *Journal of Chemical and Pharmaceutical Research* 3, 444–453.

Ashton CH, Moore PB (2011). Endocannabinoid system dysfunction in mood and related disorders. *Acta Psychiatrica Scandinavica* 124, 250–261.

Astbury J, Bruck D, Loxton D (2011). Forced sex: A critical factor in the sleep difficulties of young Australian women. *Violence and Victims* 26, 53–72.

Avila DS, Palma AS, Colle D, Scolari R, Manarin F, da Silveira AF, Nogueira CW, Rocha JBT, Soares FAA (2011). Hepatoprotective activity of a vinylic telluride against acute exposure to acetaminophen. *European Journal of Pharmacology* 661, 92–101.

Aziz N (2011). What self-immolation means to Afghan women. *Peace Review* 23, 45–51.

Babu GR (2011). In response to 'Suicide and Ethnicity in Malaysia' reply. *American Journal of Forensic Medicine and Pathology* 32, e15.

Baghaei P, Tabarsi P, Dorriz D, Marjani M, Shamaei M, Pooramiri MV, Mansouri D, Farnia P, Masjedi M, Velayati A (2011). Adverse effects of multidrug-resistant tuberculosis treatment with a standardized regimen: A report from Iran. *American Journal of Therapeutics* 18, e29–e34.

Bah A, Wilson C, Fatkin L, Atkisson C, Brent E, Horton D (2011). Computing the prevalence rate of at-risk individuals for suicide within the army. *Military Medicine* 176, 731–742.

Baldessarini RJ (2011). Suicidal risk during antidepressant treatment. *Journal of Clinical Psychiatry* 72, 722.

Bando DH, Fernandes TG, Goulart AC, Bensenor IM, Lotufo PA (2011). Income inequality and suicide in Sao Paulo, Brazil (1996 to 2009). *American Journal of Epidemiology* 173, S290.

Bansal YS, Singh D (2011). A study to establish a relationship between serum cholesterol level & unnatural fatalities among the population of the Chandigarh Zone of North West India. *Medico-Legal Update* 11, 83–85.

Barbui C (2011). Getting through the quicksand of the relationship between drugs and suicide. *Drug Safety* 34, 397–401.

Beard JD, Umbach DM, Hoppin JA, Richards M, Alavanja MC, Blair A, Sandler DP, Kamel F (2011). Suicide and pesticide use among pesticide applicators and their spouses in the agricultural health study. *Environmental Health Perspectives.* Published online: 13 July 2011. doi: http://dx.doi.org /10.1289/ehp.1103413

Besancenot JP, Thibaudon M, Cecchi L (2011). Has allergenic pollen an impact on non-allergic diseases? *European Annals of Allergy and Clinical Immunology* 43, 69–76.

Bjorkenstam E, Bjorkenstam C, Vinnerljung B, Dalman C, Hallqvist J, Ljung R (2010). Juvenile delinquency, socio-economic background and suicide. *European Journal of Public Health* 20, 49–50.

Bland P (2011). Suicide risk raised following bariatric surgery. *Practitioner* 255, 7.

Bookbinder P (2011). Suicide in Nazi Germany. *European History Quarterly* 41, 526–527.

Branas CC, Richmond TS, ten Have TR, Wiebe DJ (2011). Acute alcohol consumption, alcohol outlets, and gun suicide. *Substance Use & Misuse* 46, 1592–1603.

Bright RP, Krahn L (2011). Depression and suicide among physicians. *Current Psychiatry* 10, 16–30.

Brumby S, Chandrasekara A, McCoombe S, Kremer P, Lewandowski P (2011). Farming fit? Dispelling the Australian agrarian myth. *BMC Research Notes* 4, 89.

Bryan C, Anestis M (2011). Reexperiencing symptoms and the interpersonal-psychological theory of suicidal behavior among deployed service members evaluated for traumatic brain injury. *Journal of Clinical Psychology* 67, 856–865.

Bryan CJ, Cukrowicz KC (2011). Associations between types of combat violence and the acquired capability for suicide. *Suicide and Life-Threatening Behavior* 41, 126–136.

Butkova T, Kibrik N (2011). The analysis of suicide behaviour owing to family-sexual disharmonies. *Journal of Sexual Medicine* 8, 288.

Calandre EP, Vilchez JS, Molina-Barea R, Tovar MI, Garcia-Leiva JM, Hidalgo J, Rodriguez-Lopez CM, Rico-Villademoros F (2011). Suicide attempts and risk of suicide in patients with fibromyalgia: A survey in Spanish patients. *Rheumatology (Oxford)* 50, 1889–1893.

Callanan VJ, Davis MS (2011). Gender differences in suicide methods. *Social Psychiatry and Psychiatric Epidemiology.* Published online: 22 May 2011. doi: 10.1007/s00127-011-0393-5

Canales R (2011). Adult suicide. Early recognition of risk factors is key to prevention. *Advance for Nurse Practitioners and Physician Assistants* 2, 33–36.

Catalan J, Harding R, Sibley E, Clucas C, Croome N, Sherr L (2011). HIV infection and mental health: Suicidal behaviour — Systematic review. *Psychology, Health & Medicine* 16, 588–611.

Catassi C, Lionetti E (2011). Coeliac disease and suicide risk: Facts or artefacts? *Digestive and Liver Disease* 43, 585–586.

Cheatle MD (2011). Depression, chronic pain, and suicide by overdose: On the edge. *Pain Medicine* 12, S43–S48.

Cheikh IB, Rousseau C, Mekki-Berrada A (2011). Suicide as protest against social suffering in the Arab world. *British Journal of Psychiatry* 198, 494–495.

Chen ES, Ernst C, Turecki G (2011). The epigenetic effects of antidepressant treatment on human prefrontal cortex BDNF expression. *International Journal of Neuropsychopharmacology* 14, 427–429.

Cigrang JA, Rauch SAM, Avila LL, Bryan CJ, Goodie JL, Hryshko-Mullen A, Peterson AL (2011). Treatment of active-duty military with PTSD in primary care: Early findings. *Psychological Services* 8, 104–113.

Congdon P (2011). Spatial path models with multiple indicators and multiple causes: Mental health in US counties. *Spatial and Spatio-temporal Epidemiology* 2, 103–116.

Conner KR (2011). Clarifying the relationship between alcohol and depression. *Addiction* 106, 915–916.

Conwell Y, Van Orden K, Caine ED (2011). Suicide in older adults. *Psychiatric Clinics of North America* 34, 451–468.

Crespi F (2011). Influence of Neuropeptide Y and antidepressants upon cerebral monoamines involved in depression: An in vivo electrochemical study. *Brain Research* 1407, 27–37.

Cui H, Supriyanto I, Sasada T, Shiroiwa K, Fukutake M, Shirakawa O, Asano M, Ueno Y, Nagasaki Y, Hishimoto A (2011). Association study of EP1 gene polymorphisms with suicide completers in the Japanese population. *Progress in Neuropsychopharmacology and Biological Psychiatry* 35, 1108–1111.

Daly MC, Oswald AJ, Wilson D, Wu S (2010). Dark contrasts: The paradox of high rates of suicide in happy places. *Journal of Economic Behavior and Organization*. Published online: 22 April 2011. doi: 10.1016/j.jebo.2011.04.007

Danziger PD, Silverwood R, Koupil I (2011). Fetal growth, early life circumstances, and risk of suicide in late adulthood. *European Journal of Epidemiology* 26, 571–581.

de Haan L, Sterk B, Wouters L, Linszen DH (2011). The 5-Year course of obsessive-compulsive symptoms and obsessive-compulsive disorder in first-episode schizophrenia and related disorders. *Schizophrenia Bulletin*. Published online: 28 July 2011. doi: 10.1093/ schbul/sbr077

Denton CA, Al Otaiba S (2011). Teaching word identification to students with reading difficulties and disabilities. *Focus on Exceptional Children* 43, 1–16.

Detotto C, Sterzi V (2011). The role of family in suicide rate in Italy. *Economics Bulletin* 31, 1509–1519.

Dias AC, Araújo MR, Dunn J, Sesso RC, de Castro V, Laranjeira R (2011). Mortality rate among crack/cocaine-dependent patients: A 12-year prospective cohort study conducted in Brazil. *Journal of Substance Abuse and Treatment* 41, 273–278.

DiFulvio GT (2011). Sexual minority youth, social connection and resilience: From personal struggle to collective identity. *Social Science and Medicine* 72, 1611–1617.

Doka KJ (2011). Suicide and homicide-suicide among police. *Omega: Journal of Death and Dying* 63, 197.

Dongre AR, Deshmukh PR (2011). Farmers' suicides in the Vidarbha region of Maharashtra, India: A qualitative exploration of their causes. *Journal of Injury and Violence Research*. Published online: 16 April 2011. doi: 10.5249/jivr.v4i1.68

Emslie GJ, Kennard BD, Mayes TL (2011). Predictors of treatment response in adolescent depression. *Pediatric Annals* 40, 300–306.

Ernst C, Nagy C, Kim S, Yang JP, Deng X, Hellstrom IC, Choi KH, Gershenfeld H, Meaney MJ, Turecki G (2011). Dysfunction of astrocyte connexins 30 and 43 in dorsal lateral prefrontal cortex of suicide completers. *Biological Psychiatry* 70, 312–319.

Flensborg madsen T (2011). Alcohol use disorders and depression – The chicken or the egg? *Addiction* 106, 916–918.

Freire RC, Hallak JE, Crippa JA, Nardi AE (2011). New treatment options for panic disorder: Clinical trials from 2000 to 2010. *Expert Opinion on Pharmacotherapy* 12, 1419–1428.

Fridner A, Belkic K, Minucci D, Pavan L, Marini M, Pingel B, Putoto G, Simonato P, Lovseth LT, Schenck-Gustafsson K (2011). Work environment and recent suicidal thoughts among male university hospital physicians in Sweden and Italy: The Health and Organization Among University Hospital Physicians in Europe (HOUPE) study. *Gender Medicine* 8, 269–279.

Gao Q, Zhang J, Jia C (2011). Psychometric properties of the Dickman Impulsivity Instrument in suicide victims and living controls of rural China. *Journal of Affective Disorders* 132, 368–374.

Garssen J, Deerenberg I, Mackenbach JP, Kerkhof A, Kunst AE (2011). Familial risk of early suicide: Variations by age and sex of children and parents. *Suicide and Life-Threatening Behavior*. Published online: 4 August 2011. doi: 10.1111/j.1943-278X.2011.00050.x

Gartner A, Farewell D, Roach P, Dunstan F (2011). Rural/urban mortality differences in England and Wales and the effect of deprivation adjustment. *Social Science and Medicine* 72, 1685–1694.

Gilbert E, Adams A, Buckingham CD (2011). Examining the relationship between risk assessment and risk management in mental health. *Journal of Psychiatric and Mental Health Nursing*. Published online: 5 May 2011. doi: 10.1111/j.1365-2850.2011.01737.x

Giupponi G, Conca A, Schmidt E, Hinterhuber H, Pompili M, Pycha R (2011). Suicide in ethnic and cultural minorities — A research on literature. *Neuropsychiatrie* 25, 93–102.

Gonda X, Fountoulakis KN, Csukly G, Bagdy G, Pap D, Molnár E, Laszik A, Lazary J, Sarosi A, Faludi G, Sasvari-Szekely M, Szekely A, Rihmer Z (2011). Interaction of 5-HTTLPR genotype and unipolar major depression in the emergence of aggressive/hostile traits. *Journal of Affective Disorders* 132, 432–437.

Grall-Bronnec M, Wainstein L, Feuillet F, Bouju G, Rocher B, Vénisse JL, Sébille-Rivain V (2011). Clinical profiles as a function of level and type of impulsivity in a sample group of at-risk and pathological gamblers seeking treatment. *Journal of Gambling Studies*. Published online: 23 June 2011. doi: 10.1007/s10899-011-9258-9

Griffith J (2011). Decades of transition for the US reserves: Changing demands on reserve identity and mental well-being. *International Review of Psychiatry* 23, 181–191.

Hakko H, Wahlberg KE, Tienari P, Rasanen S (2011). Genetic vulnerability and premature death in schizophrenia spectrum disorders: A 28-year follow-up of adoptees in the Finnish Adoptive Family Study of Schizophrenia. *Nordic Journal of Psychiatry* 65, 259–265.

Harper M (2011). Taking stock: Agrarian distress in India — Poor Indian farmers, suicides and government. *Enterprise Development and Microfinance* 22, 11–16.

Hasnain M, Vieweg WV (2011). Letter by Hasnain and Vieweg regarding article, 'myocardial infarction and risk of suicide: A population-based case-control study'. *Circulation* 124, e51–352.

Henderson AF, Joseph AP (2011). Motor vehicle accident or driver suicide? Identifying cases of failed driver suicide in the trauma setting. *Injury*. Published online: 12 July 2011. doi: 10.1016/j.injury.2011.06.192

Hickie IB (2011). Antidepressants in elderly people: Careful monitoring is needed for adverse effects, particularly in the first month of treatment. *BMJ: British Medical Journal* 343, 7819.

Hirvikoski T, Jokinen J (2011). Personality traits in attempted and completed suicide. *European Psychiatry*. Published online: 20 June 2011. doi:10.1016/j.eurpsy.2011.04.004

Hjelmeland H (2011). Cultural context is crucial in suicide research and prevention. *Crisis* 32, 61–64.

Inoue K, Fukunaga T, Okazaki Y, Ono Y (2011). Report on suicidal trends in persons aged 60 or over in Japan: The need for effective prevention measures. *Medicine, Science and the Law* 51, 32–35.

Jahanshahi M, Czernecki V, Zurowski M (2011). Neuropsychological, neuropsychiatric, and quality of life issues in DBS for dystonia. *Movement Disorders* 26, s68–s83.

Jayasinghe NR, Foster JH (2011). Deliberate self-harm/poisoning, suicide trends. The link to increased alcohol consumption in Sri Lanka. *Archives of Suicide Research* 15, 223–237.

Jeon HJ (2011). Depression and suicide. *Journal of the Korean Medical Association* 54, 370–375.

Jokinen J, Chatzittofis A, Hellström C, Nordström P, Uvnäs-Moberg K, Asberg M (2011). Low CSF oxytocin reflects high intent in suicide attempters. *Psychoneuroendocrinology*. Published online: 16 August 2011. doi:10.1016/j.psyneuen.2011.07.016

Kabacs N, Memon A, Obinwa T, Stochl J, Perez J (2011). Lithium in drinking water and suicide rates across the East of England. *British Journal of Psychiatry* 198, 406–407.

Kaufman KR (2011). Antiepileptic drugs in the treatment of psychiatric disorders. *Epilepsy and Behavior* 21, 1–11.

Kelly BD (2011). Self-immolation, suicide and self-harm in Buddhist and Western traditions. *Transcultural Psychiatry* 48, 299–317.

Keyes KM, Liu XC, Cerda M (2011). The role of race/ethnicity in alcohol-attributable injury in the United States. *Epidemiologic Reviews*. Published online: 19 September 2011. doi: 10.1093/epirev/mxr018

Kharawala S, Dalal J (2011). Challenges in conducting psychiatry studies in India. *Perspectives in Clinical Research* 2, 8–12.

Kjaer TK, Jensen A, Dalton SO, Johansen C, Schmiedel S, Kjaer SK (2011). Suicide in Danish women evaluated for fertility problems. *Human Reproduction* 26, 2401–2407.

Klibert J, Langhinrichsen-Rohling J, Luna A, Robichaux M (2011). Suicide proneness in college students: Relationships with gender, procrastination, and achievement motivation. *Death Studies* 35, 625–645.

Kuo CJ, Tsai SY, Liao YT, Conwell Y, Lin SK, Chang CL, Chen CC, Chen WJ (2011). Risk and protective factors for suicide among patients with methamphetamine dependence: A nested case-control study. *Journal of Clinical Psychiatry* 72, 487–493.

Laan W, Termorshuizen F, Smeets HM, Boks MP, de Wit NJ, Geerlings MI (2011). A comorbid anxiety disorder does not result in an excess risk of death among patients with a depressive disorder. *Journal of Affective Disorders*. Published online: 20 September 2011. doi: 10.1016/j.jad.2011.08.026

Lande RG (2011). Felo de se: Soldier suicides in America's civil war. *Military Medicine* 176, 531–536.

Lankford A (2011). Could suicide terrorists actually be suicidal? *Studies in Conflict and Terrorism* 34, 337–366.

Larsen KK, Agerbo E, Sondergaard J, Christensen B, Vestergaard M (2011). Response to letter regarding article, 'Myocardial infarction and risk of suicide: A population-based case-control study'. *Circulation* 124, 53.

Lazary J, Juhasz G, Hunyady L, Bagdy G (2011). Personalized medicine can pave the way for the safe use of CB1 receptor antagonists. *Trends in Pharmacological Sciences* 32, 270–280.

Lee KM, Guo S, Manning V, Thane K, Wong KE (2011). Are the demographic and clinical features of pathological gamblers seeking treatment in Singapore changing? *Singapore Medical Journal* 52, 428–431.

Lépine JP, Briley M (2011). The increasing burden of depression. *Neuropsychiatric Disorders and Treatment* 7, 3–7.

Lett TA, Zai CC, Tiwari AK, Shaikh SA, Likhodi O, Kennedy JL, Müller DJ (2011). ANK3, CACNA1C and ZNF804A gene variants in bipolar disorders and psychosis subphenotype. *World Journal of Biological Psychiatry* 12, 392–397.

Li H, Keshavan M (2011). Risk factors of suicide: Need for more research in Asian populations. *Asian Journal of Psychiatry* 4, 1.

Li Y, Chui E (2011). China's policy on rural-urban migrants and urban social harmony. *Asian Social Science* 7, 12–22.

López-Moríñigo JD, Ramos-Ríos R, David AS, Dutta R (2011). Insight in schizophrenia and risk of suicide: A systematic update. *Comprehensive Psychiatry*. Published online: 6 August 2011. doi: 10.1016/j.comppsych.2011.05.015

Lundin A, Lundberg I, Hemmingsson T (2010). The relation between sickness absence and later unemployment and suicide in a general population in Sweden. *European Journal of Public Health* 20, 10–159.

Lung FW, Tzeng DS, Huang MF, Lee MB (2011). Association of the MAOA promoter uVNTR polymorphism with suicide attempts in patients with major depressive disorder. *BMC Medical Genetics* 12, 74.

Luo F, Florence C, Quispe-Agnoli M, Ouyang L, Crosby A (2011). Impact of business cycles on US suicide rates, 1928–2007. *American Journal of Public Health* 101, 1139–1146.

MacDermott D (2010). Psychological hardiness and meaning making as protection against sequelae in veterans of the wars in Iraq and Afghanistan. *International Journal of Emergency Mental Health* 12, 199–206.

MacFarlane E, Simpson P, Benke G, Sim MR (2011). Suicide in Australian pesticide-exposed workers. *Occupational Medicine* 61, 259–264.

Magno LA, Santana CV, Sacramento EK, Rezende VB, Cardoso MV, Maurício-da-Silva L, Neves FS, Miranda DM, De Marco LA, Correa H, Romano-Silva MA (2011). Genetic variations in FOXO3A are associated with bipolar disorder without conferring vulnerability for suicidal behaviour. *Journal of Affective Disorders* 133, 633–637.

Mahdi H, Swensen RE, Munkarah AR, Chiang S, Luhrs K, Lockhart D, Kumar S (2011). Suicide in women with gynecologic cancer. *Gynecologic Oncology* 122, 344–349.

Marjo K, Jaana S, Sami P, Laksy K, Unto H, Matti I, Helina H (2011). Five-year follow-up study of disability pension rates in first-onset schizophrenia with special focus on regional differences and mortality. *General Hospital Psychiatry* 33, 509–517.

Matson JL, Sipes M, Fodstad JC, Fitzgerald ME (2011). Issues in the management of challenging behaviours of adults with autism spectrum disorder. *CNS Drugs* 25, 597–606.

Matsumoto T, Azekawa T, Uchikado H, Ozaki S, Hasegawa N, Takekawa Y, Matsushita S (2011). Comparative study of suicide risk in depressive disorder patients with and without problem drinking. *Psychiatry and Clinical Neurosciences* 65, 529–532.

Mihalache G, Buhas C, Rahota D (2011). Medical and social implications of suicide in youth. Holistic study of cases in Bihor county 2007–2009. *Romanian Journal of Legal Medicine* 19, 69–72.

Mirabelli D, Petroni ML, Ferrante D, Merletti F (2011). Risk of suicide and bariatric surgery. *American Journal of Medicine* 124, e17.

Mohandie K, Meloy JR (2011). Suicide by cop among female subjects in officer-involved shooting cases. *Journal of Forensic Sciences* 56, 664–668.

Monteso P, Ferre C, Lleixa M, Albacar N, Aguilar C, Sanchez A, Lejeune M (2011). Depression in the elderly: Study in a rural city in southern Catalonia. *Journal of Psychiatric and Mental Health Nursing*. Published online: 1 September 2011. doi: 10.1111/j.1365-2850. 2011.01798.x

Muehlenkamp JJ, Brausch AM (2011). Body image as a mediator of non-suicidal self-injury in adolescents. *Journal of Adolescence.* Published online: 20 July 2011. doi:10.1016/j.adolescence.2011.06.010

Nakamura K, Seto H, Okino S, Ono K, Ogasawara M, Shibamoto Y, Agata T, Nakayama K (2011). Psychological stress factors related to depression in white-collar workers: Within or outside the workplace. *International Medical Journal* 18, 89–99.

Nath AS, Sudhakar C, Paniyadi N (2011). A study to determine the psychological consequences of Tsunami among Tsunami-affected people of Kollam district, Kerala. *International Journal of Nursing Education* 3, 4–7.

Nevin RL (2011). Mefloquine blockade of connexin 36 and connexin 43 gap junctions and risk of suicide. *Biological Psychiatry.* Published online: 19 August 2011. doi: 10.1016/j.biopsych.2011.07.026

Nielsen J (2011). The safety of atypical antipsychotics: Does QTc provide all the answers? *Expert Opinion of Drug Safety* 10, 341–344.

Nishioka SA, Perin EA, Sampaio AS, Cordeiro Q, Cappi C, Mastrorosa RS, Morais IA, Reis VND, do Rosario MC, Hounie AG (2011). The role of the VNTR functional polymorphism of the promoter region of the MAOA gene on psychiatric disorders. *Revista de Psiquiatria Clinica* 38, 34–42.

Nivoli AMA, Pacchiarotti I, Rosa AR, Popovic D, Murru A, Valenti M, Bonnin CM, Grande I, Sanchez-Moreno J, Vieta E, Colom F (2011). Gender differences in a cohort study of 604 bipolar patients: The role of predominant polarity. *Journal of Affective Disorders* 133, 443–449.

O'Brien CW, Agrawal N (2011). Epilepsy and its neuropsychiatric complications in older adults. *British Journal of Hospital Medicine* 72, 88–91.

Olabi B, Hall J (2010). Borderline personality disorder: Current drug treatments and future prospects. *Therapeutic Advances in Chronic Disease* 1, 59–66.

Olson LM, Wahab S, Thompson CW, Durrant L (2011). Suicide notes among Native Americans, Hispanics, and Anglos. *Qualitative Health Research* 21, 1484–1494.

Ozek E, Ekici B (2011). Asthma and suicide: Possible role of brain-derived neurotrophic factor. *Medical Hypotheses* 77, 261–262.

Pandey GN, Rizavi HS, Ren X, Fareed J, Hoppensteadt DA, Roberts RC, Conley RR, Dwivedi Y (2011). Proinflammatory cytokines in the prefrontal cortex of teenage suicide victims. *Journal of Psychiatric Research.* Published online: 8 September 2011. doi:10.1016/j.jpsychires.2011.08.006

Perroud N (2011). Suicidal ideation during antidepressant treatment: Do genetic predictors exist? *CNS Drugs* 25, 459–471.

Pelkonen M, Karlsson L, Marttunen M (2011). Adolescent suicide: Epidemiology, psychological theories, risk factors, and prevention. *Current Pediatric Reviews* 7, 52–67.

Pivac N, Pregelj P, Nikolac M, Zupanc T, Nedic G, Seler DM, Paska AV (2011). The association between catechol-O-methyl-transferase Val (108/158) Met polymorphism and suicide. *Genes, Brain & Behavior* 10, 565–569.

Pompili M, Innamorati M, Venturini P, Serafini G, Lester D, Girardi P (2011). Child abuse as a risk factor for suicide in life: A selective overview. *Minerva Psichiatrica* 52, 61–69.

Pompili M, Serafini G, Innamorati M, Lester D, Shrivastava A, Girardi P, Nordentoft M (2011). Suicide risk in first episode psychosis: A selective review of the current literature. *Schizophrenia Research* 129, 1–11.

Pompili M, Serafini G, Innamorati M, Serra G, Forte A, Lester D, Ducci G, Girardi P, Tatarelli R (2010). White matter hyperintensities, suicide risk and late-onset affective disorders: An overview of the current literature. *Clinica Terapeutica* 161, 555–563.

Prati C, Claudepierre P, Pham T, Wendling D (2011). Mortality in spondylarthritis. *Joint Bone Spine* 78, 466–470.

Queinec R, Beitz C, Contrand B, Jougla E, Leffondre K, Lagarde E, Encrenaz G (2011). Copycat effect after celebrity suicides: Results from the French national death register. *Psychological Medicine* 41, 668–671.

Randle AA, Graham CA (2011). A review of the evidence on the effects of intimate partner violence on men. *Psychology of Men and Masculinity* 12, 97–111.

Razvodovsky YE (2011). Alcohol consumption and Suicide in Belarus, 1980–2005. *Suicidology Online* 2, 1–7.

Rihmer Z, Gonda X (2011). Antidepressant-resistant depression and antidepressant-associated suicidal behaviour: The role of underlying bipolarity. *Depression Research and Treatment*. Published online: 3 April 2011. doi: 10.1155/2011/906462

Ruiz MA, Douglas KS, Edens JF, Nikolova NL, Lilienfeld SO (2011). Co-occurring mental health and substance use problems in offenders: Implications for risk assessment. *Psychological Assessment*. Published online: 25 July 2011. doi: 10.1037/a0024623

Saleh C (2011). DBS, parkinson's disease, and suicide. *Journal of Neuropsychiatry and Clinical Neurosciences* 23, E4.

Schöpfer J, Schrauzer GN (2011). Lithium and other elements in scalp hair of residents of Tokyo prefecture as investigational predictors of suicide risk. *Biological Trace Element Research*. Published online: 14 June 2011. doi: 10.1007/s12011-011-9114-x

Serafini G, Pompili M, Innamorati M, Giordano G, Tatarelli R, Lester D, Girardi P, Dwivedi Y (2011). Glycosides, depression and suicidal behaviour: The role of glycoside-linked proteins. *Molecules* 16, 2688–2713.

Shah A (2011). A replication of a possible relationship between elderly suicide rates and smoking using five-year data on suicide rates? A cross-national study. *Journal of Injury and Violence Research* 2, 35–40.

Shah A (2011). A replication of the relationship between adversity earlier in life and elderly suicide rates using five years cross-national data. *Journal of Injury and Violence Research*. Published online: 16 April 2011. doi: 10.5249/jivr.v4i1.65

Shah A (2011). Suicide rates: Age-associated trends and their correlates. *Journal of Injury and Violence Research*. Published online: 16 April 2011. doi: 10.5249/jivr.v4i2.101

Shenton B (2011). Suicide and surplus people/value. *Identities* 18, 63–68.

Shoval G, Nahshoni E, Gothelf D, Manor I, Golobchik P, Zemishlany Z, Weizman A, Zalsman G (2011). Effectiveness and safety of citalopram in hospitalized adolescents with major depression: A preliminary, 8-week, fixed-dose, open-label, prospective study. *Clinical neuropharmacology* 34, 182–185.

Shun SC, Hsiao FH, Lai YH (2011). Relationship between hope and fatigue characteristics in newly diagnosed outpatients with cancer. *Oncology Nursing Forum* 38, E81–E86.

Simon RI (2011). Assessing protective factors against suicide: Questioning assumptions. *Psychiatric Times* 28, 35–37.

Singh NK, Singh RK (2010). Comprehensive epilepsy early warning system & seizure alarm. *Springer Tracts in Advanced Robotics* 60, 89–92.

Spates K (2011). African-American women and suicide: A review and critique of the literature. *Sociology Compass* 5, 336–350.

Speldewinde PC, Cook A, Davies P, Weinstein P (2011). The hidden health burden of environmental degradation: Disease comorbidities and dryland salinity. *Ecohealth*. Published online: 21 May 2011. doi: 10.1007/s10393-011-0686-x

Spreen O (2011). Nonverbal learning disabilities: A critical review. *Child Neuropsychology* 17, 418–443.

Stack S, Kposowa AJ (2011). Religion and suicide acceptability: A cross-national analysis. *Journal for the Scientific Study of Religion* 50, 289–306.

Thompson AH, Dewa CS, Phare S (2011). The suicidal process: Age of onset and severity of suicidal behaviour. *Social Psychiatry & Psychiatric Epidemiology*. Published online: 21 September. doi: 10.1007/s00127-011-0434-0

Troisi A (2011). Low cholesterol is a risk factor for attentional impulsivity in patients with mood symptoms. *Psychiatry Research* 188, 83–87.

Underwood MD, Arango V (2011). Evidence for neurodegeneration and neuroplasticity as part of the neurobiology of suicide. *Biological Psychiatry* 70, 306–307.

Valiente C, Provencio M, Espinosa R, Chaves C, Fuentenebro F (2011). Predictors of subjective well-being in patients with paranoid symptoms: Is insight necessarily advantageous? *Psychiatry research* 189, 190–194.

van Tilburg MAL, Spence NJ, Whitehead WE, Bangdiwala S, Goldston DB (2011). Chronic pain in adolescents is associated with suicidal thoughts and behaviors. *Journal of Pain* 12, 1032–1039.

Voracek M (2011). Biological parent suicide and severe psychiatric morbidity are risk factors for suicide in adopted and non-adopted offspring. *Evidence Based Mental Health* 14, 66.

Voss Horrell SC, Holohan DR, Didion LM, Vance GT (2011). Treating traumatized OEF/OIF veterans: How does trauma treatment affect the clinician? *Professional Psychology: Research and Practice* 42, 79–86.

Vyssoki B, Praschak-Rieder N, Sonneck G, Blüml V, Willeit M, Kasper S, Kapusta ND (2011). Effects of sunshine on suicide rates. *Comprehensive Psychiatry*. Published online: 6 August 2011. doi:10.1016/j.comppsych.2011.06.003

Walsh PC (2011). Suicide risk in men with prostate-specific antigen-detected early prostate cancer: A nationwide population-based cohort study from PCBaSe Sweden. *Journal of Urology* 185, 1706–1707.

Ward K, Roncancio A, Plaxe S (2011). Women with invasive gynecologic malignancies are more than 12 times as likely to commit suicide as are women in the general population. *Gynecologic Oncology* 121, S39.

Waters K (2011). Teenage bullies: Might not right. *Phi Kappa Phi Forum* 91, 7–9.

Weiner J, Richmond TS, Conigliaro J, Wiebe DJ (2011). Military veteran mortality following a survived suicide attempt. *BMC Public Health* 11, 374.

Wilkinson PO (2011). Nonsuicidal self-injury: A clear marker for suicide risk. *Journal of the American Academy of Child & Adolescent Psychiatry* 50, 741–743.

Williams J (2011). The effect on young people of suicide reports in the media. *Mental Health Practice* 14, 34–36.

Wilson DH, Ross NA (2011). Place, gender and the appeal of video lottery terminal gambling: Unpacking a focus group study of Montreal youth. *GeoJournal* 76, 123–138.

Windfuhr K (2011). Suicide: Rates, risk factors and future directions for prevention. *British Journal of Hospital Medicine* 72, 364–365.

Wong MMC, Tsui CF, Li SW, Chan CF, Lau YM (2011). Patients committing suicide whilst under the care of the elderly suicide prevention programme of a regional hospital in Hong Kong. *East Asian Archives of Psychiatry* 21, 17–21.

Zai CC, Manchia M, De Luca V, Tiwari AK, Chowdhury NI, Zai GC, Tong RP, Yilmaz Z, Shaikh SA, Strauss J, Kennedy JL (2011). The brain-derived neurotrophic factor gene in suicidal behaviour: A meta-analysis. *International Journal of Neuropsychopharmacology* 30, 1–6.

Zarghami M (2011). Methamphetamine has changed the profile of patients utilizing psychiatric emergency services in Iran. *Iranian Journal of Psychiatry and Behavioral Sciences* 5, 1–5.

Zhang J, Jia C (2011). Suicidal intent among young suicides in rural China. *Archives of Suicide Research* 15, 127–139.

## Prevention

Alizadeh NS, Afkhamzadeh A, Mohsenpour B, Salehian B, Shamsalizadeh N (2011). Intention to die in suicide attempters by poisoning in Kurdistan province. *Journal of Mazandaran University of Medical Sciences* 20, 61–67.

Andres AR, Hempstead K (2011). Gun control and suicide: The impact of state firearm regulations in the United States, 1995–2004. *Health Policy* 101, 95–103.

Autry AE, Adachi M, Nosyreva E, Na ES, Los MF, Cheng PF, Kavalali ET, Monteggia LM (2011). NMDA receptor blockade at rest triggers rapid behavioural antidepressant responses. *Nature* 475, 91–95.

Bae SB, Woo JM (2011). Suicide prevention strategies from medical perspective. *Journal of the Korean Medical Association* 54, 386–391.

Beskovnik L, Juricic NK, Svab V (2011). Suicide index reduction in Slovenia: The impact of primary care provision. *Mental Health in Family Medicine* 8, 51–55.

Bhar SS, Brown GK (2009). Treatment of depression and suicide in older adults. *Cognitive and Behavioral Practice.* Published online: 15 April 2011. doi:10.1016/j.cbpra.2010.12.005

Bhat CS, Chang SH, Linscott JA (2010). Addressing cyberbullying as a media literacy issue. *New Horizons in Education* 58, 34.

Blignault I, Iaurel J, Nampon R, Paul M, Natuman S (2011). Establishing mental health policy and services in Vanuatu. *Asia-Pacific Psychiatry* 3, 76–79.

Bo JZ, Yang SQ, Liu ZG (2011). Application of multimedia teaching in psychological health education of college students. *Advanced Materials Research*, 271–273, 1459–1462.

Botella C, Moragrega I, Banos R, Garcia-Palacios A (2010). Online predictive tools for intervention in mental illness: The OPTIMI project. *Studies in Health Technology and Informatics* 163, 86–92.

Bowers L, Dack C, Gul N, Thomas B, James K (2010). Learning from prevented suicide in psychiatric inpatient care: An analysis of data from the National Patient Safety Agency. *International Journal of Nursing Studies.* Published online: 11 June 2011. doi:10.1016/ j.ijnurstu.2011.05.008

Brenner LA, Breshears RE, Betthauser LM, Bellon KK, Holman E, Harwood JE, Silverman MM, Huggins J, Nagamoto HT (2011). Implementation of a suicide nomenclature within two VA healthcare settings. *Journal of Clinical Psychology in Medical Settings* 18, 116–128.

Brent DA (2011). Preventing youth suicide: Time to ask how. *Journal of the American Academy of Child & Adolescent Psychiatry* 50, 738–740.

Brown L (2010). Reducing the suicide rate in the profession. *The Veterinary Record* 167, 1018.

Brumby S, Chandrasekara A, McCoombe S, Torres S, Kremer P, Lewandowski P (2011). Reducing psychological distress and obesity in Australian farmers by promoting physical activity. *BMC Public Health* 11, 362.

Chua JL (2011). Making time for the children: Self-temporalization and the cultivation of the antisuicidal subject in south India. *Cultural Anthropology* 26, 112–137.

Courtet P, Gottesman II, Jollant F, Gould TD (2011). The neuroscience of suicidal behaviors: What can we expect from endophenotype strategies? *Translational Psychiatry* 1, E7.

Doessel DP, Williams RFG (2010). The economic argument for a policy of suicide prevention. *Suicidology Online* 1, 66–75.

Donker GA, Wolters I, Schellevis F (2010). Risk factors and trends in attempting or committing suicide in Dutch general practice in 1983–2009 and tools for early recognition. *European Journal of Public Health* 20, 50.

Dwyer AJ, Morley P, Reid E, Angelatos C (2011). Distressed doctors: A hospital-based support program for poorly performing and 'at-risk' junior medical staff. *Medical Journal of Australia* 194, 466–469.

Dyrbye LN, Shanafelt TD (2011). Commentary: Medical student distress: A call to action. *Academic Medicine* 86, 801–803.

Erlangsen A, Nordentoft M, Conwell Y, Waern M, De Leo D, Lindner R, Oyama H, Sakashita T, Andersen-Ranberg K, Quinnett P, Draper B, Lapierre S (2011). Key considerations for preventing suicide in older adults. *Crisis* 32, 106–109.

Ertl V, Pfeiffer A, Schauer E, Elbert T, Neuner F (2011). Community-implemented trauma therapy for former child soldiers in Northern Uganda: A randomized controlled trial. *JAMA: Journal of the American Medical Association* 306, 503–512.

Fang CK, Lu HC, Liu SI, Sun YW (2011). Religious beliefs along the suicidal path in northern Taiwan. *Omega: Journal of Death and Dying* 63, 255–269.

Friedlander AH, Rosenbluth SC, Rubin RT (2011). The adult suicide-prone patient: A review of the medical literature and implications for oral and maxillofacial surgeons. *Journal of Oral and Maxillofacial Surgery*. Published online: 7 July 2011. doi: 10.1016/j.joms.2011. 02.024

Ghio L, Zanelli E, Gotelli S, Rossi P, Natta W, Gabrielli F (2011). Involving patients who attempt suicide in suicide prevention: A focus groups study. *Journal of Psychiatric and Mental Health Nursing* 18, 510–518.

Gibbons MM, Studer J (2011). Trainings in suicide awareness: A focus on school settings. *Journal of Professional Counseling, Practice, Theory, & Research* 38, 2–17.

Glasper A (2011). What part can nurses play in the prevention of suicide? *British Journal of Nursing* 20, 1002–1003.

Grantham D (2011). New perspectives on suicide prevention. *Behavioral Healthcare* 31, 45–50.

Ha K (2011). Can a suicide prevention law decrease the suicide rate in Korea? *Journal of the Korean Medical Association* 54, 792–794.

Hill N, Joubert L, Harvey C, Hawthorne G (2011). To waiver or not to waiver? The dilemma of informed consent in emergency department suicide prevention research. *Australasian Medical Journal* 4, 463–468.

Honda N (2011). The role of occupational physicians at workplace. *Japan Medical Association Journal* 54, 87–91.

Indelicato NA, Mirsu-Paun A, Griffin WD (2011). Outcomes of a suicide prevention gatekeeper training on a university campus. *Journal of College Student Development* 52, 350–361.

Inoue K, Fukunaga T, Abe S, Okazaki Y, Ono Y (2011). A report of suicide trends and overall suicide prevention measures in Germany: Opinion on prevention measures is important. *West Indian Medical Journal* 60, 103–104.

Inoue K, Fukunaga T, Fujita Y, Okazaki Y, Ono Y (2011). A report on the importance of further liaison between relevant organizations in implementing suicide prevention measures in Japan: A summary along with a look at areas of future study. *West Indian Medical Journal* 60, 104–105.

Inoue K, Nishimura M, Fujita Y, Ono Y (2011). Report on transition and prevention measures of suicide in Kawasaki city, Japan. *International Medical Journal* 18, 19–20.

Jamieson PE, Romer D (2011). Trends in explicit portrayal of suicidal behavior in popular U.S. Movies, 1950–2006. *Archives of Suicide Research* 15, 277–289.

Kaklauskas A, Zavadskas EK, Pruskus V, Vlasenko A, Bartkiene L, Paliskiene R, Zemeckyte L, Gerstein V, Dzemyda G, Tamulevicius G (2011). Recommended biometric stress management system. *Expert Systems with Applications* 38, 14011–14025.

Kelly C, Dale E (2011). Ethical perspectives on suicide and suicide prevention. *Advances in Psychiatric Treatment* 17, 214–219.

King KA, Strunk CM, Sorter MT (2011). Preliminary effectiveness of surviving the teens suicide prevention and depression awareness program on adolescents' suicidality and self-efficacy in performing help-seeking behaviors. *The Journal of School Health* 81, 581–590.

Lehman S, Miller JA (2010). Interest and need greatly outpace resources for youth suicide prevention. *North Carolina Medical Journal* 71, 540.

Lin JJ, Lu TH (2011). Trends in solids/liquids poisoning suicide rates in Taiwan: A test of the substitution hypothesis. *BMC Public Health* 11, 712.

Liu J, Chen X, Lewis G (2010). Childhood internalizing behaviour: Analysis and implications. *Journal of Psychiatric and Mental Health Nursing*. Published online: 20 May 2011. doi: 10.1111/j.1365-2850.2011.01743.x

Mak MHJ (2010). Quality insights of university students on dying, death, and death education- A preliminary study in Hong Kong. *Omega: Journal of Death and Dying* 62, 387–405.

Manning J, Vandeusen K (2011). Suicide prevention in the dot com era: Technological aspects of a university suicide prevention program. *Journal of American College Health* 59, 431–433.

Marvasti JA (2011). Treatment of war trauma in veterans: Pharmacotherapy and self-help proposal. *Connecticut Medicine* 75, 133–141.

McDowell AK, Lineberry TW, Bostwick JM (2011). Practical suicide risk management for the busy primary care physician. *Mayo Clinic Proceedings* 86, 792–800.

Mills PD (2011). Commentary on: Learning from prevented suicide in psychiatric inpatient care: An analysis of data from the National Patient Safety Agency and author's response. *International Journal of Nursing Studies*. Published online: 27 July 2011. doi:10.1016/j.ijnurstu.2011.07.006

Mouw I, Troth A (2011). Suicide and the parking garage. *Journal of Healthcare Protection Management* 27, 117–124.

Nadeem E, Kataoka SH, Chang VY, Vona P, Wong M, Stein BD (2011). The role of teachers in school-based suicide prevention: A qualitative study of school staff perspectives. *School Mental Health*. Published online: 20 May 2011. doi: 10.1007/s12310-011-9056-7

O'Connor SS, Beebe TJ, Lineberry TW, Jobes DA, Conrad AK (2011). The association between the Kessler 10 and suicidality: A cross-sectional analysis. *Comprehensive Psychiatry*. Published online: 12 April 2011. doi:10.1016/j.comppsych.2011.02.006

Pisani AR, Cross WF, Gould MS (2011). The assessment and management of suicide risk: State of workshop education. *Suicide and Life-Threatening Behavior* 41, 255–276.

Pitman A, Osborn DP (2011). Cross-cultural attitudes to help-seeking among individuals who are suicidal: New perspective for policy-makers. *British Journal of Psychiatry* 199, 8–10.

Poma SZ, Grossi A, Venturini M, Cristina C, Toniolo E (2011). Setting up suicide prevention plans at the local level: The methodology of focus groups with stakeholders. *Journal of Community Psychology* 39, 755–760.

Pompili M, Serafini G, Innamorati M, Ambrosi E, Telesforo L, Venturini P, Giordano G, Battuello M, Lester D, Girardi P (2011). Unmet treatment needs in schizophrenia patients: Is asenapine a potential therapeutic option? *Expert Review of Neurotherapeutics* 11, 989–1006.

Poudel-Tandukar K, Nanri A, Mizoue T, Matsushita Y, Takahashi Y, Noda M, Inoue M, Tsugane S (2011). Social support and suicide in Japanese men and women — The Japan Public Health Center (JPHC)-based prospective study. *Journal of Psychiatric Research.* Published online: 30 July 2011. doi:10.1016/j.jpsychires.2011.07.009

Rihmer Z, Gonda X (2011). The effect of pharmacotherapy on suicide rates in bipolar patients. *CNS Neuroscience and Therapeutics.* Published online: 31 July 2011. doi: 10.1111/j.1755-5949.2011.00261.x

Rutecki GW (2011). Primary care and suicide prevention. *Consultant* 51, 1.

Sachse S, Keville S, Feigenbaum J (2011). A feasibility study of mindfulness-based cognitive therapy for individuals with borderline personality disorder. *Psychology and Psychotherapy: Theory, Research and Practice* 84, 184–200.

Shabana H (2011). Clinical reminders as a screening alert: Improving universal suicide screens in primary care. *Annals of Behavioral Medicine* 41, 169.

Sher L (2011). Teaching medical professionals about suicide prevention: What's missing? *QJM.* Published online: 8 August 2011. doi: 10.1093/qjmed/hcr125

Sher L (2011). Teaching medical staff in general hospitals about suicide prevention. *Journal of the Formosan Medical Association* 110, 664.

Sher L, Yehuda R (2011). Preventing suicide among returning combat veterans: A moral imperative. *Military Medicine* 176, 601–602.

Simpson GK, Brenner LA (2011). Perspectives on suicide and traumatic brain injury. *Journal of Head Trauma Rehabilitation* 26, 241–243.

Simpson GK, Tate RL, Whiting DL, Cotter RE (2011). Suicide prevention after traumatic brain injury: A randomized controlled trial of a program for the psychological treatment of hopelessness. *Journal of Head Trauma Rehabilitation* 26, 290–300.

Skruibis P, Gailiené D, Hjelmeland H, Fartacek R, Fekete S, Knizek BL, Osvath P, Renberg ES, Rohrer RR (2010). Attitudes towards suicide among regional politicians in Lithuania, Austria, Hungary, Norway and Sweden. *Suicidology Online* 2, 79–87.

Spencer-Thomas S (2011). High performers and suicide prevention in the workplace. *Psychiatric Annals* 41, 343–344.

Stanley B, Brown GK (2010). Safety planning intervention: A brief intervention to mitigate suicide risk. *Cognitive and Behavioral Practice.* Published online: 15 April 2011. doi:10.1016/j.cbpra.2011.01.001

Stark CR, Riordan V, O'Connor R (2011). A conceptual model of suicide in rural areas. *Rural Remote Health* 11, 1622.

Steffen AM (2011). Translating research for professional development and effective clinical practice with older adults. *Cognitive and Behavioral Practice.* Published online: 22 June 2011. doi:10.1016/j.cbpra.2011.05.006

Strickland CJ, Cooper M (2011). Getting into trouble: Perspectives on stress and suicide prevention among Pacific Northwest Indian Youth. *Journal of Transcultural Nursing* 22, 240–247.

Svab V, Subelj M, Vidmar G (2011). Prescribing changes in anxiolytics and antidepressants in Slovenia. *Psychiatria Danubina* 23, 178–182.

Tam CL, Lee TH, Har WM, Chan LC (2011). Perception of suicidal attempts among college students in Malaysia. *Asian Social Science* 7, 30–41.

Tsai WP, Lin LY, Chang HC, Yu LS, Chou MC (2011). The effects of the gatekeeper suicide-awareness program for nursing personnel. *Perspectives in Psychiatric Care* 47, 117–125.

Usherwood T (2011). Peer support brings benefits for students. *Veterinary Record* 168, 658–659.

Vatan S, Gençöz F, Walker R, Lester D (2010). Lay theories of suicide in Turkish and American students. *Suicidology Online* 1, 28–33.

Waits WM, Wise J (2011). The fort Campbell high interest program. *Military medicine* 176, 359–360.

Wallace ML, Dombrovski AY, Morse JQ, Houck PR, Frank E, Alexopoulos GS, Reynolds CF 3rd, Schulz R (2011). Coping with health stresses and remission from late-life depression in primary care: A two-year prospective study. *International Journal of Geriatric Psychiatry*. Published online: 30 March 2011. doi: 10.1002/gps.2706.

Ward JE, Odegard MA (2011). A proposal for increasing student safety through suicide prevention in schools. *The Clearing House* 84, 144–149.

Warner CH, Appenzeller GN, Parker JR, Warner C, Diebold CJ, Grieger T (2011). Suicide prevention in a deployed military unit. *Psychiatry* 74, 127–141.

Yip PSF (2011). Towards evidence-based suicide prevention programs. *Crisis* 32, 117–120.

Zamorski MA (2011). Suicide prevention in military organizations. *International Review of Psychiatry* 23, 173–180.

## Postvention and bereavement

Benedek CDM (2011). Impact of soldier suicide on unit and care givers: Implications for education and training. *Psychiatry* 74, 124–126.

Bhushan B, Kumar S, Harizuka S (2011). Bereavement, cognitive-emotional processing, and coping with the loss: A study of Indian and Japanese students. *Journal of Social Work in End-Of-Life & Palliative Care* 7, 263–280.

Carr RB (2011). When a soldier commits suicide in Iraq: Impact on unit and caregivers. *Psychiatry* 74, 95–106.

Davidsen AS (2011). Response to letter to the editor and commentary to 'And then one day he'd shot himself. Then I was really shocked': General practitioners' reaction to patient suicide'. *Patient Education and Counselling*. Published online: 1 September 2011. doi: 10.1016/j.pec.2011.08.001

Dyregrov KM, Dieserud G, Hjelmeland HM, Straiton M, Rasmussen ML, Knizek BL, Leenaars AA (2011). Meaning-making through psychological autopsy interviews: The value of participating in qualitative research for those bereaved by suicide. *Death Studies* 35, 685–710.

Ellis TE, Patel AB (2011). Client suicide: What now? *Cognitive and Behavioral Practice*. Published online: 15 April 2011. doi:10.1016/j.cbpra.2010.12.004

Hadry T, Adamowski T, Kiejna A (2011). Mental disorder in Polish families: Is diagnosis a predictor of caregiver's burden? *Social Psychiatry & Psychiatric Epidemiology* 46, 363–372.

Heeb JL, Gutjahr E, Gulfi A, Dransart DAC (2011). Psychometric properties of the French version of the impact of event Scale-Revised in mental health and social professionals after a patient suicide. *Swiss Journal of Psychology* 70, 105–111.

Jones A, Meier M (2011). Growing www.parentsofsuicide: A case study of an online support community. *Social Work with Groups* 34, 101–120.

Kizza D, Hjelmeland H, Kinyanda E, Knizek BL (2011). Qualitative psychological autopsy interviews on suicide in post-conflict northern Uganda: The participants' perceptions. *Omega: Journal of Death and Dying* 63, 235–254.

Mann JJ (2011). The impact of soldier suicide on a base in Afghanistan: Lessons for prevention and postvention. *Psychiatry* 74, 121–123.

Melhem NM, Porta G, Shamseddeen W, Walker Payne M, Brent DA (2011). Grief in children and adolescents bereaved by sudden parental death. *Archives of General Psychiatry* 68, 911–916.

Nock MK (2011). A soldier's suicide: Understanding its effect on fellow soldiers. *Psychiatry* 74, 107–109.

Pearson J (2011). Implications for civilian postvention research and practice. *Psychiatry* 74, 118–120.

Rober P, Walravens G, Versteynen L (2011). 'In search of a tale they can live with': About loss, family secrets, and selective disclosure. *Journal of Marital and Family Therapy.* Published online: 27 July 2011. doi: 10.1111/j.1752-0606.2011.00237.x

Skodlar B, Welz C (2011). How a therapist survives the suicide of a patient-with a special focus on patients with psychosis. *Phenomenology and the Cognitive Sciences.* Published online: 25 April 2011. doi:10.1007/s11097-011-9205-3.

Steeves RH, Parker B, Laughon K, Knopp A, Thompson ME (2011). Adolescents' experiences with uxoricide. *Journal of the American Psychiatric Nurses Association* 17, 115–123.

VandeCreek L, Mottram K (2011). The perceived roles of god during suicide bereavement. *Journal of Psychology and Theology* 39, 155–162.

Veilleux JC (2011). Coping with client death: Using a case study to discuss the effects of accidental, undetermined, and suicidal deaths on therapists. *Professional Psychology: Research and Practice* 42, 222–228.

# NON-FATAL SUICIDAL BEHAVIOUR

## Epidemiology

Alfonso M (2011). Frequency of adolescent injury. *Annals of Behavioral Medicine* 41, s220.

Anonymous (2011). Suicidal behaviour in adolescents. *International Journal of Social Psychiatry* 57, 40–56.

Anonymous (2011). Clinical profile identified for severe form of self-injury. *Journal of Psychosocial Nursing and Mental Health Services* 49, 12.

Ackard DM, Fulkerson JA, Neurnark-Sztainer D (2011). Psychological and behavioral risk profiles as they relate to eating disorder diagnoses and symptomatology among a school-based sample of youth. *International Journal of Eating Disorders* 44, 440.

Adinkrah M (2011). Epidemiologic characteristics of suicidal behavior in contemporary Ghana. *Crisis* 32, 31–36.

Ahmed N, Ansari MA, Rehman RU (2011). Psychiatric morbidity in psychoactive substance users- A multicentre study in Hyderabad. *Journal of the Liaquat University of Medical and Health Sciences* 10, 15–18.

Aiba M, Matsui Y, Kikkawa T, Matsumoto T, Tachimori H (2011). Factors influencing suicidal ideation among Japanese adults: From the national survey by the cabinet office. *Psychiatry and Clinical Neurosciences* 65, 468–475.

Alaghehbandan R, Rastegar LA, Joghataei MT, Motavalian A (2011). A prospective population-based study of suicidal behavior by burns in two provinces in Iran. *American Journal of Epidemiology* 173, S289–S289.

Al-Maskari F, Shah SM, Al-Sharhan R, Al-Haj E, Al-Kaabi K, Khonji D, Schneider JD, Nagelkerke NJ, Bernsen RM (2011). Prevalence of depression and suicidal behaviors among male migrant workers in United Arab Emirates. *Journal of Immigrant and Minority Health*. Published online: 19 April 2011. doi: 10.1007/s10903-011-9470-9.

Andover MS, Schatten HT, Crossman DM, Donovick PJ (2011). Neuropsychological functioning in prisoners with and without self-injurious behaviors: Implications for the criminal justice system. *Criminal Justice and Behavior* 38, 1103–1114.

Archie S, Zangeneh Kazemi A, Akhtar-Danesh N (2011). Concurrent binge drinking and depression among Canadian youth: Prevalence, patterns, and suicidality. *Alcohol*. Published online: 6 August 2011. doi:10.1016/j.alcohol.2011.07.001.

Armed Forces Health Surveillance Center (AFHSC) (2011). Surveillance snapshot: Hospitalizations for suicidal ideation, active component, U.S. armed forces, 2005–2010. *Massachusetts Society for Medical Research* 18, 23.

Armey MF, Crowther JH, Miller IW (2011). Changes in ecological momentary assessment reported affect associated with episodes of nonsuicidal self-injury. *Behavior Therapy*. Published online: 29 April 2011. doi:10.1016/j.beth.2011.01.002.

Asarnow JR, Porta G, Spirito A, Emslie G, Clarke G, Wagner KD, Vitiello B, Keller M, Birmaher B, McCracken J, Mayes T, Berk M, Brent DA (2011). Suicide attempts and nonsuicidal self-injury in the treatment of resistant depression in adolescents: Findings from the TORDIA study. *Journal of the American Academy of Child and Adolescent Psychiatry* 50, 772–781.

Ayalon L (2011). The prevalence and predictors of passive death wishes in Europe: A 2-year follow-up of the survey of health, ageing, and retirement in Europe. *International Journal of Geriatric Psychiatry* 26, 923–929.

Azkunaga B, Mintegi S, Bizkarra I, Fernandez J (2011). Toxicology surveillance system of the Spanish society of paediatric emergencies: First-year analysis. *European Journal of Emergency Medicine* 18, 285–287.

Backmund M, Meyer K, Schütz C, Reimer J (2011). Factors associated with suicide attempts among injection drug users. *Substance Use & Misuse* 46, 1553–1559.

Balch CM, Oreskovich MR, Dyrbye LN, Colaiano JM, Satele DV, Sloan JA, Shanafelt TD (2011). Personal consequences of malpractice lawsuits on American surgeons. *Journal of the American College of Surgeons.* Published online: 3 September 2011. doi:10.1016/j.jamcoll-surg.2011.08.005.

Baldacara L, Nery-Fernandes F, Rocha M, Quarantini LC, Rocha GGL, Guimaraes JL, Araujo C, Oliveira I, Miranda-Scippa A, Jackowski A (2011). Is cerebellar volume related to bipolar disorder? *Journal of Affective Disorders.* Published online: 23 July 2011. doi:10.1016/j.jad.2011.06.059.

Bansal PD, Barman R (2011). Psychiatric morbidity and the socio-demographic determinants of deliberate self harm. *Journal of Clinical and Diagnostic Research* 5, 601–604.

Barrocas AL, Jenness JL, Davis TS, Oppenheimer CW, Technow JR, Gulley LD, Badanes LS, Hankin BL (2011). Developmental perspectives on vulnerability to nonsuicidal self-injury in youth. *Advances in Child Development and Behavior* 40, 301–302.

Bennett GH, Shiels WE 2nd, Young AS, Lofthouse N, Mihalov L (2011). Self-embedding behavior: A new primary care challenge. *Pediatrics* 127, e1386–e1391.

Berlin I, Covey LS, Donohue MC, Agostiv V (2011). Duration of smoking abstinence and suicide related outcomes. *Nicotine and Tobacco Research.* Published online: 26 May 2011. doi: 10.1093/ntr/ntr089.

Birch S, Cole S, Hunt K, Edwards B, Reaney E (2011). Self-harm and the positive risk taking approach. Can being able to think about the possibility of harm reduce the frequency of actual harm? *Journal of Mental Health* 20, 293–303.

Bogstrand ST, Normann PT, Rossow I, Larsen M, Morland J, Ekeberg O (2011). Prevalence of alcohol and other substances of abuse among injured patients in a Norwegian emergency department. *Drug and Alcohol Dependence* 117, 132–138.

Bowers L, Crowder M (2011). Nursing staff numbers and their relationship to conflict and containment rates on psychiatric wards- A cross sectional time series Poisson regression study. *International Journal of Nursing Studies.* Published online: 2 August 2011. doi:10.1016/j.ijnurstu.2011.07.005.

Boyd RC, Diamond GS, Ten Have TR (2011). Emotional and behavioral functioning of offspring of African American mothers with depression. *Child Psychiatry & Human Development* 42, 594–608.

Bradley B, DeFife JA, Guarnaccia C, Phifer J, Fani N, Ressler KJ, Westen D (2011). Emotion dysregulation and negative affect: Association with psychiatric symptoms. *Journal of Clinical Psychiatry* 72, 685–691.

Bradvik L, Berglund M (2011). Antidepressant therapy in severe depression may have different effects on ego-dystonic and ego-syntonic suicidal ideation. *Depression Research and Treatment.* Published online: 12 May 2011. doi: 10.1155/2011/896395

Bronsard G, Lancon C, Loundou A, Auquier P, Rufo M, Simeoni MC (2011). Prevalence rate of DSM mental disorders among adolescents living in residential group homes of the French Child Welfare System. *Children and Youth Services Review* 33, 1886–1890.

Budnitz DS, Lovegrove MC, Crosby AE (2011). Emergency department visits for overdoses of acetaminophen-containing products. *American Journal of Preventive Medicine* 40, 585–592.

Calabrese JR, Prescott M, Tamburrino M, Liberzon I, Slembarski R, Goldmann E, Shirley E, Fine T, Goto T, Wilson K, Ganocy S, Chan P, Serrano MB, Sizemore J, Galea S (2011). PTSD comorbidity and suicidal ideation associated with PTSD within the Ohio Army National Guard. *Journal of Clinical Psychiatry* 72, 1072–1078.

Capron DW, Fitch K, Medley A, Blagg C, Mallott M, Joiner T (2011). Role of anxiety sensitivity subfactors in suicidal ideation and suicide attempt history. *Depression and Anxiety.* Published online: 4 August 2011. doi: 10.1002/da.20871.

Cavanaugh CE, Messing JT, Del-Colle M, Osullivan C, Campbell JC (2011). Prevalence and correlates of suicidal behavior among adult female victims of intimate partner violence. *Suicide and Life-Threatening Behavior* 41, 372.

Chan HL, Liu CY, Chau YL, Chang CM (2011). Prevalence and association of suicide ideation among Taiwanese elderly — A population-based cross-sectional study. *Chang Gung Medical Journal* 34, 197–204.

Chan KL (2011). Association between childhood sexual abuse and adult sexual victimization in a representative sample in Hong Kong Chinese. *Child Abuse and Neglect* 35, 220–229.

Chan KL, Yan E, Brownridge DA, Tiwari A, Fong DY (2011). Childhood sexual abuse associated with dating partner violence and suicidal ideation in a representative household sample in Hong Kong. *Journal of Interpersonal Violence* 26, 1763–1784.

Chan SSM, Wong CSM, Chiu HFK (2011). The validity of proxy-based NEO-five factor inventory data in suicide research: A study of 18- to 64-year-old Hong Kong Chinese who attempted suicide. *East Asian Archives of Psychiatry* 21, 58–63.

Chan YC, Tse ML, Lau FL (2011). Hong Kong poison information centre: Annual report 2009. *Hong Kong Journal of Emergency Medicine* 18, 221–231.

Chaudieu I, Norton J, Ritchie K, Birmes P, Vaiva G, Ancelin ML (2011). Late-life health consequences of exposure to trauma in a general elderly population: The mediating role of reexperiencing posttraumatic symptoms. *The Journal of Clinical Psychiatry* 72, 929–935.

Cheng CP, Yen CF, Ko CH, Yen JY (2011). Factor structure of the center for epidemiologic studies depression scale in Taiwanese adolescents. *Comprehensive Psychiatry.* Published online: 31 May 2011. doi:10.1016/j.comppsych.2011.04.056.

Chiodo D, Crooks CV, Wolfe DA, McIsaac C, Hughes R, Jaffe PG (2011). Longitudinal prediction and concurrent functioning of adolescent girls demonstrating various profiles of dating violence and victimization. *Prevention Science.* Published online: 19 July 2011. doi: 10.1007/s11121-011-0236-3.

Chung MS, Chiu HJ, Sun WJ, Lin CN, Kuo CC, Huang WC, Chen YS, Cheng HP, Chou P (2011). A rapid screening test for depression in junior high school children. *Journal of the Chinese Medical Association* 74, 363–368.

Cleary A (2011). Suicidal action, emotional expression, and the performance of masculinities. *Social Science and Medicine.* Published online: 23 August 2011. doi:10.1016/j.socscimed.2011.08.002.

Collier R (2011). Self-injury rates indicate Canadian mental health services are inadequate. *CMA: Canadian Medical Association Journal.* Published online: 13 June 2011. doi: 10.1503/ cmaj.109-3920.

Crawford MJ, Kakad S, Rendel C, Mansour NA, Crugel M, Liu KW, Paton C, Barnes TR (2011). Medication prescribed to people with personality disorder: The influence of patient factors and treatment setting. *Acta Psychiatrica Scandinavica.* Published online: 27 June 2011. doi: 10.1111/j.1600-0447.2011.01728.x.

Cripps RA, Lee BB, Wing P, Weerts E, Mackay J, Brown D (2011). A global map for traumatic spinal cord injury epidemiology: Towards a living data repository for injury prevention. *Spinal Cord* 49, 493–501.

Cukrowicz KC, Schlegel EF, Smith PN, Jacobs MP, Van Orden KA, Paukert AL, Pettit JW, Joiner TE (2011). Suicide ideation among college students evidencing subclinical depression. *Journal of American College Health* 59, 575–581.

Cwik MF, Barlow A, Tingey L, Larzelere-Hinton F, Goklish N, Walkup JT (2011). Nonsuicidal self-injury in an American Indian reservation community: Results from the White Mountain Apache Surveillance System, 2007–2008. *Journal of the American Academy of Child and Adolescent Psychiatry* 50, 860–869.

Darke S, Campbell G, Popple G (2011). Self-harm and attempted suicide among therapeutic community admissions. *Drug and Alcohol Review.* Published online: 31 August 2011. doi: 10.1111/j.1465-3362.2011.00344.x.

de Abreu LN, Nery FG, Harkavy-Friedman JM, de Almeida KM, Gomes BC, Oquendo MA, Lafer B (2011). Suicide attempts are associated with worse quality of life in patients with bipolar disorder type I. *Comprehensive Psychiatry.* Published online 6 May 2011. doi:10.1016/j.comppsych.2011.03.003.

de Haro L, Gazin V, Aymard I, Blanc-Brisset I, Saviuc P (2011). Suicide attempts with methadone in France: A 2 year national survey since the availability of capsules in 2008. *Clinical Toxicology* 49, 14.

De Hert M, Dirix N, Demunter H, Correll CU (2011). Prevalence and correlates of seclusion and restraint use in children and adolescents: A systematic review. *European Child & Adolescent Psychiatry* 20, 221–230.

Denny SJ, Grant S, Utter J, Robinson EM, Fleming TM, Milfont TL, Crengle S, Clark T, Ameratunga SN, Dixon R, Merry S, Herd R, Watson P (2011). Health and well-being of young people who attend secondary school in Aotearoa, New Zealand: What has changed from 2001 to 2007? *Journal of Paediatrics and Child Health* 47, 191–197.

Dick K, Gleeson K, Johnstone L, Weston C (2011). Staff beliefs about why people with learning disabilities self-harm: A Q-methodology study. *British Journal of Learning Disabilities* 39, 233–242.

Dick T (2011). 'Cut yourself here': Rethinking our view of suicide. *JEMS: Journal of Emergency Medical Services* 36, 34.

Dolan MA, Fein JA, The Committee on Pediatric Emergency Medicine (2011). Technical report — Pediatric and adolescent mental health emergencies in the emergency medical services system. *Pediatrics* 127, E1356–E1366.

D'Souza R, Rajji TK, Mulsant BH, Pollock BG (2011). Use of lithium in the treatment of bipolar disorder in late-life. *Current Psychiatry Reports.* Published online: 17 August 2011. doi: 10.1007/s11920-011-0228-9.

Dumlu K, Orhon Z, Ozerdem A, Tural U, Ulas H, Tunca Z (2011). Treatment-induced manic switch in the course of unipolar depression can predict bipolarity: Cluster analysis based evidence. *Journal of Affective Disorders* 134, 91–101.

Durrani A, Deahl M (2011). Self harm on prescription: The lesser of two evils? *British Journal of Hospital Medicine* 72, 172–173.

Ekinci O, Albayrak Y, Caykoylu A (2011). Impulsivity in euthymic patients with major depressive disorder: The relation to sociodemographic and clinical properties. *Journal of Nervous & Mental Disease* 199, 454–458.

Ekinci O, Albayrak Y, Ekinci AE, Caykoylu A (2011). Relationship of trait impulsivity with clinical presentation in euthymic bipolar disorder patients. *Psychiatry Research.* Published online: 2 July 2011. doi:10.1016/j.psychres.2011.06.010.

Emet M, Beyhun NE, Uzkeser M, Cakir Z, Aslan S (2011). The main differences in oral exposures in children and adults. *Bratislava Medical Journal* 112, 346–352.

Emul M, Uzunoglu Z, Sevinç H, Güzel C, Yılmaz C, Erkut D, Arikan K (2011). The attitudes of preclinical and clinical Turkish medical students toward suicide attempters. *Crisis* 32, 128–133.

Engin E, Cuhadar D, Ozturk E (2011). Healthy life behaviors and suicide probability in university students. *Archives of Psychiatric Nursing.* Published online: 30 July 2011. doi:10.1016/j.apnu.2011.05.001.

Evren C, Cınar O, Evren B, Celik S (2011). History of suicide attempt in male substance-dependent inpatients and relationship with borderline personality features, anger, hostility and aggression. *Psychiatry Research.* Published online: 27 August 2011. doi:10.1016/ j.psychres.2011.08.002.

Evren C, Cınar O, Evren B, Celik S (2011). Self-mutilative behaviors in male substance-dependent inpatients and relationship with anger and aggression: Mediator effect of childhood trauma. *Comprehensive Psychiatry.* Published online: 31 May 2011. doi:10.1016/ j.comppsych.2011.04.061.

Fite PJ, Stoppelbein L, Greening L, Preddy TM (2011). Associations between relational aggression, depression, and suicidal ideation in a child psychiatric inpatient sample. *Child Psychiatry and Human Development.* Published online: 24 June 2011. doi: 10.1007/s10578-011-0243-4.

Fitzgerald CT, Messias E, Buysse DJ (2011). Teen sleep and suicidality: Results from the youth risk behavior surveys of 2007 and 2009. *Journal of Clinical Sleep Medicine* 7, 351–356.

Foldes-Busque G, Marchand A, Chauny JM, Poitras J, Diodati J, Denis I, Lessard MJ, Pelland MÈ, Fleet R (2011). Unexplained chest pain in the ED: Could it be panic? *American Journal of Emergency Medicine* 29, 743–751.

Forrester MB (2011). Ingestions of hydrocodone, carisoprodol, and alprazolam in combination reported to texas poison centers. *Journal of Addictive Diseases* 30, 110.

Frankenburg FR, Zanarini M (2011). Relationship between cumulative BMI and symptomatic, psychosocial, and medical outcomes in patients with borderline personality disorder. *Journal of Personality Disorders* 25, 421–431.

Friedman ES, Davis LL, Zisook S, Wisniewski SR, Trivedi MH, Fava M, Rush AJ (2011). Baseline depression severity as a predictor of single and combination antidepressant treatment outcome: Results from the CO-MED trial. *European Neuropsychopharmacology.* Published online: 14 September 2011. doi:10.1016/j.euroneuro.2011.07.010.

Fuchs J, Rauber-Lüthy C, Kupferschmidt H, Kupper J, Kullak-Ublick GA, Ceschi A (2011). Acute plant poisoning: Analysis of clinical features and circumstances of exposure. *Clinical Toxicology* 49, 671–680.

Furlanetto LM, Stefanello B (2011). Suicidal ideation in medical inpatients: Psychosocial and clinical correlates. *General Hospital Psychiatry.* Published online: 9 September 2011. doi: 10.1016/ j.genhosppsych.2011.08.002.

Gal M, Rus D, Peek-Asa C, Chereche RM, Sirlincan EO, Boeriu C, Baba CO (2011). Epidemiology of assault and self-harm injuries treated in a large Romanian Emergency Department. *European Journal of Emergency Medicine.* Published online: 22 August 2011. doi: 10.1097/MEJ.0b013e32834ada2e.

Garland EL, Carter K, Howard MO (2011). Prevalence, correlates, and characteristics of gasoline inhalation among high-risk youth: Associations with suicidal ideation, self-medication, and antisociality. *Klinik Psikofarmakoloji Bulteni* 21, 105–113.

Gladden R, Vagi K, Patel N, Lipskiy N, Benoit S, English R, Dey A, Crosby A (2011). Monitoring emergency department (ED) visits for suicide ideation and attempts during the US economic recession using biosense, 2008–2009. *American Journal of Epidemiology* 173, S291–S291.

Glenn CR, Klonsky ED (2011). Prospective prediction of nonsuicidal self-injury: A 1-year longitudinal study in young adults. *Behavior Therapy.* Published online: 12 June 2011. doi:10.1016/j.beth.2011.04.005.

Glenn CR, Klonsky ED (2011). One-Year test-retest reliability of the Inventory of Statements about Self-Injury (ISAS). *Assessment*. Published online: 10 June 2011. doi: 10.1177/107319 1111411669.

Gretton HM, Clift RJW (2011). The mental health needs of incarcerated youth in British Columbia, Canada. *International Journal of Law and Psychiatry* 34, 109–115.

Greydanus DE, Apple RW (2011). The relationship between deliberate self-harm behavior, body dissatisfaction, and suicide in adolescents: Current concepts. *Journal of Multidisciplinary Healthcare* 4, 183–189.

Guillaume S, Jaussent I, Olié E, Genty C, Bringer J, Courtet P, Schmidt U (2011). Characteristics of suicide attempts in anorexia and bulimia nervosa: A case-control study. *PLoS ONE* 6, e23578.

Gwini SM, Shaw D, Iqbal M, Spaight A, Siriwardena AN (2011). Exploratory study of factors associated with adverse clinical features in patients presenting with non-fatal drug overdose/self-poisoning to the ambulance service. *Emergency Medicine Journal* 28, 892–894.

Håkansson A, Bradvik L, Schlyter F, Berglund M (2011). Variables associated with repeated suicide attempt in a criminal justice population. *Suicide and Life-Threatening Behavior* 41, 517–531.

Hamdulay AK, Mash R (2011). The prevalence of substance use and its associations amongst students attending high school in Mitchells Plain, Cape Town. *South African Family Practice* 53, 83–90.

Harrison-Woolrych M, Ashton J (2011). Psychiatric adverse events associated with varenicline. *Drug Safety* 34, 763–772.

Hart T, Brenner L, Clark AN, Bogner JA, Novack TA, Chervoneva I, Nakase-Richardson R, Arango-Lasprilla JC (2011). Major and minor depression after traumatic brain injury. *Archives of Physical Medicine and Rehabilitation* 92, 1211–1219.

Heba YS, Omneya IY, Fawzi MM (2011). Demographic and clinical parameters of digitalis intoxicated pediatric patients during years 2009–2010. *Indian Journal of Forensic Medicine and Toxicology* 5, 58–62.

Hirsch JK, Webb JR, Jeglic EL (2011). Forgiveness, depression, and suicidal behavior among a diverse sample of college students. *Journal of Clinical Psychiatry* 67, 896–906.

Hodge FS, Nandy K (2011). Predictors of wellness and American Indians. *Journal of Health Care for the Poor and Underserved* 22, 791–803.

Howard LM, Flach C, Mehay A, Sharp D, Tylee A (2011). The prevalence of suicidal ideation identified by the Edinburgh Postnatal Depression Scale in postpartum women in primary care: findings from the RESPOND trial. *BMC Pregnancy and Childbirth*. Published online: 3 August 2011. doi:10.1186/1471-2393-11-57.

Hybels CF, Landerman LR, Blazer DG (2011). Age differences in symptom expression in patients with major depression. *International Journal of Geriatric Psychiatry*. Published online: 19 July 2011. doi: 10.1002/gps.2759.

Hysinger EB, Callahan ST, Caples TL, Fuchs DC, Shelton R, Cooper WO (2011). Suicidal behavior differs among early and late adolescents treated with antidepressant agents. *Pediatrics* 128, 447–454.

Im MY, Kim YJ (2011). A phenomenological study of suicide attempts in elders. *Journal of Korean Academy of Nursing* 41, 61–71.

Inoue K, Fukunaga T, Fujita Y, Ono Y (2011). The current state of ten high-ranking causes of death in recent years in Japan: Prevention measures. *West Indian Medical Journal* 60, 103.

Jayasinghe SS, Pathirana KD (2011). Effects of deliberate ingestion of organophosphate or paraquat on brain stem auditory-evoked potentials. *Journal of Medical Toxicology.* Published online: 11 August 2011. doi: 10.1007/s13181-011-0173-3.

Jegannathan B, Kullgren G (2011). Gender differences in suicidal expressions and their determinants among young people in Cambodia, a post-conflict country. *BMC Psychiatry.* Published online: 21 March 2011. doi: 10.1186/1471-244X-11-47.

Jones CJ, Creedy DK, Gamble JA (2011). Australian midwives' knowledge of antenatal and postpartum depression: A national survey. *Journal of Midwifery and Women's Health* 56, 353–361.

Kahumoku EP, Vazsonyi AT, Pagava K, Phagava H, Alsaker FD, Michaud PA (2011). Objectified body consciousness and mental health in female adolescents: Cross-cultural evidence from Georgian and Swiss national samples. *Journal of Adolescent Health* 49, 141–147.

Kann L, Olsen EO, McManus T, Kinchen S, Chyen D, Harris WA, Wechsler H; Division of Adolescent and School Health, National Center for Chronic Disease Prevention and Health Promotion, CDC (2011). Sexual identity, sex of sexual contacts, and health-risk behaviors among students in grades 9–12 — Youth risk behavior surveillance, selected sites, United States, 2001–2009. *Morbidity & Mortality Weekly Report: Surveillance Summaries* 60, 1–133.

Katirci Y, Kandis H, Aslan S, Kirpinar I (2011). Neuropsychiatric disorders and risk factors in carbon monoxide intoxication. *Toxicology and Industrial Health* 27, 397–406.

Kavita R, Girish N, Gururaj G (2011). Burden, characteristics, and outcome of injury among females: Observations from Bengaluru, India. *Women's Health Issues* 21, 320–326.

Keller S, Sarchiapone M, Zarrilli F, Tomaiuolo R, Carli V, Angrisano T, Videtic A, Amato F, Pero R, Di Giannantonio M, Iosue M, Lembo F, Castaldo G, Chiariotti L (2011). TrkB gene expression and DNA methylation state in Wernicke area does not associate with suicidal behavior. *Journal of Affective Disorders.* Published online: 29 July 2011. doi:10.1016/j.jad. 2011.07.003.

Khade A, Borkar R, Bashir MSM (2011). Profile of medicolegal cases in northern tribal region of Andhra Pradesh. *Medico-Legal Update* 11, 1–4.

Khan A, Khan SR, Hobus J, Faucett J, Mehra V, Giller EL, Rudolph RL (2011). Differential pattern of response in mood symptoms and suicide risk measures in severely ill depressed patients assigned to citalopram with placebo or citalopram combined with lithium: Role of lithium levels. *Journal of Psychiatric Research.* Published online: 12 July 2011. doi:10.1016/j.jpsychires.2011.06.016.

Ki S (2011). Lifetime prevalence of suicidal-related behaviors and its relationship with alcohol use problems in Chungcheongnam- Do province, Republic of Korea. *Alcohol & Alcoholism* 46, 53–53.

Kim HG, Geppert J, Quan T, Bracha Y, Lupo V, Cutts DB (2011). Screening for postpartum depression among low-income mothers using an interactive voice response system. *Maternal & Child Health Journal.* Published online: 17 May 2011. doi: 10.1007/s10995-011-0817-6.

Kim YJ, Moon SS, Kim MJ (2011). Physical and psycho-social predictors of adolescents' suicide behaviors. *Child and Adolescent Social Work Journal.* Published online: 5 June 2011. doi: 10.1007/s10560-011-0241-1.

Kleespies PM, AhnAllen CG, Knight JA, Presskreischer B, Barrs KL, Boyd BL, Dennis JP (2011). A study of self-injurious and suicidal behavior in a veteran population. *Psychological Services* 8, 236–250.

Ko KD, Lee KY, Cho B, Park MS, Son KY, Ha JH, Park SM (2011). Disparities in health-risk behaviors, preventive health care utilizations, and chronic health conditions for people with disabilities: The Korean national health and nutrition examination survey. *Archives of Physical Medical and Rehabilitation* 92, 1230–1237.

Kokkevi A, Rotsika V, Arapaki A, Richardson C (2011). Adolescents' self-reported suicide attempts, self-harm thoughts and their correlates across 17 European countries. *Journal of

*Child Psychology and Psychiatry.* Published online: 5 September 2011. doi: 10.1111/j.1469-7610.2011.02457.x.

Krivoy A, Malka L, Fischel T, Weizman A, Valevski A (2011). Predictors of clozapine discontinuation in patients with schizophrenia. *International Clinical Psychopharmacology* 26, 311–315.

Kurimoto A, Awata S, Ohkubo T, Tsubota-Utsugi M, Asayama K, Takahashi K, Suenaga K, Satoh H, Imai Y (2011). Reliability and validity of the Japanese version of the abbreviated Lubben Social Network Scale. *Japanese Journal of Geriatrics* 48, 149–157.

Larkin GL, Beautrais AL (2011). A preliminary naturalistic study of low-dose ketamine for depression and suicide ideation in the emergency department. *International Journal of Neuropsychopharmacology* 14, 1127–1131.

Le LC, Blum RW (2011). Intentional injury in young people in Vietnam: Prevalence and social correlates. *MEDICC review* 13, 23–28.

Lebeau R, Coulibaly A, Kountele Gona S, Koffi Gnangoran M, Kouakou B, Yapo P, Assohoun T, Kanga Miessan JB (2011). Isolated gastric outlet obstruction due to corrosive ingestion. *Journal of visceral surgery* 148, 59–63.

Li C, Martin BC (2011). Trends in emergency department visits attributable to acetaminophen overdoses in the United States: 1993–2007. *Pharmacoepidemiology and Drug Safety* 20, 810–818.

Li D, Zhang W, Li X, Li N, Ye B (2011). Gratitude and suicidal ideation and suicide attempts among Chinese adolescents: Direct, mediated, and moderated effects. *Journal of Adolescence.* Published online: 19 July 2011. doi:10.1016/j.adolescence.2011.06.005.

Liang KY, Meg Tseng MC (2011). Impulsive behaviors in female patients with eating disorders in a university hospital in northern Taiwan. *Journal of the Formosan Medical Association* 110, 607–610.

Liang S, Friedman LS (2011). Analysis of suspected suicides using poison center data. *Archives of Suicide Research* 15, 185–194.

Lin YR, Wu TK, Liu TA, Chou CC, Wu HP (2011). Poison exposure and outcome of children admitted to a pediatric emergency department. *World Journal of Pediatrics* 7, 143–149.

Lukaschek K, Baumert J, Ladwig KH (2011). Behaviour patterns preceding a railway suicide: Explorative study of German Federal Police officers' experiences. *BMC Public Health.* Published online: 4 August 2011. doi:10.1186/1471-2458-11-620.

Madianos MG, Sarhan AL, Koukia E (2011). Posttraumatic stress disorders comorbid with major depression in west bank, Palestine: A general population cross sectional study. *European Journal of Psychiatry* 25, 19–31.

Maharaj R, Gillies D, Andrew S, O'Brien L (2011). Characteristics of patients referred by police to a psychiatric hospital. *Journal of Psychiatric Mental Health Nursing* 18, 205–212.

Mariu KR, Merry SN, Robinson EM, Watson PD (2011). Seeking professional help for mental health problems, among New Zealand secondary school students. *Clinical Child Psychology and Psychiatry.* Published online: 18 August 2011. doi: 10.1177/1359104511404176.

Marshal MP, Dietz LJ, Friedman MS, Stall R, Smith HA, McGinley J, Thoma BC, Murray PJ, D'Augelli AR, Brent DA (2011). Suicidality and depression disparities between sexual minority and heterosexual youth: A meta-analytic review. *Journal of Adolescent Health* 49, 115–123.

Marshall M, Rathbone J (2011). Early intervention for psychosis. *Cochrane Database of Systematic Reviews* 6, 4718–4718.

May A, Klonsky DE (2011). Validity of suicidality items from the youth risk behavior survey in a high school sample. *Assessment* 18, 379–381.

McCabe I, Acree M, O'Mahony F, McCabe J, Kenny J, Twyford J, Quigley K, McGlanaghy E (2011). Male street prostitution in Dublin: A psychological analysis. *Journal of Homosexuality* 58, 998–1021.

McClure CK, Patrick TE, Katz KD, Kelsey SF, Weiss HB (2011). Birth outcomes following self-inflicted poisoning during pregnancy, California, 2000 to 2004. *Journal of Obstetric, Gynecology & Neonatal Nursing* 40, 292–301.

McKetin R, Lubman DI, Lee NM, Ross JE, Slade TN (2011). Major depression among methamphetamine users entering drug treatment programs. *Medical Journal of Australia* 195, S51–S55.

Mekonnen D, Kebede Y (2011). The prevalence of suicidal ideation and attempts among individuals attending an adult psychiatry out-patient clinic in Gondar, Ethiopia. *African Health Sciences* 11, 103–107.

Mendez RC, Perez RS, Munoz MS, Hernandez MI, Fortunez PR, Hernandez MH, Sirvent JG, Rodriguez DL, Sosa AJ, Badia MD B (2011). Study of prevalence and suicide risk factors in HIV patients: Preliminary results. *Journal of Psychosomatic Research* 70, 586–586.

Mills PD, Watts BV, Derosier JM, Tomolo AM, Bagian JP (2011). Suicide attempts and completions in the emergency department in Veterans Affairs Hospitals. *Emergency Medicine Journal.* Published online: 13 April 2011. doi:10.1136/emj.2010.105239.

Molnar S, Mihanovic M, Grah M, Kezic S, Filakovic P, Degmecic D (2011). Comparative study on gene tags of the neurotransmission system in schizophrenic and suicidal subjects. *Collegium Antropologicum* 34, 1427–1432.

Mosotho L, Louw D, Calitz, FJW (2011). Schizophrenia among Sesotho speakers in South Africa. *African Journal of Psychiatry* 14, 50–55.

Muralidhara Yadiyal B, Aruna G (2011). Psychopathology among suicide attempters: A cross-sectional study. *Indian Journal of Forensic Medicine and Toxicology* 5, 5–8.

Nath Y, Paris J, Thombs B, Kirmayer L (2011). Prevalence and social determinants of suicidal behaviours among college youth in India. *International Journal of Social Psychiatry.* Published online: 1 June 2011. doi: 10.1177/0020764011401164.

Olguin HJ, Garduño LB, Pérez JF, Bastida MA, Pérez CF (2011). Frequency of suicide attempts by ingestion of drugs seen at a tertiary care pediatric hospital in Mexico. *Candian Journal of Clinical Pharmacology* 18, e161–e165.

Olino TM, Klein DN, Farmer RF, Seeley JR, Lewinsohn PM (2011). Examination of the structure of psychopathology using latent class analysis. *Comprehensive Psychiatry.* Published online: 12 Jul 2011. doi:10.1016/j.comppsych.2011.05.008

Oluwole OSA (2011). Incidence and risk factors of early post-traumatic seizures in Nigerians. *Brain Injury* 25, 980–988.

Ougrin D, Zundel T, Kyriakopoulos M, Banarsee R, Stahl D, Taylor E (2011). Adolescents with suicidal and nonsuicidal self-harm: Clinical characteristics and response to therapeutic assessment. *Psychological Assessment* Published online: 22 August 2011. E-publication.

Pagura J, Katz LY, Mojtabai R, Druss BG, Cox B, Sareen J (2011). Antidepressant use in the absence of common mental disorders in the general population. *Journal of Clinical Psychiatry* 72, 494–501.

Palma-Coca O, Hernandez-Serrato MI, Villalobos-Hernandez A, Unikel-Santoncini C, Olaiz-Fernandez G, Bojorquez-Chapela I (2011). Association of socioeconomic status, problem behaviors, and disordered eating in Mexican adolescents: Results of the Mexican National Health and Nutrition Survey 2006. *Journal of Adolescent Health* 49, 400–406.

Pan LA, Batezati-Alves SC, Almeida JR, Segreti A, Akkal D, Hassel S, Lakdawala S, Brent DA, Phillips ML (2011). Dissociable patterns of neural activity during response inhibition in depressed adolescents with and without suicidal behaviour. *Journal of the American Academy of Child & Adolescent Psychiatry* 50, 602–611.

Park C, McDermott B, Loy J, Dean P (2011). Adolescent admissions to adult psychiatric units: Patterns and implications for service provision. *Australasian Psychiatry* 19, 345–349.

Patil S, Shivakumar C (2011). A study of deliberate self-harm patients attending tertiary care teaching hospitals in South India. *Australasian Medical Journal* 4, 277–279.

Peleg K, Jaffe DH (2011). Characteristics of unintentional and intentional injuries in Israel between the years 2000–2006. *Harefuah* 149, 418–421.

Perroud N, Baud P, Mouthon D, Courtet P, Malafosse A (2011). Impulsivity, aggression and suicidal behavior in unipolar and bipolar disorders. *Journal of Affective Disorders* 134, 112–118.

Peterson J, Skeem J, Manchak S (2011). If you want to know, consider asking: How likely is it that patients will hurt themselves in the future? *Psychological Assessment* 23, 626–34.

Pettit JW, Green KL, Grover KE, Schatte DJ, Morgan ST (2011). Domains of chronic stress and suicidal behaviors among inpatient adolescents. *Journal of Clinical Child and Adolescent Psychology* 40, 494–499.

Pinder RJ, Iversen AC, Kapur N, Wessely S, Fear NT (2011). Self-harm and attempted suicide among UK Armed Forces personnel: Results of a cross-sectional survey. *International Journal of Social Psychiatry*. Published online: 21 June 2011. doi: 10.1177/0020764011 408534

Polazarevska M, Manchevska S, Filipovska A, Gerazova V (2011). Ten-year epidemiological study on suicide attempts in Skopje, Republic of Macedonia. *Medical Archives* 65, 38–41.

Potera C (2011). YouTube self-harm videos under scrutiny. *American Journal of Nursing* 111, 20.

Poynter BA, Hunter JJ, Coverdale JH, Kempinsky CA (2011). Hard to swallow: A systematic review of deliberate foreign body ingestion. *General Hospital Psychiatry* 33, 518–524.

Reed SC, Bell JF, Edwards TC (2011). Adolescent well-being in Washington state military families. *American Journal of Public Health* 101, 1676–1682.

Rees S, Silove D, Chey T, Ivancic L, Steel Z, Creamer M, Teesson M, Bryant R, McFarlane AC, Mills KL, Slade T, Carragher N, O'Donnell M, Forbes D (2011). Lifetime prevalence of gender-based violence in women and the relationship with mental disorders and psychosocial function. *Journal of the American Medical Association* 306, 513–521.

Rezaie L, Khazaie H, Soleimani A, Schwebel DC (2011). Self-immolation a predictable method of suicide: A comparison study of warning signs for suicide by self-immolation and by self-poisoning. *Burns*. Published online: 13 May 2011. doi:10.1016/j.burns.2011. 04.006.

Riedel M, Moller HJ, Obermeier M, Adli M, Bauer M, Kronmüller K, Brieger P, Laux G, Bender W, Heuser I, Zeiler J, Gaebel W, Schennach-Wolff R, Henkel V, Seemüller F (2011). Clinical predictors of response and remission in inpatients with depressive syndromes. *Journal of Affective Disorders* 133, 137–149.

Rissanen ML, Kylma J, Laukkanen E (2011). A systematic literature review: Self-mutilation among adolescents as a phenomenon and help for it-what kind of knowledge is lacking? *Issues in Mental Health Nursing* 32, 575–583.

Roe-Sepowitz D, Hickle K (2011). Comparing boy and girl arsonists: Crisis, family, and crime scene characteristics. *Legal and Criminological Psychology* 16, 277–288.

Rost K, Hsieh YP, Xu S, Harman J (2011). Gender differences in hospitalization after emergency room visits for depressive symptoms. *Journal of Women's Health* 20, 719–724.

Rybakowski, Janusz K (2011). Lithium in neuropsychiatry: A 2010 update. *World Journal of Biological Psychiatry* 12, 340–348.

Saha S, Scott JG, Johnston AK, Slade TN, Varghese D, Carter GL, McGrath JJ (2011). The association between delusional-like experiences and suicidal thoughts and behaviour. *Schizophrenia Research*. Published online: 1 August 2011. doi:10.1016/j.schres.2011.07.012.

Saitta P, Keehan P, Yousif J, Way BV, Grekin S, Brancaccio R (2011). An update on the presence of psychiatric comorbidities in acne patients, Part 2: Depression, anxiety, and suicide. *Cutis* 88, 92–97.

Sansone RA, Dittoe N, Hahn HS, Wiederman MW (2011). The prevalence of self-harm behaviors in a consecutive sample of cardiac stress test patients. *International Journal of Psychiatry in Medicine* 41, 123–126.

Sansone RA, Lam C, Wiederman MW (2011). The relationship between illegal behaviors and borderline personality symptoms among internal medicine outpatients. *Comprehensive Psychiatry.* Published online: 5 May 2011. doi:10.1016/j.comppsych.2011.03.006.

Sansone RA, Lam C, Wiederman MW (2011). History of attempted suicide and the medical review of systems. *International Medical Journal* 41, 511.

Sarin E, Samson L, Sweat M, Beyrer C (2011). Human rights abuses and suicidal ideation among male injecting drug users in Delhi, India. *International Journal Drug of Policy* 22, 161–166.

Schennach-Wolff R, Obermeier M, Seemüller F, Jager M, Messer T, Laux G, Pfeiffer H, Naber D, Schmidt LG, Gaebel W, Klosterkötter J, Heuser I, Maier W, Lemke MR, Rüther E, Klingberg S, Gastpar M, Möller HJ, Riedel M (2011). Evaluating depressive symptoms and their impact on outcome in schizophrenia applying the Calgary Depression Scale. *Acta Psychiatrica Scandinavica* 123, 228–238.

Seoighe DM, Conroy F, Hennessy G, Meagher P, Eadie P (2011). Self-inflicted burns in the Irish National Burns Unit. *Burns* 37, 1229–1232.

Shakya DR (2010). Psychiatric morbidity profiles of child and adolescent psychiatry out-patients in a tertiary-care hospital. *Journal of Nepal Paediatric Society* 30, 79–84.

Shakya DR (2010). Clinico-demographic profiles in obsessive compulsive disorders. *Journal of the Nepal Medical Association* 49, 133–138.

Simkin S, Hawton K, Kapur N, Gunnell D (2011). What can be done to reduce mortality from paracetamol overdoses? A patient interview study. *Quarterly Journal of Medicine.* Published online: 19 August 2011. doi:10.1093/qjmed/hcr135.

Singh N, Gupta RK, Margekar SL (2011). Myocardial injury in celphos poisoning. *Journal, Indian Academy of Clinical Medicine* 12, 54–55.

Sivasubramanian M, Mimiaga MJ, Mayer KH, Anand VR, Johnson CV, Prabhugate P, Safren SA (2011). Suicidality, clinical depression, and anxiety disorders are highly prevalent in men who have sex with men in Mumbai, India: Findings from a community-recruited sample. *Psychology, Health & Medicine* 16, 450–462.

Solano P, Pizzorno E, Gallina AM, Mattei C, Gabrielli F, Kayman J (2011). Employment status, inflation and suicidal behaviour: An analysis of a stratified sample in Italy. *International Journal of Social Psychiatry.* Published online: 3 August 2011. doi: 10.1177/002076 4011408651.

Sonal Sekhar M, Adheena Mary C, Anju PG, Hamsa NA (2011). Study on drug related hospital admissions in a tertiary care hospital in South India. *Saudi Pharmaceutical Journal* 19, 273–278.

Starkstein S, Dragovic M, Jorge R, Brockman S, Merello M, Robinson RG, Bruce D, Wilson M (2011). Diagnostic criteria for depression in Parkinson's disease: A study of symptom patterns using latent class analysis. *Movement Disorders.* Published online: 7 July 2011. doi:10.1002/mds.23836.

Taheri MS, Noori M, Shakiba M, Jalali AH (2011). Brain CT-scan findings in unconscious patients after poisoning. *International Journal of Biomedical Science* 7, 1–5.

Takayama Y, Miura E, Miura K, Ono S, Ohkubo C (2011). Condition of depressive symptoms among Japanese dental students. *Odontology* 99, 179–187.

Tanaka M, Kinney DK (2011). An evolutionary hypothesis of suicide: Why it could be biologically adaptive and is so prevalent in certain occupations. *Psychological Reports* 108, 977–992.

Tektonidou MG, Dasgupta A, Ward MM (2011). Suicidal ideation among adults with arthritis: Prevalence and subgroups at highest risk. *Arthritis Care & Research* 63, 1322–1333.

Terada S, Matsumoto Y, Sato T, Okabe N, Kishimoto Y, Uchitomi Y (2011). Suicidal ideation among patients with gender identity disorder. *Psychiatry Research*. Published online: 25 May 2011. doi:10.1016/j.psychres.2011.04.024.

Tindle HA, Kuller LH, Courcoulas A, Marcus M, Omalu B, Hammers J (2011). Risk of suicide and bariatric surgery reply. *American Journal of Medicine*. Published online: 12 June 2011. doi:10.1016/j.amjmed.2011.02.028.

Topp T, Muller T, Kiriazidis I, Lefering R, Ruchholtz S, Kuhne CA (2011). Multiple blunt trauma after suicidal attempt: An analysis of 4,754 multiple severely injured patients. *European Journal of Trauma and Emergency Surgery*. Published online: 12 May 2011. doi:10.1007/s00068-011-0114-5.

Trivedi MH, Wisniewski SR, Morris DW, Fava M, Gollan JK, Warden D, Nierenberg AA, Gaynes BN, Husain MM, Luther JF, Zisook S, Rush AJ (2011). Concise health risk tracking scale: A brief self-report and clinician rating of suicidal risk. *Journal of Clinical Psychiatry* 72, 757–764.

Trivedi MH, Wisniewski SR, Morris DW, Fava M, Kurian BT, Gollan JK, Nierenberg AA, Warden D, Gaynes BN, Luther JF, Rush AJ (2011). Concise associated symptoms tracking scale: A brief self-report and clinician rating of symptoms associated with suicidality. *Journal of Clinical Psychiatry* 72, 765–774.

Tsai MH, Chen YH, Chen CD, Hsiao CY, Chien CH (2011). Deliberate self-harm by Taiwanese adolescents. *Acta Paediatrica* 100, e223–e226.

Tsaousides T, Cantor JB, Gordon WA (2011). Suicidal ideation following traumatic brain injury: Prevalence rates and correlates in adults living in the community. *Journal of Head Trauma Rehabilitation* 26, 265–275.

Tsiouris JA, Kim SY, Brown WT, Cohen IL (2011). Association of aggressive behaviours with psychiatric disorders, age, sex and degree of intellectual disability: A large-scale survey. *Journal of Intellectual Disability Research* 55, 636–649.

Tsirigotis K, Gruszczy ski W, Tsirigotis-Woloszczak M (2011). Gender differentiation in methods of suicide attempts. *Medical Science Monitor* 17, PH65–70.

Uebelacker LA, German NM, Gaudiano BA, Miller IW (2011). Patient health questionnaire depression scale as a suicide screening instrument in depressed primary care patients: A cross-sectional study. *Primary Care Companion to the Journal of Clinical Psychiatry* 13, e1–e6.

Varma A (2011). Deliberate self-harm in children — A growing problem. *Indian Pediatrics* 48, 361–362.

von Soest T, Kvalem IL, Wichstrøm L (2011). Predictors of cosmetic surgery and its effects on psychological factors and mental health: A population-based follow-up study among Norwegian females. *Psychological Medicine*. Published online: 25 July 2011. doi:10.1017/S0033291711001267.

Weber NS, Fisher JA, Cowan DN, Postolache TT, Page WF, Niebuhr DW (2011). Descriptive epidemiology and underlying psychiatric conditions among suicide attempters in the national hospital discharge survey (NHDS). *American Journal of Epidemiology* 173, S289.

Weinberg A, Klonsky ED (2011). The effects of self-injury on acute negative arousal: A laboratory simulation. *Motivation and Emotion*. Published online: 28 June 2011. doi:10.1007/s11031-011-9233-x.

Weisler RH, Khan A, Trivedi MH, Yang H, Eudicone JM, Pikalov A, Tran QV, Berman RM, Carlson BX (2011). Analysis of suicidality in pooled data from 2 double-blind, placebo-controlled aripiprazole adjunctive therapy trials in major depressive disorder. *Journal of Clinical Psychiatry* 72, 548–555.

Wheatley MA, Shah BB, Morgan BW, Houry D, Kazzi ZN (2011). Injury secondary to antiretroviral agents: Retrospective analysis of a regional poison center database. *Western Journal of Emergency Medicine* 12, 293–295.

Whipple R, Fowler JC (2011). Affect, relationship schemas, and social cognition: Self-Injuring borderline personality disorder inpatients. *Psychoanalytic Psychology* 28, 183–195.

Wilcox HC, Arria AM, Caldeira KM, Vincent KB, Pinchevsky GM, O'Grady KE (2011). Longitudinal predictors of past-year non-suicidal self-injury and motives among college students. *Psychological Medicine.* Published online: 12 September 2011. doi: 10.1017/S0033291711001814.

Yan SM, Yi SG (2011). Death and suicidal ideation among nursing home residents in a Chinese city — A pilot study. China *Journal of Social Work* 4, 127–135.

Yang F, Li Y, Xie D, Shao C, Ren J, Wu W, Zhang N, Zhang Z, Zou Y, Zhang J, Qiao D, Gao C, Li Y, Hu J, Deng H, Wang G, Du B, Wang X, Liu T, Gan Z, Peng J, Wei B, Pan J, Chen H, Sun S, Jia H, Liu Y, Chen Q, Wang X, Cao J, Lv L, Chen Y, Ha B, Ning Y, Chen Y, Kendler KS, Flint J, Shi S (2011). Age at onset of major depressive disorder in Han Chinese women: Relationship with clinical features and family history. *Journal of Affective Disorders.* Published online: 22 July 2011. doi:10.1016/j.jad.2011.06.056.

Yurgelun-Todd DA, Bueler CE, McGlade EC, Churchwell JC, Brenner LA, Lopez-Larson MP (2011). Neuroimaging correlates of traumatic brain injury and suicidal behavior. *Journal of Head Trauma Rehabilitation* 26, 276–289.

ZamZam R, Chuan CY, Aziz SA, Yahya B, Syed Mokhtar SS, Yong CK, Muhammad Dain NAB (2011). National mental health registry for schizophrenia in Malaysia: A preliminary assessment on service utilization. *Asia-Pacific Psychiatry* 3, 151–156.

Zhang Y, Law CK, Yip PS (2011). Psychological factors associated with the incidence and persistence of suicidal ideation. *Journal of Affective Disorders* 133, 584–590.

Zhao Q, Zhao J, Li X, Fang X, Zhao G, Lin X, Zhang L (2011). Household displacement and health risk behaviors among HIV/AIDS-affected children in rural China. *AIDS Care* 23, 866–872.

## Risk and protective factors

Abreu LN (2011). Study identifies potential markers for suicidal behavior. *Psychiatric Annals* 41, 355.

Ahn JH, Patkar AA (2011). Escitalopram for the treatment of major depressive disorder in youth. *Expert Opinion on Pharmacotherapy* 12, 2235–2244.

Akiyama K, Saito A, Shimoda K (2011). Chronic methamphetamine psychosis after long-term abstinence in Japanese incarcerated patients. *American Journal on Addictions* 20, 240–249.

Alberdi-Sudupe J, Pita-Fernandez S, Gomez-Pardinas SM, Iglesias-Gil-de-Bernabe F, Garcia-Fernandez J, Martinez-Sande G, Lantes-Louzao S, Pertega-Diaz S (2011). Suicide attempts and related factors in patients admitted to a general hospital: A ten-year cross-sectional study (1997–2007). *BMC Psychiatry.* Published online 31 March 2011. doi:10.1186/1471-244X-11-51.

Alfonso M (2011). Using segmentation analysis to identify youth at risk for self injury. *Annals of Behavioral Medicine* 41, S169.

Allen JG (2011). Understanding nonsuicidal self-injury: Origins, assessment, and treatment. *Journal of Trauma & Dissociation* 12, 105–106.

Altamura AC, Buoli M, Dell'osso B, Albano A, Serati M, Colombo F, Pozzoli S, Angst J (2011). The impact of brief depressive episodes on the outcome of bipolar disorder and major depressive disorder: A 1-year prospective study. *Journal of Affective Disorders* 134, 133–137.

Anderson J, Allan DB (2011). Vertebral fracture secondary to suicide attempt: Demographics and patient outcome in a Scottish spinal rehabilitation unit. *Journal of Spinal Cord Medicine* 34, 380–387.

Anestis MD, Silva C, Lavender JM, Crosby RD, Wonderlich SA, Engel SG, Joiner TE (2011). Predicting nonsuicidal self-injury episodes over a discrete period of time in a sample of women diagnosed with bulimia nervosa: An analysis of self-reported trait and ecological momentary assessment based affective lability and previous suicide attempts. *International Journal of Eating Disorders*. Published online: 8 July 2011. doi:10.1002/eat.20947.

Anonymous (2011). Don't miss emergencies in 'challenging' teens psych complaints are rising. *Emergency Department Nursing* 14, 40–41.

Anonymous (2011). Increased risk of attempted suicide in patients taking isotretinoin. *Australian Journal of Pharmacy* 92, 69.

Anonymous (2011). This issue: Pediatric and adolescent depression. *Pediatric Annals* 40, 290–291.

Appelbaum PS (2011). SSRIs, Suicide, and liability for failure to warn of medication risks. *Psychiatric Services* 62, 347–349.

April C, Sandkuhl H, Torok G (2011). Warning: ED is 'risky' for suicidal people. *Emergency Department Nursing* 14, 54–55.

Aronen ET, Simola P, Soininen M (2011). Motor activity in depressed children. *Journal of Affective Disorders* 133, 188–196.

Bacher I, Houle S, Xu X, Zawertailo L, Soliman A, Wilson AA, Selby P, George TP, Sacher J, Miler L, Kish SJ, Rusjan P, Meyer JH (2011). Monoamine oxidase a binding in the prefrontal and anterior cingulate cortices during acute withdrawal from heavy cigarette smoking. *Archives of General Psychiatry* 68, 817–826.

Badiee J, Moore DJ, Atkinson JH, Vaida F, Gerard M, Duarte NA, Franklin D, Gouaux B, McCutchan JA, Heaton RK, McArthur J, Morgello S, Simpson D, Collier A, Marra CM, Gelman B, Clifford D, Grant I (2011). Lifetime suicidal ideation and attempt are common among HIV+ individuals. *Journal of Affective Disorders*. Published online: 22 Jule 2011. doi:10.1016/ j.jad.2011.06.044.

Baek JH, Park DY, Choi J, Kim JS, Choi JS, Ha K, Kwon JS, Lee D, Hong KS (2011). Differences between bipolar I and bipolar II disorders in clinical features, comorbidity, and family history. *Journal of Affective Disorders* 131, 59–67.

Baetz M, Bowen R (2011). Suicidal ideation, affective lability, and religion in depressed adults. *Mental Health, Religion & Culture* 14, 633–641.

Bedi S, Nelson EC, Lynskey MT, McCutcheon VV, Heath AC, Madden PAF, Martin NG (2011). Risk for suicidal thoughts and behavior after childhood sexual abuse in women and men. *Suicide and Life-Threatening Behavior* 41, 406–415.

Beekrum R, Valjee SR, Codings SJ (2011). An emic perspective on the dynamics of non-fatal suicidal behaviour in a sample of South African Indian women. *South African Journal of Psychology* 41, 63–73.

Ben-Efraim YJ, Wasserman D, Wasserman J, Sokolowski M (2011). Gene-environment interactions between CRHR1 variants and physical assault in suicide attempts. *Genes, Brain & Behavior* 10, 663–672.

Benoit Ratcliff M, Jenkins TM, Reiter-Purtill J, Noll JG, Zeller MH (2011). Risk-taking behaviors of adolescents with extreme obesity: Normative or not? *Pediatrics* 127, 827–834.

Bitter I, Filipovits D, Czobor P (2011). Adverse reactions to duloxetine in depression. *Expert Opinion of Drug Safety*. Published online: 5 May 2011. doi:10.1517/14740338.2011.582037.

Bjørngaard JH, Bjerkeset O, Romundstad P, Gunnell D (2011). Sleeping problems and suicide in 75,000 Norwegian adults: A 20 year follow-up of the HUNT I study. *Sleep* 34, 1155–1159.

Blasco-Fontecilla H, Alegria AA, Lopez-Castroman J, Legido-Gil T, Saiz-Ruiz J, de Leon J, Baca-Garcia E (2011). Short self-reported sleep duration and suicidal behavior: A cross-sectional study. *Journal of Affective Disorders* 133, 239–246.

Blasczyk-Schiep S, Kazén M, Kuhl J, Grygielski M (2011). Appraisal of suicidal risk among adolescents and young adults through the Rorschach test. *Journal of Personality Assessment* 93, 518–526.

Bohnert AS, Roeder KM, Ilgen MA (2011). Suicide attempts and overdoses among adults entering addictions treatment: Comparing correlates in a U.S. national study. *Drug and Alcohol Dependence*. Published online: 28 June 2011. doi:10.1016/j.drugalcdep.2011.05.032.

Bond DJ, Lang DJ, Noronha MM, Kunz M, Torres IJ, Su W, Honer WG, Lam RW, Yatham LN (2011). The association of elevated body mass index with reduced brain volumes in first-episode mania. *Biological Psychiatry* 70, 381–387.

Booij L, Turecki G, Leyton M, Gravel P, Lopez De Lara C, Diksic M, Benkelfat C (2011). Tryptophan hydroxylase(2) gene polymorphisms predict brain serotonin synthesis in the orbitofrontal cortex in humans. *Molecular Psychiatry*. Published online: 12 July 2011. doi:10.1038/mp.2011.79.

Borges G, Azrael D, Almeida J, Johnson RM, Molnar BE, Hemenway D, Miller M (2011). Immigration, suicidal ideation and deliberate self-injury in the Boston youth survey 2006. *Suicide and Life-Threatening Behavior* 41, 193–202.

Borrill J, Fox P, Roger D (2011). Religion, ethnicity, coping style, and self-reported self-harm in a diverse non-clinical UK population. *Mental Health, Religion & Culture* 14, 259–269.

Bosse C, Preville M, Vasiliadis HM, Beland SG, Lapierre S (2011). Suicidal ideation, death thoughts, and use of benzodiazepines in the elderly population. *Canadian Journal of Community Mental Health* 30, 1–13.

Bowen R, Baetz M, Leuschen C, Kalynchuk LE (2011). Predictors of suicidal thoughts: Mood instability versus neuroticism. *Personality and Individual Differences* 51, 1034–1038.

Bragança M, Palha A (2011). Depression and neurocognitive performance in Portuguese patients infected with HIV. *AIDS and Behavior*. Published online: 20 May 2011. doi:10.1007/s10461-011-9973-3.

Brausch AM, Decker KM, Hadley AG (2011). Risk of suicidal ideation in adolescents with both self-asphyxial risk-taking behavior and non-suicidal self-injury. *Suicide and Life-Threatening Behavior* 41, 424–34

Breau L, Camfield C, Camfield P (2010). The pain behaviour of children with neuronal ceroid lupofiscinosis: Variation due to child factors and pain history. *Journal of Pain Management* 3, 293–300.

Brenner LA, Betthauser LM, Homaifar BY, Villarreal E, Harwood JE, Staves PJ, Huggins JA (2011). Posttraumatic stress disorder, traumatic brain injury, and suicide attempt history among veterans receiving mental health services. *Suicide and Life-Threatening Behavior* 41, 416–423.

Brent D (2011). Nonsuicidal self-injury as a predictor of suicidal behavior in depressed adolescents. *American Journal of Psychiatry* 168, 452–454.

Brewin CR, Garnett R, Andrews B (2011). Trauma, identity and mental health in UK military veterans. *Psychological Medicine* 41, 1733–1740.

Brown DL, Jewell JD, Stevens AL, Crawford JD, Thompson R (2011). Suicidal risk in adolescent residential treatment: Being female is more important than a depression diagnosis. *Journal of Child and Family Studies*. Published online: 9 April 2011. doi: 10.1007/s10826-011-9485-9.

Bryan CJ, Corso KA (2011). Depression, PTSD, and suicidal ideation among active duty veterans in an integrated primary care clinic. *Psychological Services* 8, 94–103.

Burton CZ, Vella L, Weller JA, Twamley EW (2011). Differential effects of executive functioning on suicide attempts. *Journal of Neuropsychiatry and Clinical Neurosciences* 23, 173–179.

Cahill S, Rakow T (2011). Assessing risk and prioritizing referral for self-harm: When and why is my judgement different from yours? *Clinical Psychology and Psychotherapy*. Published online: 19 May 2011. doi:10.1002/cpp.754.

Cannon DM, Klaver JK, Gandhi SK, Solorio G, Peck SA, Erickson K, Savitz N Akula J, Eckelman WC, Furey ML, Sahakian BJ, McMahon FJ, Drevets WC (2011). Genetic variation in cholinergic muscarinic-2 receptor gene modulates M2 receptor binding in vivo and accounts for reduced binding in bipolar disorder. *Molecular Psychiatry* 16, 407–418.

Carlborg A, Jokinen J, Nordström AL, Jönsson EG, Nordström P (2011). Early death and CSF monoamine metabolites in schizophrenia spectrum psychosis. *Nordic Journal of Psychiatry* 65, 101–105.

Carli V, Mandelli L, Postuvan V, Roy A, Bevilacqua L, Cesaro C, Baralla F, Marchetti M, Serretti A, Sarchiapone M (2011). Self-harm in prisoners. *CNS Spectrums* 16. Published online: 1 March 2011. E-publication.

Carpenter DJ (2011). St. John's wort and S-adenosyl methionine as 'natural' alternatives to conventional antidepressants in the era of the suicidality boxed warning: What is the evidence for clinically relevant benefit? *Alternative Medicine Review* 16, 17–39.

Castle K, Conner K, Kaukeinen K, Tu X (2011). Perceived racism, discrimination, and acculturation in suicidal ideation and suicide attempts among black young adults. *Suicide and Life-Threatening Behavior* 41, 342–351.

Chandra P, Deo RM, Singh BK (2011). A study of psychiatric co-morbidity in cases of renal failure, undergoing hemodialysis. *Indian Journal of Public Health Research and Development* 2, 68–70.

Chang SS, Page A, Gunnell D (2011). Internet searches for a specific suicide method follow its high-profile media coverage. *American Journal of Psychiatry* 168, 855–857.

Chartrand H, Cox B, El-Gabalawy R, Clara I (2011). Social anxiety disorder subtypes and their mental health correlates in a nationally representative canadian sample. *Canadian Journal of Behavioural Science* 43, 89–98.

Chattopadhyay S, Daneshgar F (2011). A study on suicidal risks in psychiatric adults. *International Journal of Biomedical Engineering and Technology* 5, 390–408.

Chaveepojnkamjorn W, Pichainarong N (2011). Current drinking and health-risk behaviors among male high school students in central Thailand. *BMC Public Health*. Published online: 14 April 2011. doi: 10.1186/1471-2458-11-233.

Chemtob CM, Madan A, Berger P, Abramovitz R (2011). Adolescent exposure to the World Trade Center attacks, PTSD symptomatology, and suicidal ideation. *Journal of Traumatic Stress 24, 526–529.*

Chen WJ, Chen CC, Ho CK, Chou FH, Lee MB, Lung F, Lin GG, Teng CY, Chung YT, Wang YC, Sun FC (2011). The relationships between quality of life, psychiatric illness, and suicidal ideation in geriatric veterans living in a veterans' home: A structural equation modeling approach. *American Journal of Geriatric Psychiatry* 19, 597–601.

Clark L, Dombrovski AY, Siegle GJ, Butters MA, Shollenberger CL, Sahakian BJ, Szanto K (2011). Impairment in risk-sensitive decision-making in older suicide attempters with depression. *Psychology and Aging* 26, 321–330.

Coleman PK (2011). Abortion and mental health: Quantitative synthesis and analysis of research published 1995–2009. *British Journal of Psychiatry* 199, 180–186.

Congdon P (2011). Latent variable model for suicide risk in relation to social capital and socio-economic status. *Social Psychiatry and Psychiatric Epidemiology.* Published online: 28 August 2011. doi: 10.1007/s00127-011-0429-x.

Coupland C, Dhiman P, Barton G, Morriss R, Arthur A, Sach T, Hippisley-Cox J (2011). A study of the safety and harms of antidepressant drugs for older people: A cohort study using a large primary care database. *Health Technology Assessment* 15, 1–202.

Coupland C, Dhiman P, Morriss R, Arthur A, Barton G, Hippisley-Cox J (2011). Antidepressant use and risk of adverse outcomes in older people: Population based cohort study. *British Medical Journal.* Published online: 2 August 2011. doi:10.1136/bmj.d4551.

Darke S, Torok M, McKetin R, Kaye S, Ross J (2011). Patterns of psychological distress related to regular methamphetamine and opioid use. *Addiction Research & Theory* 19, 121–127.

De Leon J, Mallory P, Maw L, Susce MT, Perez-Rodriguez MM, Baca-Garcia E (2011). Lack of replication of the association of low serum cholesterol and attempted suicide in another country raises more questions. *Annals of Clinical Psychiatry* 23, 163–170.

Dell'osso L, Carmassi C, Rucci P, Ciapparelli A, Conversano C, Marazziti D (2011). Complicated grief and suicidality: The impact of subthreshold mood symptoms. *CNS Spectrums.* Published online: 15 Janurary 2011. E-publication.

DelMastro K, Hellem T, Kim N, Kondo D, Sung YH, Renshaw PF (2011). Incidence of major depressive episode correlates with elevation of substate region of residence. *Journal of Affective Disorders* 129, 376–379.

Demirbas H, Ilhan IO, Dogan YB (2011). Assessment of the mode of anger expression in alcohol dependent male inpatients. *Alcohol and Alcoholism.* Published online: 23 May 2011. doi:10.1093/ alcalc/agr056.

Denis J, Van den Noortgate W, Maes B (2011). Self-injurious behavior in people with profound intellectual disabilities: A meta-analysis of single-case studies. *Research in Developmental Disabilities* 32, 911–923.

Devries K, Watts C, Yoshihama M, Kiss L, Schraiber LB, Deyessa N, Heise L, Durand J, Mbwambo J, Janssen H, Berhane Y, Ellsberg M, Garcia-Moreno C (2011). Violence against women is strongly associated with suicide attempts: Evidence from the WHO multi-country study on women's health and domestic violence against women. *Social Science & Medicine* 73, 79–86.

Diamond GM, Shilo G, Jurgensen E, D'Augelli A, Samarova V, White K (2011). How depressed and suicidal sexual minority adolescents understand the causes of their distress. *Journal of Gay and Lesbian Mental Health* 15, 130–151.

Distefano AS, Cayetano RT (2011). Health care and social service providers' observations on the intersection of HIV/AIDS and violence among their clients and patients. *Qualitative Health Research* 21, 884–899.

Dodd S (2011). Antidepressants and suicidal thought. *Current Drug Safety* 6, 114.

Donev R, Gantert D, Alawam K, Edworthy A, Haessler F, Meyer-Lindenberg A, Dressing H, Thome J (2011). Comorbidity of schizophrenia and adult attention-deficit hyperactivity disorder. *World Journal of Biological Psychiatry* 12, 52–56.

Dore G, Mills K, Murray R, Teesson M, Farrugia P (2011). Post-traumatic stress disorder, depression and suicidality in inpatients with substance use disorders. *Drug and Alcohol Review.* Published online: 26 April 2011. doi:10.1111/j.1465-3362.2011.00314.x.

Dufrasne S, Roy M, Galvez M, Rosenblatt DS (2011). Experience over fifteen years with a protocol for predictive testing for Huntington disease. *Molecular Genetics and Metabolism* 102, 494–504.

Dyrbye LN, Schwartz A, Downing SM, Szydlo DW, Sloan JA, Shanafelt TD (2011). Efficacy of a brief screening tool to identify medical students in distress. *Academic Medicine* 86, 907–914.

Eady A, Dobinson C, Ross LE (2011). Bisexual people's experiences with mental health services: A qualitative investigation. *Community Mental Health Journal* 47, 378–389.

Eaton DK, Foti K, Brener ND, Crosby AE, Flores G, Kann L (2011). Associations between risk behaviors and suicidal ideation and suicide attempts: Do racial/ethnic variations in associations account for increased risk of suicidal behaviors among Hispanic/Latina 9th- to 12th-grade female students? *Archives of Suicide Research* 15, 113–126.

Eytan A, Haller DM, Wolff H, Cerutti B, Sebo P, Bertrand D, Niveau G (2011). Psychiatric symptoms, psychological distress and somatic comorbidity among remand prisoners in Switzerland. *International Journal of Law and Psychiatry* 34, 13–19.

Fedyszyn IE, Harris MG, Robinson J, Edwards J, Paxton SJ (2011). Characteristics of suicide attempts in young people undergoing treatment for first episode psychosis. *Australia and New Zealand Journal of Psychiatry* 45, 838–845.

Fiedorowicz JG, Mills JA, Ruggle A, Langbehn D, Paulsen JS (2011). Suicidal behavior in prodromal Huntington disease. *Neurodegenerative Diseases* 8, 483–490.

Fisher J (2011). Sensorimotor approaches to trauma treatment. *Advances in Psychiatric Treatment* 17, 171–177.

Franklin JC, Hessel ET, Prinstein MJ (2011). Clarifying the role of pain tolerance in suicidal capability. *Psychiatry Research* 189, 362–367.

Fung YL, Chan ZC (2011). A systematic review of suicidal behaviour in old age: A gender perspective. *Journal of Clinical Nursing* 20, 2109–2124.

Galfalvy H, Mann JJ (2011). Cerebrospinal fluid biomarkers in suicide attempters. *Acta Psychiatrica Scandinavica* 124, 4–5.

Gan Z, Li Y, Xie D, Shao C, Yang F, Shen Y, Zhang N, Zhang G, Tian T, Yin A, Chen C, Liu J, Tang C, Zhang Z, Liu J, Sang W, Wang X, Liu T, Wei Q, Xu Y, Sun L, Wang S, Li C, Hu C, Cui Y, Liu Y, Li Y, Zhao X, Zhang L, Sun L, Chen Y, Zhang Y, Ning Y, Shi S, Chen Y, Kendler KS, Flint J, Zhang J (2011). The impact of educational status on the clinical features of major depressive disorder among Chinese women. *Journal of Affective Disorders*. Published online: 6 August 2011. doi:10.1016/j.jad.2011.06.046.

Gaskill A, Foley FW, Kolzet J, Picone MA (2011). Suicidal thinking in multiple sclerosis. *Disability and Rehabilitation* 33, 1528–1536.

Gentile S (2011). Suicidal mothers. *Journal of Injury and Violence Research* 3, 90–97.

Gibson CE, Caplan JP (2011). Zolpidem-associated parasomnia with serious self-injury: A shot in the dark. *Psychosomatics* 52, 88–91.

Giegling I, Calati R, Porcelli S, Hartmann AM, Moller HJ, De Ronchi D, Rujescu D, Serretti A (2011). NCAM1, TACR1 and NOS genes and temperament: A study on suicide attempters and controls. *Neuropsychobiology* 64, 32–37.

Gilbert AM, Garno JL, Braga RJ, Shaya Y, Goldberg TE, Malhotra AK, Burdick KE (2011). Clinical and cognitive correlates of suicide attempts in bipolar disorder: Is suicide predictable? *Journal of Clinical Psychiatry* 72, 1027–1033.

Girardi P, Pompili M, Innamorati M, Serafini G, Berrettoni C, Angeletti G, Koukopoulos A, Tatarelli R, Lester D, Roselli D, Primiero FM (2011). Temperament, post-partum depression, hopelessness, and suicide risk among women soon after delivering. *Women's Health* 51, 511–524.

Givon L, Porter S, Padmanabhan B, Goren J, Cohen PA (2011). Levetiracetam, seizures, and suicidality. *Harvard Review of Psychiatry* 19, 47–55.

Glenn CR, Blumenthal TD, Klonsky ED, Hajcak G (2011). Emotional reactivity in nonsuicidal self-injury: Divergence between self-report and startle measures. *International Journal of Psychophysiology* 80, 166–170.

Godet-Mardirossian H, Jehel L, Falissard B (2011). Suicidality in male prisoners: Influence of childhood adversity mediated by dimensions of personality. *Journal of Forensic Sciences* 56, 942–949.

Goldstein TR, Obreja M, Shamseddeen W, Iyengar S, Axelson DA, Goldstein BI, Monk K, Hickey MB, Sakolsky D, Kupfer DJ, Brent DA, Birmaher B (2011). Risk for suicidal ideation among the offspring of bipolar parents: Results from the Bipolar Offspring Study (BIOS). *Archives of Suicide Research.* 15, 207–222.

Gomez J, Miranda R, Polanco L (2011). Acculturative stress, perceived discrimination, and vulnerability to suicide attempts among emerging adults. *Journal of Youth and Adolescence.* Published online: 30 June 2011. doi:10.1007/s10964-011-9688-9.

Gonzalez-Pinto A, Barbeito S, Alonso M, Alberich S, Haidar MK, Vieta E, Tabares-Seisdedos R, Zorrilla I, Gonzalez-Pinto MA, Lopez P (2011). Poor long-term prognosis in mixed bipolar patients: 10-Year outcomes in the Vitoria prospective naturalistic study in Spain. *Journal of Clinical Psychiatry* 72, 671–676.

Goodman M, Hazlett EA, Avedon JB, Siever DR, Chu KW, New AS (2011). Anterior cingulate volume reduction in adolescents with borderline personality disorder and co-morbid major depression. *Journal of Psychiatric Research* 45, 803–807.

Gradus JL, Street AE, Resick PA (2011). Stressful deployment events and post-deployment suicidal behaviour in veterans of the Afghanistan and Iraq wars. *American Journal of Epidemiology* 173 S319

Grall-Bronnec M, Wainstein L, Augy J, Bouju G, Feuillet F, Vénisse JL, Sébille-Rivain V (2011). Attention deficit hyperactivity disorder among pathological and at-risk gamblers seeking treatment: A hidden disorder. *European Addiction Research* 17, 231–240.

Greene PK (2011). Suicidal behaviour. *Bulletin of the Menninger Clinic* 75, 97–98.

Guilhoto LMFF, Loddenkemper T, Gooty VD, Rotenberg A, Takeoka M, Duffy FH, Coulter D, Urion D, Bourgeois BF, Kothare SV (2011). Experience with lacosamide in a series of children with drug-resistant focal epilepsy. *Pediatric Neurology* 44, 414–419.

Gulbas LE, Zayas LH, Nolle AP, Hausmann-Stabile C, Kuhlberg JA, Baumann AA, Pena JB (2011). Family relationships and Latina teen suicide attempts: Reciprocity, asymmetry, and detachment. *Families in Society* 92, 317–323.

Gunja N (2011). Teenage toxins: Recreational poisoning in the adolescent. *Journal of Paediatrics and Child Health.* Published online: 29 April 2011. doi:10.1111/j.1440-1754.2011.02082.x.

Gunter TD, Chibnall JT, Antoniak SK, Philibert RA, Hollenbeck N (2011). Predictors of suicidal ideation, suicide attempts, and self-harm without lethal intent in a community corrections sample. *Journal of Criminal Justice* 39, 238–245.

Hahm HC, Kolaczyk E, Lee Y, Jang J, Ng L (2011). Do Asian-American women who were maltreated as children have a higher likelihood for HIV risk behaviors and adverse mental health outcomes? *Women's Health Issues.* Published online: 26 August 2011. doi:10.1016/j.whi.2011.07.003.

Hakansson A, Schlyter F, Berglund M (2011). Associations between polysubstance use and psychiatric problems in a criminal justice population in Sweden. *Drug and Alcohol Dependence* 118, 5–11.

Hanley AJ, Gibb BE (2011). Verbal victimization and changes in hopelessness among elementary school children. *Journal of Clinical Child and Adolescent Psychology* 40, 772–776.

Hassiotis A, Gazizova D, Akinlonu L, Bebbington P, Meltzer H, Strydom A (2011). Psychiatric morbidity in prisoners with intellectual disabilities: Analysis of prison survey data for England and Wales. *British Journal of Psychiatry.* Published online: 4 May 2011. doi:10.1192/bjp.bp.110.088039.

Havaki-Kontaxaki BJ, Papalias E, Kontaxaki MEV, Papadimitriou GN (2011). Seasonality, suicidality and melatonin. *Psychiatrike* 21, 324–331.

Hayes J, Koo J (2011). Depression and acitretin: A true association or a class labeling? *Journal of Drugs in Dermatology* 10, 409–412.

Hecimovic H, Salpekar J, Kanner AM, Barry JJ (2011). Suicidality and epilepsy: A neuropsychobiological perspective. *Epilepsy & Behaviour* 22, 77–84.

Hennink MM, Cunningham SA (2011). Health of home-based sex workers and their children in rural Andhra Pradesh, India. *Asian Population Studies* 7, 157–173.

Hess EA, Becker MA, Pituch KA, Saathoff AK (2011). Mood states as predictors of characteristics and precipitants of suicidality among college students. *Journal of College Student Psychotherapy* 25, 145–155.

Hewamanne S (2010). Suicide narratives and in-between identities among Sri Lanka's factory workers. *Ethnology* 49, 1–22.

Hightow-Weidman LB, Phillips G, Jones KC, Outlaw AY, Fields SD, Smith JC, For The YMSM of Color SPNS Initiative Study Group JC (2011). Racial and sexual identity-related maltreatment among minority YMSM: Prevalence, perceptions, and the association with emotional distress. *AIDS Patient Care and STDS.* Published online: 15 August 2011. doi:10.1089/apc.2011.9877.

Hill RM, Castellanos DA, Pettit JW (2011). Suicide-related behaviors and anxiety in children and adolescents: A review. *Clinical Psychology Review* 31, 1133–1144.

Hirsch JK, Barton AL (2011). Positive social support, negative social exchanges, and suicidal behavior in college students. *Journal of American College Health* 59, 393–398.

Hodge F, Nandy K (2011). Factors associated with American Indian cigarette smoking in rural settings. *International Journal of Environmental Research and Public Health* 8, 944–954.

Hong J, Reed C, Novick D, Haro JM, Aguado J (2011). Clinical and economic consequences of medication non-adherence in the treatment of patients with a manic/mixed episode of bipolar disorder: Results from the European Mania in Bipolar Longitudinal Evaluation of Medication (EMBLEM) Study. *Psychiatry Research.* Published online: 14 May 2011. doi:10.1016/ j.psychres.2011.04.016.

Hopwood CJ, Morey LC, Skodol AE, Sanislow CA, Grilo CM, Ansell EB, McGlashan TH, Markowitz JC, Pinto A, Yen S, Shea MT, Gunderson JG, Zanarini MC, Stout RL (2011). Pathological personality traits among patients with absent, current, and remitted substance use disorders. *Addictive Behaviors* 36, 1087–1090.

Howes OD, Falkenberg I (2011). Early detection and intervention in bipolar affective disorder: Targeting the development of the disorder. *Current Psychiatry Reports.* Published online: 18 August 2011. doi: 10.1007/s11920-011-0229-8.

Huffman JC, Mastromauro CA, Sowden GL, Wittmann C, Rodman R, Januzzi JL (2011). A collaborative care depression management program for cardiac inpatients: Depression characteristics and in-hospital outcomes. *Psychosomatics* 52, 26–33.

Iliceto P, Pompili M, Lester D, Gonda X, Niolu C, Girardi N, Rihmer Z, Candilera G, Girardi P (2011). Relationship between temperament, depression, anxiety, and hopelessness in adolescents: A structural equation model. *Research and Treatment*. Published online: 21 July 2011. *Depression* doi:10.1155/2011/160175.

Jakobsen IS, Christiansen E, Larsen KJ, Waaktaar T (2011). Differences between youth with a single suicide attempt and repeaters regarding their and their parents history of psychiatric illness. *Archives of Suicide Research* 15, 265–276.

Jakupcak M, Hoerster KD, Varra A, Vannoy S, Felker B, Hunt S (2011). Hopelessness and suicidal ideation in Iraq and Afghanistan war veterans reporting subthreshold and threshold posttraumatic stress disorder. *Journal of Nervous & Mental Disease* 199, 272–275.

Jamieson LM, Paradies YC, Gunthorpe W, Cairney SJ, Sayers SM (2011). Oral health and social and emotional well-being in a birth cohort of Aboriginal Australian young adults. *BMC Public Health*. Published online: 19 August 2011. doi: 10.1186/1471-2458-11-656.

Jenkins M, Winefield H, Sarris A (2011). Consequences of being accused of workplace bullying: an exploratory study. *International Journal of Workplace Health Management* 4, 33–47.

Jimenez-Castro L, Raventos-Vorst H, Escamilla M (2011). Substance use disorder and schizophrenia: Prevalence and sociodemographic characteristics in the Latin American population. *Actas Espanolas De Psiquiatria* 39, 123–130.

Joiner Jr TE, Ribeiro JD (2011). Assessment and management of suicidal behavior in teens. *Psychiatric Annals* 41, 220–225.

Jurgens TP, Gaul C, Lindwurm A, Dresler T, Paelecke-Habermann Y, Schmidt-Wilcke T, Lurding R, Henkel K, Leinisch E (2011). Impairment in episodic and chronic cluster headache. *Cephalalgia* 31, 671–682.

Kahalley LS, Robinson LA, Tyc VL, Hudson MM, Leisenring W, Stratton K, Mertens AC, Zeltzer L, Robison LL, Hinds PS (2011). Risk factors for smoking among adolescent survivors of childhood cancer: A report from the childhood cancer survivor study. *Pediatric Blood & Cancer*. Published online: 25 May 2011. doi:10.1002/pbc.23139.

Kanner AM (2011). Are antiepileptic drugs used in the treatment of migraine associated with an increased risk of suicidality? *Current Pain and Headache Reports* 15, 164–169.

Kao YC, Liu YP, Cheng TH, Chou MK (2011). Cigarette smoking in outpatients with chronic schizophrenia in Taiwan: Relationships to socio-demographic and clinical characteristics. *Psychiatry Research*. Published online 31 May 2011. doi:10.1016/j.psychres.2011.05.016.

Karanges E, Li KM, Motbey C, Callaghan PD, Katsifis A, McGregor IS (2011). Differential behavioural and neurochemical outcomes from chronic paroxetine treatment in adolescent and adult rats: A model of adverse antidepressant effects in human adolescents? *The International Journal of Neuropsychopharmacology* 14, 491–504.

Katsiki N, Hatzitolios AI, Mikhailidis DP (2011). Naltrexone sustained-release (SR) + bupropion SR combination therapy for the treatment of obesity: 'A new kid on the block'? *Annals of Medicine* 43, 249–258.

Kazim SF, Shamim MS, Tahir MZ, Enam SA, Waheed S (2011). Management of penetrating brain injury. *Journal of Emergencies, Trauma and Shock* 4, 395–402.

Kenedi CA, Goforth HW (2011). A systematic review of the psychiatric side-effects of efavirenz. *AIDS and Behavior*. Published online: 12 April 2011. doi:10.1007/s10461-011-9939-5.

Keskin G, Engin E (2011). The evaluation of depression, suicidal ideation and coping strategies in haemodialysis patients with renal failure. *Journal of Clinical Nursing* 20, 2721–2732.

Keyvanara M, Haghshenas A (2011). Sociocultural contexts of attempting suicide among Iranian youth: A qualitative study. *Eastern Mediterranean Health Journal* 17, 529–535.

Khasakhala L, Sorsdahl KR, Harder VS, Williams DR, Stein DJ, Ndetei DM (2011). Lifetime mental disorders and suicidal behaviour in South Africa. *African Journal of Psychiatry* 14, 134–139.

Kim DS (2011). Increasing effect of body weight perception on suicidal ideation among young Korean women: Findings from the Korea National Health and Nutrition Examination Survey 2001 and 2005. *Diabetes, Metabolic Syndrome and Obesity* 4, 17–22.

Kim TS, Jeong SH, Kim JB, Lee MS, Kim JM, Yim HW, Jun TY (2011). The clinical research center for depression study: Baseline characteristics of a Korean long-term hospital-based observational collaborative prospective cohort study. *Psychiatry Investigation* 8, 1–8.

Kisely S, Campbell LA, Cartwright J, Bowes MJ, Jackson L (2011). Factors associated with not seeking professional help or disclosing intent prior to suicide: A study of medical examiners' records in Nova Scotia. *Canadian Journal of Psychiatry* 56, 436–440.

Klomek AB, Kleinman M, Altschuler E, Marrocco F, Amakawa L, Gould MS (2011). High School bullying as a risk for later depression and suicidality. *Suicide and Life-Threatening Behavior* 41, 501–516.

Klomek AB, Sourander A, Gould MS (2011). Bullying and suicide detection and intervention. *Psychiatric Times* 28, 27–31.

Knowles S, Townsend E, Anderson M (2011). Factors associated with self-harm in community-based young offenders: The importance of psychological variables. *Journal of Forensic Psychiatry and Psychology* 22, 479–495.

Kok R, Kirsten DK, Botha KFH (2011). Exploring mindfulness in self-injuring adolescents in a psychiatric setting. *Journal of Psychology in Africa* 21, 185–195.

Krause JS, Saunders LL, Bombardier C, Kalpakjian C (2011). Confirmatory factor analysis of the Patient Health Questionnaire-9: A study of the participants from the spinal cord injury model systems. *PM & R: The Journal of Injury, Function, and Rehabilitation* 3, 533–540.

Kuba T, Yakushi T, Fukuhara H, Nakamoto Y, Singeo ST, Tanaka O, Kondo T (2011). Suicide-related events among child and adolescent patients during short-term antidepressant therapy. *Psychiatry and Clinical Neurosciences* 65, 239–245.

Lamis DA, Malone PS (2011). Alcohol-related problems and risk of suicide among college students: The mediating roles of belongingness and burdensomeness. *Suicide and Life-Threatening Behavior* 41, 543–553.

Langan SM, Batchelor JM (2011). Acne, isotretinoin and suicide attempts: A critical appraisal. *British Journal of Dermatology* 164, 1183–1185.

Langhinrichsen-Rohling J, Snarr JD, Slep AM, Heyman RE, Foran HM (2011). Risk for suicidal ideation in the U.S. Air Force: An ecological perspective. *Journal of Consulting and Clinical Psychology* 79, 600–612.

Lapierre S, Boyer R, Desjardins S, Dubé M, Lorrain D, Préville M, Brassard J (2011). Daily hassles, physical illness, and sleep problems in older adults with wishes to die. *International Psychogeriatric*. Published online: 16 August 2011. doi:10.1017/S1041610211001591.

Larson MJ, Clayson PE (2011). Suicide, psychopathology, and performance monitoring: Electrophysiological indices of suicide risk? *Psychophysiology* 48, S73–S73.

Lau JTF, Gu J, Tsui H, Chen H, Wang R, Hu X (2011). How likely are HIV-positive female sex workers in China to transmit HIV to others? *Sexual health* 8, 399–406.

Lee TS, Shen HC, Wu WH, Huang CW, Yen MY, Wang BE, Chuang P, Shih CY, Chou YC, Liu YL (2011). Clinical characteristics and risk behavior as a function of HIV status among heroin users enrolled in methadone treatment in northern Taiwan. *Substance Abuse Treatment, Prevention and Policy*. Published online: 8 April 2011. doi:10.1186/1747-597X-6-6.

Lester D, Iliceto P, Pompili M, Girardi P (2011). Depression and suicidality in obese patients. *Psychological Reports* 108, 367–368.

Lin D, Li X, Fan X, Fang X (2011). Child sexual abuse and its relationship with health risk behaviors among rural children and adolescents in Hunan, China. *Child Abuse and Neglect* 35, 680–687.

Ling VJ, Lester D, Mortensen PB, Langenberg PW, Postolache TT (2011). Toxoplasma gondii seropositivity and suicide rates in women. *Journal of Nervous & Mental Disease* 199, 440–444.

Lundh LG, Wångby-Lundh M, Bjärehed J (2011). Deliberate self-harm and psychological problems in young adolescents: Evidence of a bidirectional relationship in girls. *Scandinavian Journal of Psychology* 52, 476–483.

Lundin A, Lundberg I, Allebeck P, Hemmingsson T (2011). Psychiatric diagnosis in late adolescence and long-term risk of suicide and suicide attempt. *Acta Psychiatrica Scandinavica.* Published online: 13 August 2011. doi:10.1111/j.1600-0447.2011.01752.x.

Lung FW, Tzeng DS, Huang MF, Lee MB (2011). Association of the MAOA promoter uVNTR Polymorphism with suicide attempts in patients with major depressive disorder. *BMC Medical Genetics.* Published online: 24 May 2011. doi: 10.1186/1471-2350-12-74.

Luxton DD, Greenburg D, Ryan J, Niven A, Wheeler G, Mysliwiec V (2011). Prevalence and isact of short sleep duration in redeployed OIF soldiers. *Sleep* 34, 1189–1195.

Lynam DR, Miller JD, Miller DJ, Bornovalova MA, Lejuez CW (2011). Testing the relations between impulsivity-related traits, suicidality, and nonsuicidal self-injury: A test of the incremental validity of the UPPS model. *Personality Disorders: Theory, Research, and Treatment* 2, 151–160.

Lyne JP, O'Donoghue B, Clancy M, O'Gara C (2011). Comorbid psychiatric diagnoses among individuals presenting to an addiction treatment program for alcohol dependence. *Substance Use & Misuse* 46, 351–358.

Maalouf FT, Atwi M, Brent DA (2011). Treatment-resistant depression in adolescents: Review and updates on clinical management. *Depression and Anxiety.* Published online: 2 September 2011. doi: 10.1002/da.20884

Mackay K, Taylor M, Bajaj N (2011). The adverse consequences of mephedrone use: A case series. *Psychiatrist* 35, 203–205.

Madsen T, Nordentoft M (2011). Suicidal changes in patients with first episode psychosis: clinical predictors of increasing suicidal tendency in the early treatment phase. Early *Intervention in Psychiatry.* Published online: 31 August 2011. doi: 10.1111/j.1751-7893.2011.00284.x.

Malloy-Diniz LF, Neves FS, de Moraes PH, De Marco LA, Romano-Silva MA, Krebs MO, Correa H (2011). The 5-HTTLPR polymorphism, impulsivity and suicide behavior in euthymic bipolar patients. *Journal of Affective Disorders* 133, 221–226.

Mansfield AJ, Bender RH, Hourani LL, Larson GE (2011). Suicidal or self-harming ideation in military personnel transitioning to civilian life. *Suicide and Life-Threatening Behavior* 41, 392–405.

Marchand WR, Lee JN, Garn C, Thatcher J, Gale P, Kreitschitz S, Johnson S, Wood N (2011). Striatal and cortical midline activation and connectivity associated with suicidal ideation and depression in bipolar II disorder. *Journal of Affective Disorders* 133, 638–645.

Marcinko D, Bilic V, Pivac N, Tentor B, Franic T, Loncar M, Marcinko VM, Jakovljevic M (2011). Serum cholesterol concentration and structured individual psychoanalytic psychotherapy in suicidal and non-suicidal male patients suffering from borderline personality disorder. *Collegium Antropologicum* 35, 219–223.

Maremmani AG, Rovai L, Pani PP, Pacini M, Lamanna F, Rugani F, Schiavi E, Dell'Osso L, Maremmani I (2011). Do methadone and buprenorphine have the same impact on psychopathological symptoms of heroin addicts? *Annals of General Psychiatry.* Published online: 15 May 2011. doi:10.1186/1744-859X-10-17.

Margolis DJ (2011). Commentary: Acne, isotretinoin and suicide attempts. *British Journal of Dermatology* 164, 1186–1187.

Marshall BD, Galea S, Wood E, Kerr T (2011). Injection methamphetamine use is associated with an increased risk of attempted suicide: A prospective cohort study. *Drug and Alcohol Dependence*. Published online: 14 June 2011. doi:10.1016/j.drugalcdep.2011.05.012.

Marshall BDL, Galea S, Wood E, Kerr T (2011). Methamphetamine use increases the risk of attempted suicide among injection drug users: A prospective cohort study. *American Journal of Epidemiology* 173, S323

Martinez JM, Garakani A, Yehuda R, Gorman JM (2011). Proinflammatory and 'resiliency' proteins in the CSF of patients with major depression. *Depression and Anxiety*. Published online: 2 September 2011. doi:10.1002/da.20876.

Mathias CW, Dougherty DM, James LM, Richard DM, Dawes MA, Acheson A, Hill-Kapturczak N (2011). Intolerance to delayed reward in girls with multiple suicide attempts. *Suicide and Life-Threatening Behavior* 41, 277–286.

McAuliffe C (2011). Likelihood of later hospital admission for deliberate self-harm may be influenced by various risk factors in young people smoking. *Evidence-Based Mental Health*. Published online: 13 March 2011. doi:10.1136/ebmh1151

McCall WV (2011). Insomnia is a risk factor for suicide-what are the next steps? *Sleep* 34, 1149–1150.

McCartan FM, Law H, Murphy M, Bailey S (2011). Child and adolescent females who present with sexually abusive behaviours: A 10-year UK prevalence study. *The Journal of Sexual Aggression* 17, 4–14.

McChargue DE, Drevo S, Herrera MJ, Doran N, Salvi S, Klanecky AK (2011). Trait-impulsivity moderates the relationship between rumination and number of major depressive episodes among cigarette smokers. *Mental Health and Substance Use: Dual Diagnosis* 4, 96–104.

McDonald SA, Hershey AD, Pearlman E, Lewis D, Winner PK, Rothner D, Linder SL, Runken MC, Richard NE, Derosier FJ (2011). Long-term evaluation of sumatriptan and naproxen sodium for the acute treatment of migraine in adolescents. *Headache: The Journal of Head and Face Pain* 51, 1374–1387.

McKay D, Andover M (2011). Should nonsuicidal self-injury be a putative obsessive-compulsive-related condition? A critical appraisal. *Behavioral Modification*. Published online: 1 September 2011. doi:10.1177/0145445511417707.

McKnight-Eily LR, Eaton DK, Lowry R, Croft JB, Presley-Cantrell L, Perry GS (2011). Relationships between hours of sleep and health-risk behaviors in US adolescent students. *Preventive Medicine*. Published online: 5 August 2011. doi:10.1016/j.ypmed.2011.06.020.

Mee S, Bunney BG, Bunney WE, Hetrick W, Potkin SG, Reist C (2011). Assessment of psychological pain in major depressive episodes. *Journal of Psychiatric Research*. Published online: 9 August 2011. doi:10.1016/j.jpsychires.2011.06.011.

Melissa-Halikiopoulou Ca, Tsiga Eb, Khachatryan Rac, Papazisis Gad (2011). Suicidality and depressive symptoms among nursing students in northern Greece. *Health Science Journal* 5, 90–97.

Miller LJ, LaRusso EM (2011). Preventing postpartum depression. *Psychiatric Clinics of North America* 34, 53–56.

Mojtabai R (2011).The public health impact of antidepressants: An instrumental variable analysis. *Journal of Affective Disorders* 134, 188–197.

Mordal J, Holm B, Gossop M, Romoren M, Morland J, Bramness JG (2011). Psychoactive substance use among patients admitted to an acute psychiatric ward: Laboratory findings and associations with clinical characteristics. *Nordic Journal of Psychiatry* 65, 208–215.

Morina N, von Lersner U, Prigerson HG (2011). War and bereavement: Consequences for mental and physical distress. *PLoS ONE.* Published online: 12 July 2011. doi:10.1371/journal.pone.0022140.

Mott J (2011). Suicide assessment in the school setting. *NASN School Nurse* 26, 102–108.

Mrnak-Meyer J, Tate SR, Tripp JC, Worley MJ, Jajodia A, McQuaid JR (2011). Predictors of suicide-related hospitalization among U.S. veterans receiving treatment for comorbid depression and substance dependence: Who is the riskiest of the risky? *Suicide and Life-Threatening Behavior* 41, 532–542.

Murphy TM, Ryan M, Foster T, Kelly C, McClelland R, O'Grady J, Corcoran E, Brady J, Reilly M, Jeffers A, Brown K, Maher A, Bannan N, Casement A, Lynch D, Bolger S, Tewari P, Buckley A, Quinlivan L, Daly L, Kelleher C, Malone KM (2011). Risk and protective genetic variants in suicidal behaviour: Association with SLC1A2, SLC1A3, 5-HTR1B & NTRK2 polymorphisms. *Behavioral and Brain Functions.* Published online: 28 June 2011. doi:10.1186/1744-9081-7-22

Nada-Raja S, Skegg K (2011). Victimization, posttraumatic stress disorder symptomatology, and later nonsuicidal self-harm in a birth cohort. *Journal of Interpersonal Violence.* Published online: 20 May 2011, doi: 10.1177/0886260511403757.

Nelson C, Cyr KS, Corbett B, Hurley E, Gifford S, Elhai JD, Donald Richardson J (2011). Predictors of posttraumatic stress disorder, depression, and suicidal ideation among Canadian Forces personnel in a National Canadian Military Health Survey. *Journal of Psychiatric Research.* Published online: 12 July 2011. doi:10.1016/j.jpsychires.2011.06.014.

Nemoto T (2011). Social support, exposure to violence and transphobia, and correlates of depression among male-to-female transgender women with a history of sex work. *American Journal of Public Health.* Published online: 14 April 2011. doi:10.2105/AJPH. 2010.197285.

Nickels SJ, Walls NE, Laser JA, Wisneski H (2011). Differences in motivations of cutting behavior among sexual minority youth. *Child and Adolescent Social Work Journal.* Published online: 4 August 2011. doi:10.1007/s10560-011-0245-x.

Nicolosi GT, Falcão DV, Batistoni SS, Lopes A, Cachioni M, Neri AL, Yassuda MS (2011). Depressive symptoms in old age: relations among sociodemographic and self-reported health variables. *International Psychogeriatrics* 23, 941–949.

Nierenberg AA, Leon AC, Price LH, Shelton RC, Trivedi MH (2011). Crisis of confidence: Antidepressant risk versus benefit. *The Journal of Clinical Psychiatry* 72, 3.

Nobile CG, Flotta D, Nicotera G, Pileggi C, Angelillo IF (2011). Self-reported health status and access to health services in a sample of prisoners in Italy. *BMC Public Health.* Published online: 4 July 2011. doi:10.1186/1471-2458-11-529.

Nugent KL, Daniels AM, Azur MJ (2011). Correlates of schizophrenia spectrum disorders in children and adolescents cared for in community settings. *Child and Adolescent Mental Health.* Published online: 5 August 2011. doi: 10.1111/j.1475-3588.2011.00618.x.

Obando Medina CM, Herrera A, Kullgren G (2011). Suicidal expression in adolescents in Nicaragua in relation to Youth Self-Report (YSR) syndromes and exposure to suicide. *Clinical Practice and Epidemology in Mental Health* 7, 89–96.

O'Donnell S, Meyer I, Schwartz S (2011). Increased risk of suicide attempts among black and latino lesbians, gay men, and bisexuals. *American Journal of Public Health.* Published online: 14 April. doi: 10.2105/AJPH.2010.300032.

Oh SH, Park KN, Jeong SH, Kim HJ (2011). Deliberate self-poisoning: Factors associated with recurrent self-poisoning. *American Journal of Emergency Medicine* 29, 908–912.

Okuno K, Yoshimura R, Ueda N, Ikenouchi-Sugita A, Umene-Nakano W, Hori H, Hayashi K, Katsuki A, Chen HI, Nakamura J (2011). Relationships between stress, social adaptation, personality traits, brain-derived neurotrophic factor and 3-methoxy-4-hydroxyphenylglycol plasma concentrations in employees at a publishing company in Japan. *Psychiatry Research* 186, 326–332.

Okusaga O, Langenberg P, Sleemi A, Vaswani D, Giegling I, Hartmann AM, Konte B, Friedl M, Groer MW, Yolken RH, Rujescu D, Postolache TT (2011). Toxoplasma gondii antibody titers and history of suicide attempts in patients with schizophrenia. *Schizophrenia Research.* Published online: 3 September 2011. doi:10.1016/j.schres.2011.08.006.

Oliffe JL, Han CS, Ogrodniczuk JS, Phillips JC, Roy P (2011). Suicide from the perspectives of older men who experience depression: A gender analysis. *American Journal of Men's Health.* Published online: 3 August 2011. doi: 10.1177/1557988311408410.

Oliver C, Petty J, Ruddick L, Bacarese-Hamilton M (2011). The association between repetitive, self-injurious and aggressive behavior in children with severe intellectual disability. *Journal of Autism and Developmental Disorders.* Published online: 1 July 2011. doi: 10.1007/s10803-011-1320-z.

Oliver C, Petty J, Ruddick L, Bacarese-Hamilton M (2011). The association between repetitive, self-injurious and aggressive behavior in children with severe intellectual disability. *Journal of Autism and Developmental Disorders.* Published online: 1 July 2011. doi: 10.1007/s10803-011-1320-z.

Outlaw AY, Phillips G, Hightow-Weidman LB, Fields SD, Hidalgo J, Halpern-Felsher B, Green-Jones And The Young Msm Of Color Spns Initiative Study Group M (2011). Age of MSM sexual debut and risk factors: Results from a multisite study of racial/ethnic minority YMSM living with HIV. *AIDS Patient Care and STDS* 25, S23–S9.

Owusu A, Hart P, Oliver B, Kang M (2011). The association between bullying and psychological health among senior high school students in Ghana, West Africa. *Journal of School Health* 81, 231–238.

Özdemir M, Stattin H (2011). Bullies, victims, and bully-victims: A longitudinal examination of the effects of bullying-victimization experiences on youth well-being. *Journal of Aggression, Conflict and Peace Research* 3, 97–102.

Pacchiarotti I, Mazzarini L, Kotzalidis GD, Valenti M, Nivoli AMA, Sani G. Torrent C, Murru A, Sanchez-Moreno J, Patrizi B, Girardi P, Vieta E, Colom F (2011). Mania and depression. Mixed, not stirred. *Journal of Affective Disorders* 133, 105–113.

Padgett CL (2010). The potential association between isotretinoin treatment, depression and suicidal behaviors: A review. *Current Psychiatry Reviews* 6, 234–243.

Page RM, Dennis M, Lindsay GB, Merrill RM (2011). Psychosocial distress and substance use among adolescents in four countries: Philippines, China, Chile, and Namibia. *Youth & Society* 43, 900–930.

Paley B, Auerbach BE (2010). Children with fetal alcohol spectrum disorders in the dependency court system: Challenges and recommendations. *Journal of Psychiatry and Law* 38, 507–558.

Pan X, Zhang C, Shi Z (2011). Soft drink and sweet food consumption and suicidal behaviors among Chinese adolescents. *Acta Paediatrica.* Published online: 31 May 2011. doi:10.1111/j.1651-2227.2011.02369.x

Parron T, Requena M, Hernandez AF, Alarcon R (2011). Association between environmental exposure to pesticides and neurodegenerative diseases. *Toxicology and Applied Pharmacology.* Published online: 13 May 2011. doi:10.1016/j.taap.2011.05.006

Pasko L, Mayeda DT (2011). Pathways and predictors of juvenile justice involvement for native Hawaiian and Pacific Islander youths: A focus on gender. *Journal of Ethnic & Cultural Diversity in Social Work* 20, 114–130.

Patel MN, Bhaju J, Thompson MP, Kaslow NJ (2011). Life stress as mediator of the childhood maltreatment — Intimate partner violence link in low-income, African American women.

*Journal of School Nursing.* Published online: 8 Setpember 2011. doi: 10.1007/s10896-011-9398-9

Peña JB, Kuhlberg JA, Zayas LH, Baumann AA, Gulbas L, Hausmann-Stabile C, Nolle AP (2011). Familism, family environment, and suicide attempts among Latina youth. *Suicide and Life-Threatening Behavior* 41, 330–341.

Phillips KA, Menard W (2011). Olfactory reference syndrome: Demographic and clinical features of imagined body odor. *General Hospital Psychiatry* 33, 398–406.

Quelopana AM, Champion JD, Reyes-Rubilar T (2011). Factors associated with postpartum depression in Chilean women. *Health care for Women International* 32, 939–949.

Rasic D, Kisely S, Langille DB (2011). Protective associations of importance of religion and frequency of service attendance with depression risk, suicidal behaviours and substance use in adolescents in Nova Scotia, Canada. *Journal of Affective Disorders* 132, 389–395.

Rasmussen KA, Wingate LR (2011). The role of optimism in the interpersonal-psychological theory of suicidal behavior. *Suicide and Life-Threatening Behavior* 41, 137–148.

Rathod S, Mistry M, Ibbotson B, Kingdon D (2011). Stress in psychiatrists: Coping with a decade of rapid change. *Psychiatrist* 35, 130–134.

Reyes JA, Elias MJ (2011). Fostering social-emotional resilience among Latino youth. *Psychology in the Schools* 48, 723–737.

Reyes JC, Robles RR, Cólon HM, Negrón JL, Matos TD, Calderón JM (2011). Polydrug use and attempted suicide among Hispanic adolescents in Puerto Rico. *Archives of Suicide Research* 15, 151–159.

Rhodes AE, Boyle MH, Tonmyr L, Wekerle C, Goodman D, Leslie B, Mironova P, Bethell J, Manion I (2011). Sex differences in childhood sexual abuse and suicide-related behaviors. *Suicide and Life-Threatening Behavior* 41, 235–254.

Riordan DV, Morris C, Hattie J, Stark C (2011). Family size and perinatal circumstances, as mental health risk factors in a Scottish birth cohort. *Social Psychiatry & Psychiatric Epidemiology.* Published online: 11 June 2011. doi: 10.1007/s00127-011-0405-5

Rosenstein DL (2011). Depression and end-of-life care for patients with cancer. *Dialogues in Clinical Neuroscience* 13, 101–108.

Roy A, Carli V, Sarchiapone M (2011). Resilience mitigates the suicide risk associated with childhood trauma. *Journal of Affective Disorders* 133, 591–594.

Ruljancic N, Mihanovic M, Bakliza A, Cepelak I (2011). Serum levels of cytokines in depressed patients with or without suicidal behavior. *Clinical Chemistry and Laboratory Medicine* 49, S854.

Russell ST, Ryan C, Toomey RB, Diaz RM, Sanchez J (2011). Lesbian, gay, bisexual, and transgender adolescent school victimization: Implications for young adult health and adjustment. *Journal of School Health* 81, 223–230.

Sadiq KT, Moghal A, Mahadun P (2011). Section 136 assessments in Trafford borough of Manchester. *Clinical Governance* 16, 29–34.

Samuels J (2011). Personality disorders: Epidemiology and public health issues. *International Review of Psychiatry* 23, 223–233.

Sansone RA, Farukhi S, Wiederman MW (2011). Utilization of primary care physicians in borderline personality. *General Hospital Psychiatry* 33, 343–646.

Sansone RA, Sansone LA (2011). Gender patterns in borderline personality disorder. *Innovations in Clinical Neuroscience* 8, 16–20.

Sansone RA, Wiederman MW, Schumacher D, Routsong-Weichers L (2011). The relationship between suicide attempts and borderline personality in gastric surgery candidates. *Primary Care Companion to the Journal of Clinical Psychiatry* 13, e1–e2.

Scheyen HK, Vaaler AE, Auestad BH, Malt UF, Melle I, Andreassen OA, Morken G (2011). Despite clinical differences, bipolar disorder patients from acute wards and outpatient clinics have similar educational and disability levels compared to the general population. *Journal of Affective Disorders* 132, 209–215.

Schoenleber M, Berenbaum H (2011). Shame regulation in personality pathology. *Journal of Abnormal Psychology*. Published online: 5 September 2011. doi: 10.1037/a0025281.

Scuderi G, Pompili M, Innamorati M, Pasquale N, Pontremolesi S, Erbuto D, Mazzeo F, Venturini P, Lester D, Serafini G, Tatarelli R, Girardi P (2011). Affective temperaments are associated with higher hopelessness and perceived disability in patients with open-angle glaucoma. *International Journal of Clinical Practice* 65, 976–984.

Segal DL, Marty MA, Meyer WJ, Coolidge FL (2011). Personality, suicidal ideation, and reasons for living among older adults. *Journals of Gerontology Series B: Psychological Sciences and Social Sciences*. Published online: 16 July 2011. doi: 10.1093/geronb/gbr080.

Sher L (2011). Brain-derived neurotrophic factor and suicidal behavior in patients with posttraumatic stress disorder. *Revista Brasileira de Psiquiatria* 33, 105–106.

Shim EJ, Hahm BJ (2011). Anxiety, helplessness/hopelessness and 'desire for hastened death' in Korean cancer patients. *European Journal of Cancer Care* 20, 395–402.

Sillito CL, Salari S (2011). Child outcomes and risk factors in U.S. homicide-suicide cases 1999–2004. *Journal of Family Violence* 26, 285–279.

Simic A, Milicevic MS, Seskar SS, Ilic G, Milosavljevic B, Vujovic M, Flaten TP (2011). Fatal pesticides-related self-poisonings in the southeastern region of Serbia-Alarming increase in suicides calls for restrictions. *Toxicology Letters* 205, S234.

Simms VM, Higginson IJ, Harding R (2011). What palliative care-related problems do patients experience at HIV diagnosis? A systematic review of the evidence. *Journal of Pain and Symptom Management*. Published online: 25 May 2011. doi:10.1016/j.jpainsymman.2011.02.014

Simpson A (2011). Flesh wounds? New ways of understanding self injury. *Nursing Ethics* 18, 277.

Siris SG, Acosta FJ (2011). Qualitative content of auditory hallucinations and suicidal behavior in schizophrenia. *Schizophrenia Research*. Published online: 21 September 2011. doi:10.1016/j.schres.2011.08.016

Sjostrom N, Hetta J, Waern M (2011). Sense of coherence and suicidality in suicide attempters: A prospective study. *Journal of Psychiatric and Mental Health Nursing*. Published online: 30 May 2011. doi: 10.1111/j.1365-2850.2011.01755.

Skoog I (2011). Psychiatric disorders in the elderly. *Canadian Journal of Psychiatry* 56, 387–397.

Slama F, Merle S, Ursulet G, Charles-Nicolas A, Ballon N (2011). Prevalence of and risk factors for lifetime suicide attempts among Caribbean people in the French West Indies. *Psychiatry Research*. Published online: 7 September 2011. doi:10.1016/j.psychres.2011.08.007.

Slotboom AM, Kruttschnitt C, Bijleveld C, Menting B (2011). Psychological well-being of incarcerated women in the Netherlands: Importation or deprivation? *Punishment and Society* 13, 176–197.

Song JI, Shin DW, Choi JY, Kang J, Baek YJ, Mo HN, Seo MJ, Hwang YH, Lim YK, Lee OK (2011). Quality of life and mental health in the bereaved family members of patients with terminal cancer. *Psycho-Oncology*. Published online: 7 August 2011. doi: 10.1002/pon.2027 2011

Souery D, Zaninotto L, Calati R, Linotte S, Sentissi O, Amital D, Moser U, Kasper S, Zohar J, Mendlewicz J, Serretti A (2011). Phenomenology of psychotic mood disorders: Lifetime and major depressive episode features. *Journal of Affective Disorders*. Published online 31 August 2011. doi: 10.1016/j.jad.2011.07.027.

Spendelow JS (2011). Assessment of behavioral and psychiatric problems in people with prader-willi syndrome: A review of the literature. *Journal of Policy and Practice in Intellectual Disabilities* 8, 104–112.

Staubli S, Killias M (2011). Long-term outcomes of passive bullying during childhood: Suicide attempts, victimization and offending. *European Journal of Criminology* 8, 377–385.

Stefanello S, Marín-Léon L, Fernandes PT, Li LM, Botega NJ (2011). Depression and anxiety in a community sample with epilepsy in Brazil. *Arquivos de Neuro-Psiquiatria* 69, 342–348.

Steinberg JR, Becker D, Henderson JT (2011). Does the outcome of a first pregnancy predict depression, suicidal ideation, or lower self-esteem? Data from the national comorbidity survey. *American Journal of Orthopsychiatry* 81, 193–201.

Stinson JD, Robbins SB, Crow CW (2011). Self-regulatory deficits as predictors of sexual, aggressive, and self-harm behaviors in a psychiatric sex offender population. *Criminal Justice and Behavior* 38, 885–895.

Subhi N, Mohamad SM, Sarnon N, Nen S, Hoesni SM, Alavi K, Chong ST (2011). Intrapersonal conflict between christianity and homosexuality: The personal effects faced by gay men and lesbians. *e-BANGI* 6, 193–205.

Sublette ME, Galfalvy HC, Fuchs D, Lapidus M, Grunebaum MF, Oquendo MA, John Mann J, Postolache TT (2011). Plasma kynurenine levels are elevated in suicide attempters with major depressive disorder. *Brain, Behavior, and Immunity* 25, 1272–1278.

Sundström A, Alfredsson L, Sjölin-Forsberg G, Gerdén B, Bergman U, Jokinen J (2011). Response to acne, isotretinoin and suicide attempts: A critical appraisal. *British Journal of Dermatology* 164, 1185–1186.

Suris A, Link-Malcolm J, North CS (2011). Predictors of suicidal ideation in veterans with PTSD related to military sexual trauma. *Journal of Traumatic Stress* 24, 605–608.

Suzuki Y, Tsutsumi A, Fukasawa M, Honma H, Someya T, Kim Y (2011). Prevalence of mental disorders and suicidal thoughts among community-dwelling elderly adults 3 years after the Niigata-Chuetsu earthquake. *Journal of Epidemiology* 21, 144–150.

Swahn MH, Ali B, Bossarte RM, Van Dulmen M, Crosby A, Strine T, Raskin S (2010). Self-harm and its link to peer and dating violence among adolescents in a high-risk urban community. *Suicidology Online* 1, 53–65.

Swahn MH, Bossarte RM, Choquet M, Hassler C, Falissard B, Chau N (2011). Early substance use initiation and suicide ideation and attempts among students in France and the United States. *International Journal of Public Health.* Published online: 27 April 2011. doi: 10.1007/s00038-011-0255-7

Swann AC, Lijffijt M, Lane SD, Kjome KL, Steinberg JL, Moeller FG (2011). Criminal conviction, impulsivity, and course of illness in bipolar disorder. *Bipolar Disorders* 13, 173–181.

Symons FJ (2011). Self-injurious behavior in neurodevelopmental disorders: Relevance of nociceptive and immune mechanisms. *Neuroscience and Biobehavioral Reviews* 35, 1266–1274.

Symons FJ, Wolff JJ, Stone LS, Lim TKY, Bodfish JW (2011). Salivary biomarkers of HPA axis and autonomic activity in adults with intellectual disability with and without stereotyped and self-injurious behavior disorders. *Journal of Neurodevelopmental Disorders* 3, 144–151.

Takusari E, Suzuki M, Nakamura H, Otsuka K (2011). Mental health, suicidal ideation, and related factors among workers from medium-sized business establishments in Northern Japan: Comparative study of sex differences. *Industrial Health* 49, 452–63.

Taliaferro LA, Eisenberg ME, Johnson KE, Nelson TF, Neumark-Sztainer D (2011). Sport participation during adolescence and suicide ideation and attempts. *International Journal of Adolescent Medicine and Health* 23, 3–10.

Tang WK, Lu JY, Mok V, Ungvari GS, Wong KS (2011). Is fatigue associated with suicidality in stroke? *Archives of Physical Medical and Rehabilitation* 92, 1336–1338.

Taverner T, Closs SJ, Briggs M (2011). Painful leg ulcers: Community nurses' knowledge and beliefs, a feasibility study. *Primary Health Care Research & Development* 12, 379–392.

Taylor PJ, Gooding PA, Wood AM, Johnson J, Tarrier N (2011). Prospective predictors of suicidality: Defeat and entrapment lead to changes in suicidal ideation over time. *Suicide and Life-Threatening Behavior* 41, 297–306.

Taylor PJ, Gooding PA, Wood AM, Tarrier N (2011). The role of defeat and entrapment in depression, anxiety, and suicide. *Psychological Bulletin* 137, 391–420.

Taylor RJ, Chatters LM, Joe S (2011). Religious involvement in suicidal behaviour among African Americans and black Caribbeans. *Journal of Nervous & Mental Disease* 199, 478–486.

Thangathurai D, Mogos M (2011). Ketamine alleviates fear, depression, and suicidal ideation in terminally ill patients. *Journal of Palliative Medicine* 14, 389.

Theunissen MJ, Jansen M, van Gestel A (2011). Are mental health and binge drinking associated in Dutch adolescents? Cross-sectional public health study. *BMC Research Notes* 4, 100.

Thobaben M, Kozlak JB (2011). Suicidal clients in the home. *Home Health Care Management and Practice* 23, 149–151.

Thompson R, Proctor LJ, English DJ, Dubowitz H, Narasimhan S, Everson MD (2011). Suicidal ideation in adolescence: Examining the role of recent adverse experiences. *Journal of Adolescence.* Published online: 8 April 2011. doi:10.1016/j.adolescence.2011.03.003 |

Torres-Platas SG, Hercher C, Davoli MA, Maussion G, Labonté B, Turecki G, Mechawar N (2011). Astrocytic hypertrophy in anterior cingulate white matter of depressed suicides. *Neuropsychopharmacology.* Published online: 3 August 2011. doi:10.1038/npp.2011.154

Tovilla-Zarate C, Juarez-Rojop I, Ramon-Frias T, Villar-Soto M, Pool-Garcia S, Camarena Medellin B, Genis AD, Lopez Narvaez L, Humberto N (2011). No association between COMT val158met polymorphism and suicidal behavior: Meta-analysis and new data. *BMC Psychiatry* 11, 151.

Tsai HC, Lu MK, Yang YK, Huang MC, Yeh TL, Chen WJ, Lu RB, Kuo PH (2011). Empirically derived subgroups of bipolar I patients with different comorbidity patterns of anxiety and substance use disorders in Han Chinese population. *Journal of Affective Disorders.* Published online: 7 September 2011. doi:10.1016/j.jad.2011.08.015

Tsai MH, Fang KC, Lu CH, Chen CD, Hsieh CP, Chen TT (2011) Positive attitudes and self-harming behavior of adolescents in a juvenile detention house in Taiwan. *European Child & Adolescent Psychiatry* 20, 413–418.

Tundo A, Cavalieri P, Navari S, Marchetti F (2011). Treating bipolar depression — antidepressants and alternatives: A critical review of the literature. *Acta Neuropsychiatrica* 23, 94–105.

Ugurlu GK, Ekinci O, Albayrak Y, Arslan M, Caykoylu A (2011). The relationship between cognitive insight, clinical insight, and depression in patients with schizophrenia. *Comprehensive Psychiatry.* Published online: 11 April 2011. doi:10.1016/j.comppsych.2011. 02.010

Väänänen A, Ahola K, Koskinen A, Pahkin K, Kouvonen A (2011). Organisational merger and psychiatric morbidity: A prospective study in a changing work organisation. *Journal of Epidemiology & Community Health* 65, 682–687.

Valenti M, Pacchiarotti I, Rosa AR, Bonnin CM, Popovic D, Nivoli AMA, Murru A, Grande I, Colom F, Vieta E (2011). Bipolar mixed episodes and antidepressants: A cohort study of bipolar I disorder patients. *Bipolar Disorders* 13, 145–154.

van de Loo-Neus GHH, Rommelse N, Buitelaar JK (2011). To stop or not to stop? How long should medication treatment of attention-deficit hyperactivity disorder be extended? *European Neuropsychopharmacology* 21, 584–599.

Van Orden KA, Cukrowicz KC, Witte TK, Joiner TE (2011). Thwarted belongingness and perceived burdensomeness: Construct validity and psychometric properties of the interpersonal needs questionnaire. *Psychological Assessment.* Published online: 19 September 2011. E-publication.

Vander Stoep A, Adrian M, Mc Cauley E, Crowell SE, Stone A, Flynn C (2011). Risk for suicidal ideation and suicide attempts associated with co-occurring depression and conduct problems in early adolescence. *Suicide and Life-Threatening Behavior* 41, 316–329.

Vera M, Reyes-Rabanillo ML, Huertas S, Juarbe D, Pe ez-Pedrogo C, Huertas A, Peña M (2011). Suicide ideation, plans, and attempts among general practice patients with chronic health conditions in Puerto Rico. *International Journal of General Mecidine* 4, 197–205.

Vitiello B, Emslie G, Clarke G, Wagner KD, Asarnow JR, Keller MB, Birmaher B, Ryan ND, Kennard B, Mayes TL, DeBar L, Lynch F, Dickerson J, Strober M, Suddath R, McCracken JT, Spirito A, Onorato M, Zelazny J, Porta G, Iyengar S, Brent DA (2011). Long-term outcome of adolescent depression initially resistant to selective serotonin reuptake inhibitor treatment: A follow-up study of the TORDIA sample. *Journal of Clinical Psychiatry* 72, 388–396.

Vivekananda K, Telley A, Trethowan S (2011). A five year study on psychological distress within a university counselling population. *Journal of the Australian and New Zealand Student Services Association* 37, 39–57.

Voelker R (2011). Community a factor in suicide attempts by lesbian, gay, and bisexual teens. *JAMA: Journal of the American Medical Association.* 305, 1951.

Vrshek-Schallhorn S, Czarlinski J, Mineka S, Zinbarg RE, Craske M (2011). Prospective predictors of suicidal ideation during depressive episodes among older adolescents and young adults. *Personality and Individual Differences.* 50, 1202–1207.

Vyssoki B, Bluml V, Gleiss A, Friedrich F, Kogoj D, Walter H, Zeiler J, Hofer P, Lesch OM, Erfurth A (2011). The impact of temperament in the course of alcohol dependence. *Journal of Affective Disorders* Published online: 12 August 2011. doi:10.1016/j.jad.2011. 07.007.

Walls NE, Laser J, Nickels SJ, Wisneski H (2011). Correlates of cutting behavior among sexual minority youths and young adults. *Social Work Research* 34, 213–226.

Wan YH, Hu CL, Hao JH, Sun Y, Tao FB (2011). Deliberate self-harm behaviors in Chinese adolescents and young adults. *European Child & Adolescent Psychiatry.* Published online: 29 August 2011. doi: 10.1007/s00787-011-0213-1

Webb RT, Langstrom N, Runeson B, Lichtenstein P, Fazel S (2011). Violent offending and IQ level as predictors of suicide in schizophrenia: National cohort study. *Schizophrenia Research* 130, 143–147.

West LM, Davis TA, Thompson MP, Kaslow NJ (2011). Let me count the ways: Fostering reasons for living among low-income, suicidal, African American women. *Suicide and Life-Threatening Behavior* 41, 491–500.

Weston K, Mutiso S, Mwangi JW, Qureshi Z, Beard J, Venkat P (2011). Depression among women with obstetric fistula in Kenya. *International Journal of Gynaecology & Obstetrics* 115, 31–33.

Wetzel HH, Gehl CR, Dellefave-Castillo L, Schiffman JF, Shannon KM, Paulsen JS (2011). Suicidal ideation in Huntington disease: The role of comorbidity. *Psychiatry Research* 188, 372–276.

White R, Barber C, Azrael D, Mukamal KJ, Miller M (2011). History of military service and the risk of suicidal ideation: Findings from the 2008 National Survey on Drug Use and Health. *Suicide and Life-Threatening Behavior* 5, 554–561.

Williams JM, Steinberg MB, Steinberg ML, Gandhi KK, Ulpe R, Foulds J (2011). Varenicline for tobacco dependence: Panacea or plight? *Expert Opinion on Pharmacotherapy* 12, 1799–1812.

Williams KA, Chapman MV (2011). Comparing health and mental health needs, service use, and barriers to services among sexual minority youths and their peers. *Health & Social Work* 36, 197–206.

Williams KL, Ruekert L, Lum C (2011). Treatment of bipolar disorder: A focus on medication therapy for mania. *Formulary* 46, 82–97.

Wong SP, Wang C, Meng M, Phillips MR (2011). Understanding self-harm in victims of intimate partner violence: A qualitative analysis of calls made by victims to a crisis hotline in China. *Violence Against Women*. Published online: 8 April 2011. doi: 10.1177/10778012 11404549.

Wong YJ, Brownson C, Schwing AE (2011). Risk and protective factors associated with Asian American students' suicidal ideation: A multicampus, national study. *Journal of College Student Development* 52, 396–408.

Wong YJ, Koo K, Tran KK, Chiu YC, Mok Y (2011). Asian American college students' suicide ideation: A mixed-methods study. *Journal of Counseling Psychology* 58, 197–209.

Wong YJ, Maffini CS (2011). Predictors of Asian American adolescents' suicide attempts: A Latent class regression analysis. *Journal of Youth & Adolescence*. Published online: 5 August 2011. doi: 10.1007/s10964-011-9701-3

Wright SCD, Mwinituo PP (2010). Lived experiences of Ghanaian women diagnosed with HIV and AIDS. *Africa Journal of Nursing and Midwifery* 12, 36–47.

Xie LF, Chen PL, Pan HF, Tao JH, Li XP, Zhang YJ, Zhai Y, Ye DQ (2011). Prevalence and correlates of suicidal ideation in SLE inpatients: Chinese experience. *Rheumatology International*. Published online: 27 July 2011. doi: 10.1007/s00296-011-2043-3

Yim HW, Jeong H, Jung YE, Wang HR, Kim SY (2011). Management of depression and suicide. *Journal of the Korean Medical Association.* 54, 275–283.

You J, Leung F (2011). The role of depressive symptoms, family invalidation and behavioral impulsivity in the occurrence and repetition of non-suicidal self-injury in Chinese adolescents: A 2-year follow-up study. *Journal of Adolescence*. Published online: 18 Aug 2011. doi:10.1016/j.adolescence.2011.07.020

Zayas LH, Hausmann-Stabile C, Kuhlberg J (2011) Can better mother-daughter relations reduce the chance of a suicide attempt among latinas? *Depression Research and Treatment*. Published online: 28 June 2011. doi: 10.1155/2011/403602

Zhang J, Wieczorek WF, Conwell Y, Tu XM (2011). Psychological strains and youth suicide in rural China. *Social Science and Medicine* 72, 2003–2010.

Zonda T, Nagy G, Lester D (2011). Panic disorder and suicidal behavior. *Crisis* 32, 169–172.

Zucker N, Von Holle A, Thornton LM, Strober M, Plotnicov K, Klump KL, Brandt H, Crawford S, Crow S, Fichter MM, Halmi KA, Johnson C, Kaplan AS, Keel P, LaVia M, Mitchell JE, Rotondo A, Woodside DB, Berrettini WH, Kaye WH, Bulik CM (2011). The significance of repetitive hair-pulling behaviors in eating disorders. *Journal of Clinical Psychiatry* 67, 391–403.

## Prevention

Anonymous (2011). Some antipsychotics and adjunctive antidepressants may minimize the risk of suicide in patients with schizophrenia. *Drugs & Therapy Perspectives* 27, 15–18.

Bjorkdahl A, Nyberg U, Runeson B, Omerov P (2011). The development of the Suicidal Patient Observation Chart (SPOC): Delphi study. *Journal of Psychiatric and Mental Health Nursing* 18, 558–561.

Brent D (2011). Prevention of self harm in adolescents. *British Medical Journal*. Published online: 1 April 2011. doi:10.1136/bmj.d682.

Cross WF, Seaburn D, Gibbs D, Schmeelk-Cone K, White AM, Caine ED (2011). Does practice make perfect? A randomized control trial of behavioral rehearsal on suicide prevention gatekeeper skills. *Journal of Primary Prevention* 32, 195–211.

de Wilde EJ, van de Looij P, Goldschmeding J, Hoogeveen C (2011). Self-report of suicidal thoughts and behavior vs. school nurse evaluations in Dutch high-school students. *Crisis* 32, 121–127.

Dyrbye LN, Shanafelt TD (2011). Medical student distress: A call to action. *Academic Medicine* 86, 801–803.

Lee S-Y (2011). Reasons for living and their moderating effects on Korean adolescents' suicidal ideation. *Death Studies* 35, 711–728.

Lu YJ, Chang HJ, Tung YY, Hsu MC, Lin MF (2011). Alleviating psychological distress of suicide survivors: Evaluation of a volunteer care programme. *Journal of Psychiatric and Mental Health Nursing* 18, 449–456.

Masters KJ (2011). Temporary tattoos: Alternative to adolescent self-harm? *Current Psychiatry* 10, 89–90.

McGorry PD, Goldstone S (2011). Is this normal? Assessing mental health in young people. *Australian Family Physician* 40, 94–97.

Melamed BG, Castro C (2011). Observations and insights about strengthening our soldiers (SOS). *Journal of Clinical Psychology in Medical Settings* 18, 210–223.

Sivakumar S, Weiland TJ, Gerdtz MF, Knott J, Jelinek GA (2011). Mental health-related learning needs of clinicians working in Australian emergency departments: A national survey of self-reported confidence and knowledge. *Emergency Medicine Australasia*. Published online: 10 August 2011. doi:10.1111/j.1742-6723.2011.01472.x.

Taur FM, Chai S, Chen MB, Hou JL, Lin S, Tsai SL (2011). Evaluating the suicide risk-screening scale used by general nurses on patients with chronic obstructive pulmonary disease and lung cancer: A questionnaire survey. *Journal of Clinical Nursing*. Published online: 1 August 2011. doi:10.1111/j.1365-2702.2011.03808.x.

Tsutsumi A, Maruyama T, Nagata M (2011). Psychiatric knowledge and skills required of occupational physicians: Priorities in the Japanese setting. *Journal of Occupational Health*. Published online: 5 August 2011. doi:10.1539/joh.11-0022-FS.

## Care and Support

Alegria CA (2011). Transgender identity and health care: Implications for psychosocial and physical evaluation. *Journal of the American Academy of Nurse Practitioners* 23, 175–182.

Anonymous (2011). Pediatric and adolescent mental health emergencies in the emergency medical services system. *Pediatrics* 127, 1356.

Anonymous (2011). A follow-up report on preventing suicide. *Joint Commission perspectives. Joint Commission on Accreditation of Healthcare Organizations* 31, 1–15.

Anonymous (2011). DBT for nonsuicidal self-injury: A 'middle path' example. *Current Psychiatry* 10, 3.

Anonymous (2011). Suicide assessment team in the ED. *Hospital Peer Review* 36, 30–31.

Bendit N (2011). Chronic suicidal thoughts and implicit memory: Hypothesis and practical implications. *Australasian Psychiatry* 19, 25–29.

Brecht S, Desaiah D, Marechal ES, Santini AM, Podhorna J, Guelfi JD (2011). Efficacy and safety of duloxetine 60 mg and 120 mg daily in patients hospitalized for severe depression: A double-blind randomized trial. *Journal of Clinical Psychiatry* 72, 1086–1094.

Broadbent E (2011). Working with people who self-harm: What does the service user need? *Wounds UK* 7, 78–84.

Chen EY, Tang JY, Hui CL, Chiu CP, Lam MM, Law CW, Yew CW, Wong GH, Chung DW, Tso S, Chan KP, Yip KC, Hung SF, Honer WG (2011). Three-year outcome of phase-specific early intervention for first-episode psychosis: A cohort study in Hong Kong. *Early Intervention in Psychiatry*. Published online: 4 July 2011. doi: 10.1111/j.1751-7893.2011. 00279.x.

Chen S, Conwell Y, Xu B, Chiu H, Tu X, Ma Y (2011). Depression care management for late-life depression in China primary care: Protocol for a randomized controlled trial. *Trials* 12, 121.

Chu JP, Hsieh KY, Tokars DA (2011). Help-seeking tendencies in Asian Americans with suicidal ideation and attempts. *Asian American Journal of Psychology* 2, 25–38.

Coetzee RH (2010). A clinical reflection: Why does deliberate self-harm pose such a challenge for doctors? *Journal of the Royal Naval Medical Service* 96, 139–145.

Corcoran J, Dattalo P, Crowley M, Brown E, Grindle L (2011). A systematic review of psychosocial interventions for suicidal adolescents. *Children and Youth Services Review* 33, 2112–2118.

Daniel SS, Goldston DB (2011). Hopelessness and lack of connectedness to others as risk factors for suicidal behavior across the lifespan: Implications for cognitive-behavioral treatment. *Cognitive and Behavioral Practice*. Published online: 14 June 2011. doi:10.1016/j.cbpra.2011.05.003.

Day CA, Islam MM, White A, Reid SE, Hayes S, Haber PS (2011). Development of a nurse-led primary healthcare service for injecting drug users in inner-city Sydney. *Australian Journal of Primary Health* 17, 10–15.

Dickinson T, Hurley M (2011). Exploring the antipathy of nursing staff who work within secure healthcare facilities across the United Kingdom to young people who self-harm. *Journal of Advanced Nursing*. Published online: 29 June 2011. doi: 10.1111/j.1365-2648. 2011.05745.x.

Dunn M, Makowski S, Reidy J, DuBeau C (2011). Is hospice appropriate after a failed suicide attempt? *Journal of the American Geriatrics Society* 59, S118–S119.

Eddleston M, Buckley NA (2011). A strategy for changing plasma pralidoxime kinetics and, perhaps, effect in organophosphorus insecticide poisoning. *Critical Care Medicine* 39, 908–909.

Esposito-Smythers C, Walsh A, Spirito A, Rizzo C, Goldston DB, Kaminer Y (2011). Working with the suicidal client who also abuses substances. *Cognitive and Behavioral Practice*. Published online: 31 March 2011. doi:10.1016/j.cbpra.2010.11.004.

Färdig R, Lewander T, Melin L, Folke F, Fredriksson A (2011). A randomized controlled trial of the illness management and recovery program for persons with schizophrenia. *Psychiatric Services* 62, 606–612.

Fisher P, Johnstone L, Williamson K (2011). Patients' perceptions of the process of consenting to electroconvulsive therapy. *Journal of Mental Health* 20, 347–354.

Furiak NM, Ascher-Svanum H, Klein RW, Smolen LJ, Lawson AH, Montgomery W, Conley RR (2011). Cost-effectiveness of olanzapine long-acting injection in the treatment of patients with schizophrenia in the United States: A micro-simulation economic decision model. *Current Medical Research and Opinion* 27, 713–730.

Gabler T, Yudelowitz B, Mahomed A (2011). Overdose with HAART — Are we managing these patients adequately? *SAMJ: South African Medical Journal* 101, 520–521.

Garcia C, Hermann D, Bartels A, Matamoros P, Dick-Olson L, de Patino JG (2011). Development of project wings home visits, a mental health intervention for Latino families using community-based participatory research. *Health Promotion Practice*. Published online: 8 April 2011. doi:10.1177/ 1524839911404224.

Ghahramanlou-Holloway M, Cox DW, Greene FN (2011). Post-admission cognitive therapy: A brief intervention for psychiatric inpatients admitted after a suicide attempt. *Cognitive and Behavioral Practice*. Published online 31 March 2011. doi:10.1016/j.cbpra.2010.11.006.

Gilat I, Tobin Y, Shahar G (2011). Offering support to suicidal individuals in an online support group. *Archives of Suicide Research* 15, 195–206.

Giles DC, Newbold J (2011). Self- and other-diagnosis in user-led mental health online communities. *Qualitative Health Research* 21, 419–428.

Gipson P, King C (2011). Health behavior theories and research: Implications for suicidal individuals' treatment linkage and adherence. *Cognitive and Behavioral Practice*. Published online: 31 March 2011. doi:10.1016/j.cbpra.2010.11.005.

Greydanus DE (2011). Treating self-harm in children and adolescents a complex conundrum for the clinician. *Psychiatric Times* 28, 32.

Griffin R, McGwin G Jr (2011). The effect of trauma care in the temporal distribution of homicide and suicide mortality. *American Journal of Epidemiology* 173, S287.

Gros DF, Veronee K, Strachan M, Ruggiero KJ, Acierno R (2011). Managing suicidality in home-based telehealth. *Journal of Telemedicine and Telecare* 17, 332–335.

Groves S, Backer HS, van den Bosch W, Miller A (2011). Dialectical Behaviour Therapy with adolescents: A review. *Child and Adolescent Mental Health*. Published online: 20 June 2011. doi: 10.1111/j.1475-3588.2011.00611.x.

Guptill J (2011). After an attempt: Caring for the suicidal patient on the medical-surgical unit. *Medsurg Nursing* 20, 163–167.

Hatcher S, Coupe N, Durie M, Elder H, Tapsell R, Wikiriwhi K, Parag V (2011). Te Ira Tangata: A Zelen randomised controlled trial of a treatment package including problem solving therapy compared to treatment as usual in Maori who present to hospital after self harm. *Trials 12,* 117.

Hatcher S, Sharon C, House A, Collings S, Parag V, Collins N (2011). The ACCESS study a Zelen randomised controlled trial of a treatment package including problem solving therapy compared to treatment as usual in people who present to hospital after self-harm: Study protocol for a randomised controlled trial. *Trials* 12, 125.

Heath DS (2011). Inpatient care in the 21st century: Who needs it? Letter. *Psychiatric Services* 62, 563–563.

Hindi F, Dew MA, Albert SM, Lotrich FE, Reynolds CF (2011). Preventing depression in later life: State of the art and science circa. *Psychiatric Clinics of North America* 34, 67.

Holm AL, Severinsson E (2011). Struggling to recover by changing suicidal behaviour: Narratives from women with borderline personality disorder. *International Journal of Mental Health Nursing* 20, 165–173.

Horwitz SM, Heinberg LJ, Storfer-Isser A, Barnes DH, Smith M, Kapur R, Findling R, Currier G, Wilcox HC, Wilkens K (2011). Teaching physicians to assess suicidal youth presenting to the emergency department. *Pediatric Emergency Care* 27, 601–605.

Huisman A, Kerkhof AJ, Robben PB (2011). Suicides in users of mental health care services: Treatment characteristics and hindsight reflections. *Suicide and Life-Threatening Behavior* 41, 41–49.

Husain N, Chaudhry N, Durairaj SV, Chaudhry I, Khan S, Husain M, Nagaraj D, Naeem F, Waheed W (2011). Prevention of self harm in British South Asian women: Study protocol of an Exploratory RCT of culturally adapted manual assisted Problem Solving Training (C-MAP). *Trials* 12, 159.

Husain N, Fayyaz H, Chaudhry N, Afsar S, Husain M, Rahman R, Hamirani M, Memon R, Chaudhry I, Naeem B (2011). Culturally Adapted Manual Assisted Problem Solving Training

(C-MAPS) for prevention of self harm: An RCT from a low income country. *Journal of Psychosomatic Research* 70, 595–595.

Inckle K (2011). The first cut is the deepest: A harm-reduction approach to self-injury. *Social Work in Mental Health* 9, 364–378.

Jincy J, Linu SG, Binil V (2011). Effectiveness of an informational booklet on care of attempted suicide patients. *International Journal of Nursing Education* 3, 71–73.

Jo SJ, Lee MS, Yim HW, Kim HJ, Lee K, Chung HS, Cho J, Choi SP, Seo YM (2011). Factors associated with referral to mental health services among suicide attempters visiting emergency centers of general hospitals in Korea: Does history of suicide attempts predict referral? *General Hospital Psychiatry* 33, 294–299.

Johnson RM, Frank EM, Ciocca M, Barber CW (2011). Training mental healthcare providers to reduce at-risk patients' access to lethal means of suicide: Evaluation of the CALM project. *Archives of Suicide Research* 15, 259–264.

Joiner Jr TE, Ribeiro JD (2011). Assessment and management of suicidal behavior in children and adolescents. *Pediatric Annals* 40, 319–324.

Kasckow J, Appelt C, Haas G, Huegel S, Fox L, Gurklis J, Daley D (2011). Development of a recovery manual for suicidal patients with schizophrenia. *Schizophrenia Research* 130, 287–288.

Kasckow J, Montross L, Prunty L, Fox L, Zisook S (2011). Suicidal behavior in the older patient with schizophrenia. *Aging Health* 7, 379–393.

Kayser S, Bewernick BH, Grubert C, Hadrysiewicz BL, Axmacher N, Schlaepfer TE (2011). Antidepressant effects, of magnetic seizure therapy and electroconvulsive therapy, in treatment-resistant depression. *Journal of Psychiatric Research* 45, 569–576.

Kennerley H, Walsh BW (2011). Treating self-injury: A practical guide. *Behavioural and Cognitive Psychotherapy* 39, 376–377.

Kim SW, Stewart R, Kim JM, Shin IS, Yoon JS, Jung SW, Lee MS, Yim HW, Jun TY (2011). Relationship between a history of a suicide attempt and treatment outcomes in patients with depression. *Journal of Clinical Psychopharmacology* 31, 449.

Klein DA, Miller AL (2011). Dialectical behavior therapy for suicidal adolescents with borderline personality disorder. *Child & Adolescent Psychiatric Clinics of North America* 20, 205–216.

Kondo DG, Sung YH, Hellem TL, Fiedler KK, Shi X, Jeong EK, Renshaw PF (2011). Open-label adjunctive creatine for female adolescents with SSRI-resistant major depressive disorder: A 31-phosphorus magnetic resonance spectroscopy study. *Journal of Affective Disorders.* Published online: 9 August 2011. doi:10.1016/j.jad.2011.07.010.

Lapalme-Remis S, Tremblay-Jolicoeur C, Amse R, Henry M, Greenfield B (2011). Effect of research questionnaires on satisfaction with treatment care in suicidal adolescents and their parents. *Journal of the Canadian Academy of Child and Adolescent Psychiatry* 20, 107–111.

Lee BK, Jeung KW, Lee HY, Lim JH (2011). Outcomes of therapeutic hypothermia in unconscious patients after near-hanging. *Emergency Medicine Journal.* Published online: 19 September 2011. doi: 10.1136/emermed-2011-200493.

Linden M, Baumann K, Lieberei B, Lorenz C, Rotter M (2011). Treatment of posttraumatic embitterment disorder with cognitive behaviour therapy based on wisdom psychology and hedonia strategies. *Psychotherapy & Psychosomatics* 80, 199–205.

Lindholm T, Bjärehed J, Lundh LG (2011). Functions of nonsuicidal self-injury among young women in residential care: A pilot study with the Swedish version of the inventory of statements about self-injury. *Cognitive Behavioral Therapy* 40, 183–189.

Lorillard S, Schmitt L, Andreoli A (2011). How to treat deliberate self-harm: From clinical research to effective treatment choice? Part 1: An update treatment efficacy among unselected patients referred to emergency room with deliberate self-harm. *Annales Medico-Psychologiques* 169, 221–228.

Lorillard S, Schmitt L, Andreoli A (2011). How to treat suicide attempt? Part 2: A review of treatments and their efficiency among borderline personality disorder patients. *Annales Medico-Psychologiques* 169, 229–236.

Lubman DI, Hall K, Pennay A, Rao S (2011). Managing borderline personality disorder and substance use: An integrated approach. *Australian Family Physician* 40, 376–381.

Luoma JB, Villatte JL (2011). Mindfulness in the treatment of suicidal individuals. *Cognitive and Behavioral Practice*. Published online: 15 April 2011. doi:10.1016/j.cbpra.2010.12.003.

Maclay T (2011). Implementation of a suicide protocol in critical care. *Clinical Nurse Specialist* 25, 147.

McAllister M (2011). Assessment following self-harm: Nurses provide comparable risk assessment to psychiatrists but are less likely to admit for in-hospital treatment. *Evidence-Based Nursing* 14, 83–84.

McCauley K, Barnfield J (2011). Caring for clients after suicide attempt. *International Journal of Mental Health Nursing* 20, 11–12.

McFetridge M, Coakes J (2010). The longer-term clinical outcomes of a DBT-informed residential therapeutic community: An evaluation and reunion. *Therapeutic Communities: The International Journal for Therapeutic and Supportive Organizations* 31, 406–416.

Morgan JJ, Mancl DB, Kaffar BJ, Ferreira D (2011). Creating safe environments for students with disabilities who identify as lesbian, gay, bisexual, or transgender. *Intervention in School and Clinic* 47, 3–13.

Mynhier CR, Glenn LL (2011). Antipathy towards self-harm patients and nurse education. *International Emergency Nursing*. Published online: 5 August 2011. doi: 10.1016/j.ienj.2011.02.003

Nielsen AC, Alberdi F, Rosenbaum B (2011). Collaborative assessment and management of suicidality method shows effect. *Danish Medical Bulletin* 58, 8.

Ougrin D (2011). Adding group psychotherapy to routine care does not improve outcomes in adolescents who repeatedly self-harm. *Evidence Based Mental Health* 14, 84.

Ougrin D, Latif S (2011). Specific psychological treatment versus treatment as usual in adolescents with self-harm. *Crisis* 32, 74–80.

Palmu R, Suominen K, Vuola J, Isometsa E (2011). Psychiatric consultation and care after acute burn injury: A 6-month naturalistic prospective study. *General Hospital Psychiatry* 33, 16–22.

Patrick V, Hebert C, Green S, Ingram CL (2011). Integrated multidisciplinary treatment teams: A mental health model for outpatient settings in the military. *Military Medicine* 176, 986–990.

Penzias A, Sandkuhl H, Torok G (2011). Patient is suicidal? Inform all others. *Emergency Department Nursing* 14, 81.

Perepletchikova F, Axelrod SR, Kaufman J, Rounsaville BJ, Douglas-Palumberi H, Miller AL (2011). Adapting dialectical behaviour therapy for children: Towards a new research agenda for paediatric suicidal and non-suicidal self-injurious behaviours. *Child and Adolescent Mental Health* 16, 116–121.

Piek E, van der Meer K, Penninx BW, Verhaak PF, Nolen WA (2011). Referral of patients with depression to mental health care by Dutch general practitioners: An observational study. *BMC Family Practice* 12, 41.

Ramluggun P (2011). Beyond observation: Self-harm in prisons. *Mental Health Practice* 14, 18–20.

Rathbone P (2011). Antidepressant prescribing. *The British Journal of General Practice: The Journal of the Royal College of General Practitioners* 61, 221.

Richard-Devantoy S, Annweiler C, Le Gall D, Garre JB, Olie JP, Beauchet O (2011). Cognitive Inhibition in suicidal depressed elderly: A case-control pilot study. *Journal of Clinical Psychiatry* 72, 871–872.

Roggenbaum S, Christy A, Leblanc A (2011). Suicide assessment and prevention during and after emergency commitment. *Community Mental Health Journal.* Published online: 17 June 2011. doi: 10.1007/s10597-011-9428-3.

Rostagno C, Pastorelli F, Domenichetti S, Gensini GF (2011). Cardio-vascular risks associated with clozapine treatment. *Current Psychiatry Reviews* 7, 170–176.

Ruberman L (2011). Girls who cut: Treatment in an outpatient psychodynamic psychotherapy practice with adolescent girls and young adult women. *American Journal of Psychotherapy* 65, 117–132.

Salsman NL, Arthur R (2011). Adapting dialectical behavior therapy to help suicidal adolescents. *Current Psychiatry* 10, 18–33.

Scott A, Doughty C, Kahi H (2011). 'Having those conversations': The politics of risk in peer support practice. *Health Sociology Review* 20, 187–201.

Shoirah H, Hamoda HM (2011). Electroconvulsive therapy in children and adolescents. *Expert review of neurotherapeutics* 11, 127–137.

Smith C, Taylor RR (2011). Using the intentional relationship model in the treatment of medically complicated depression. *Journal of Psychiatric Intensive Care* 7, 41–43.

Smithson J, Sharkey S, Hewis E, Jones RB, Emmens T, Ford T, Owens C (2011). Membership and boundary maintenance on an online self-harm forum. *Qualitative Health Research.* Published online: 29 June 2011. doi: 10.1177/1049732311413784.

Sorgaard KW, Nivison M, Hansen V, Oiesvold T (2011). Acknowledging illness and treatment needs in first-time admitted psychiatric patients. *European Psychiatry* 26, 446–451.

Spirito A, Esposito-Smythers C, Wolff J, Uhl K (2011). Cognitive-behavioral therapy for adolescent depression and suicidality. *Child & Adolescent Psychiatric Clinics of North America* 20, 191–204.

Sun FK (2011). A concept analysis of suicidal behavior. *Public Health Nursing.* Published online: 9 May 2011. doi: 10.1111/j.1525-1446.2011.00939.x.

Tapolaa V, Lappalainen R, Wahlstrom J (2010). Brief intervention for deliberate self harm: An exploratory study. *Suicidology Online* 1, 95–108.

Thiermann H, Steinritz D, Worek F, Radtke M, Eyer P, Eyer F, Felgenhauer N, Zilker T (2011). Atropine maintenance dosage in patients with severe organophosphate pesticide poisoning. *Toxicology Letters* 206, 77–83.

Tiwari R, Srivastava M (2011). Assessment of the attitudes of clinicians in the emergency setting towards an act of parasuicide. *Indian Journal of Public Health Research and Development* 2, 48–51.

Todd JR, Zaman K, Bayat A (2011). Innovative treatment for extensive self harm scarring through simultaneous use of a single layer skin substitute and a split thickness skin graft with negative pressure wound therapy. *Wound Repair and Regeneration* 19, A57.

Tondo L, Baldessarini RJ (2011). Can suicide be prevented? The role of lithium and other psychotropics. *Psychiatric Times* 28, 22.

Vitiello B (2011). Prevention and treatment of child and adolescent depression: Challenges and opportunities. *Epidemiology and psychiatric science* 20, 37–43.

Wagner KD (2011). Pediatric and adolescent depression. *Pediatric Annals* 40, 290–291.

Wells KC, Heilbron N (2011). Family-based cognitive-behavioral treatments for suicidal adolescents and their integration with individual treatment. *Cognitive and Behavioral Practice.* Published online: 29 June 2011. doi:10.1016/j.cbpra.2011.06.004.

Wilkinson B (2011). Current trends in remediating adolescent self-injury: An integrative review. *Journal of School Nursing* 27, 120–128.

Yonkers KA, Vigod S, Ross LE (2011). Diagnosis, pathophysiology, and management of mood disorders in pregnant and postpartum women. *Obstetrics & Gynecology* 117, 961–977.

## CASE REPORTS

Abarca-Olivas J, Concepcion-Aramendia LA, Bano-Ruiz E, Caminero-Canas MA, Navarro-Moncho JA, Botella-Asuncion C (2011). Perforating brain injury from a speargun. A case report. *Neurocirugia* 22, 271–275.

Abdelraheem M, Ali ET, Hussien R, Zijlstra E (2011). Paraphenylene diamine hair dye poisoning in an adolescent. *Toxicology and Industrial Health*. Published online: 4 May 2011. doi:10.1177/0748233711399321

Abeyasinghe NL, Perera HJ, Weerasinghe DS (2011). Case report — Death by subcutaneous injection of cyanide in Sri Lanka. *Journal of Forensic and Legal Medicine* 18, 182–183.

Afandiyev IN (2011). Fatal suicidal poisoning by injection of vipera lebetina snake venom. *Clinical Toxicology* 49, 58.

Agarwal LJ, Berger CE, Gill L (2011). Naltrexone for severe self-harm behavior: A case report. *The American Journal of Psychiatry* 168, 437–438.

Akcan R, Arslan MM, Çekin N, Karanfil R (2011). Unexpected suicide and irrational thinking in adolescence: A case report. *Journal of Forensic and Legal Medicine* 18, 288–290.

Akoglu H, Akan B, Piskinpasa S, Karaca O, Dede F, Erdem D, Albayrak MD, Odabas AR (2011). Metformin-associated lactic acidosis treated with prolonged hemodialysis. *American Journal of Emergency Medicine* 29, 575.

Alberici A, Cottini E, Cosseddu M, Borroni B, Padovani A (2011). Suicide risk in frontotemporal lobe degeneration: To be considered, to be prevented. *Alzheimer Disease and Associated Disorders*. Published online: 9 June 2011. doi: 10.1097/WAD.0b013e3182223254.

Ananda Kumar L, Subba RK, Obulesu IC, Reshma SI, Sureswar RM, Krishna PS (2011). A case report of suicidal death of a female prisoner consuming formalin in rims hospital, Kadapa — How far hospital administration is responsible? *Medico-Legal Update* 11, 16.

Ardhanari A, Srivastava U, Kumar A, Saxena S (2011). Management of a case of prallethrin poisoning- An unusual agent for suicidal ingestion. *Sri Lankan Journal of Anaesthesiology* 19, 51–52.

Atwood GE (2011). Philosophy and psychotherapy part 2: Ethics-the question of the good. *International Journal of Psychoanalytic Self Psychology* 6, 269–274.

Awsakulsutthi S (2010). Result of esophageal reconstruction using supercharged interposition colon in corrosive and Boehave's injury: Thammasat University Hospital experience. *Journal of the Medical Association of Thailand* 93, 303–306.

Badger JM, Ekman Ladd R (2011). Conflicting voices: Withhold treatment or not for a patient with chronic self-destructive behavior? *JONA's Healthcare Law, Ethics & Regulation* 13, 79–83.

Bailey AR, Sathianathan VJ, Chiew AL, Paterson AD, Chan BS, Arora S (2011). Comparison of intermittent haemodialysis, prolonged intermittent renal replacement therapy and continuous renal replacement haemofiltration for lithium toxicity: A case report. *Critical Care and Resuscitation* 13, 120–122.

Bode DV, Roberts TA (2011). Self-injurious behavior in an adolescent. *American Family Physician* 83, 609–611.

Buchade DD, Dere RC, Savardekar RR (2011). An unusual case of suicidal cut throat- A case report. *Medico-Legal Update* 11, 23–24.

Campbell J, Rondon J, Galway K, Leavey G (2011). Meeting the needs of vulnerable young men: A study of service provider views. *Children and Society*. Published online: 26 April 2011. doi: 10.1111/j.1099-0860.2011.00372.x

Capuano A, Ruggiero S, Vestini F, Ianniello B, Rafaniello C, Rossi F, Mucci A (2011). Survival from coma induced by an intentional 36-g overdose of extended-release quetiapine. *Drug and Chemical Toxicology* 34, 475–477.

Castaing N, Benali L, Ducint D, Molimard M, Gromb S, Titier K (2011). Suicide with cisatracurium and thiopental: Forensic and analytical aspects. *Journal of Analytical Toxicology* 35, 375–380.

Celano CM, Torri A, Seiner S (2011). Takotsubo cardiomyopathy after electroconvulsive therapy: A case report and review. *Journal of ECT* 27, 221–223.

Chacko J, Brar G, Elangovan A, Moorthy R (2011). Apical ballooning syndrome after attempted suicidal hanging. *Indian Journal of Critical Care Medicine* 15, 43.

Chakraborty J, Nagri SK, Gupta AN, Bansal A (2011). An uncommon but lethal poisoning – Amitraz. *Australasian Medical Journal* 4, 439–441.

Chien J (2011). Ethosuximide-induced mania in a 10-year-old boy. *Epilepsy and Behavior* 21, 483–485.

Contrada E (2011). CE Test 2.6 Hours: Care of the suicidal pediatric patient in the ED: A case study. *The American Journal of Nursing* 111, 44–45.

Demirci S, Dogan KH, Koc S (2011). Fatal injury by an unmodified blank pistol: A case report and review of the literature. *Journal of Forensic and Legal Medicine* 18, 237.

Deyle S, Exadaktylos AK, Kneubuehl BP, Buck U, Thali MJ, Voisard MX (2011). Collateral damage-penetrating head injury and orbital injury: A case report. *American Journal of Forensic Medicine and Pathology* 32, 215–218.

Duband S, Govin A, Dumollard JM, Forest F, Basset T, Peoc'h M (2011). Laryngeal teflonoma identified by Fourier-transform infrared microspectroscopy after forensic autopsy: An interesting tool for foreign material identification in forensic cases. *Forensic Science International.* Published online: 10 August 2011. doi:10.1016/j.forsciint.2011.07.036

Dyer C (2011). Psychiatrist is accused of undermining stability of 14 year old. *BMJ: British Medical Journal.* Published online: 28 April 2011. doi: 10.1136/bmj.d2773

Eizadi-Mood N, Sabzghabaee AM, Gheshlaghi F, Yaraghi A (2011). Amitraz poisoning treatment: Still supportive? *Iranian Journal of Pharmaceutical Research* 10, 155–158.

Emre H, Keles M, Uyanik A, Emet M, Bilen Y, Bayraktutan D (2011). Rhabdomyolysis and acute renal failure as a result of bentazone intoxication. *Eastern Journal of Medicine* 16, 59–61.

Facchi L, Gattoni T, Cemmi C, Straticò E (2011). Murder and madness: A case study of the criminogenesis and psychodynamics of a dual murder. *International Journal of Offender Therapy & Comparative Criminology* 55, 799–815.

Fanton L, Karger B (2010). Suicide with two shots to the head inflicted by a captive-bolt gun. *Journal of Forensic and Legal Medicine.* Published online: 5 August 2011. doi:10.1016/j.jflm.2011.07.010

Fathallah N, Zamy M, Slim R, Fain O, Hmouda H, Bouraoui K, Salem CB, Biour M (2011). Acute pancreatitis in the course of meprobamate poisoning. *Journal of the Pancreas* 12, 404–406.

Findikcioglu K, Findikcioglu F (2011). An unusual suicide attempt with injection of paint thinner in the dorsum of the hand. *Journal of Hand Surgery (European Volume)* 36, 609–610.

Freitas C, Pearlman C, Pascual-Leone A (2011). Treatment of auditory verbal hallucinations with transcranial magnetic stimulation in a patient with psychotic major depression: One-year follow-up. *Neurocase* 25, 1–9.

Fujita Y, Fujino Y, Onodera M, Kikuchi S, Kikkawa T, Inoue Y, Niitsu H, Takahashi K, Endo S (2011). A fatal case of acute hydrogen sulfide poisoning caused by hydrogen sulfide: Hydroxocobalamin therapy for acute hydrogen sulfide poisoning. *Journal of Analytical Toxicology* 35, 119–123.

Gabeli T, Adamec I, Mr en A, Radoš M, Brinar VV, Habek M (2011). Psychotic reaction as a manifestation of multiple sclerosis relapse treated with plasma exchange. *Neurological Sciences.* Published online: 27 July 2011. doi:10.1007/s10072-011-0712-3

Garaci FG, Bazzocchi G, Velari L, Gaudiello F, Goldstein AL, Manenti G, Floris R, Simonetti G (2009). Cryptogenic stroke in hanging: A case report. *Neuroradiology Journal* 22, 386–390.

Garcia-Cabeza I, De Blas MMM, Epifanio MM, De Chavez MG (2011). Cognitive deterioration after venlafaxine overdose. *Journal of Emergency Medicine* 40, 103–106.

Ghahramanlou-Holloway M (2011). Lessons learned from a soldier's suicide in Iraq. *Psychiatry* 74, 115–117.

Gloger ER (2011). Breakdown and development — A clinical case study. *Psychoanalytic Psychotherapy* 25, 157–175.

Gormley NJ, Bronstein AC, Rasimas JJ, Pao M, Wratney AT, Sun J, Austin HA, Suffredini AF (2011). The rising incidence of intentional ingestion of ethanol-containing hand sanitizers. *Critical Care Medicine.* Published online: 15 September 2011. doi: 10.1097/CCM.0b013e31822f09c0

Hanbury A, Wallace LM, Clark M (2011). Multiple outcome measures and mixed methods for evaluating the effectiveness of theory-based behaviour-change interventions: A case study targeting health professionals' adoption of a national suicide prevention guideline. *Psychology, Health & Medicine* 16, 291–303.

Harding BE, Sullivan LM, Adams S, Middleberg RA, Wolf BC (2011). multidisciplinary investigation of an unusual apparent homicide/suicide. *American Journal of Forensic Medicine and Pathology* 32, 208–212.

Harmandayan M, Romanowicz M, Sola C (2011). Successful use of ECT in post-stroke depression. *General Hospital Psychiatry.* Published online: 19 September 2011. doi:10.1016/ j.genhosppsych.2011.08.006

Harner H, Burgess AW (2011). Using a trauma-informed framework to care for incarcerated women. *JOGNN — Journal of Obstetric Gynecologic and Neonatal Nursing* 40, 469–476.

Hejna P, Safr M, Zatopkova L (2010). The ability to act — Multiple suicidal gunshot wounds. *Journal of Forensic and Legal Medicine.* Published online: 31 July 2011. doi:10.1016/ j.jflm.2011.06.017

Ho JD, Clinton JE, Lappe MA, Heegaard WG, Williams MF, Miner JR (2011). Introduction of the conducted electrical weapon into a hospital setting. *The Journal of Emergency Medicine* 41, 317–323.

Hofer KE, Trachsel C, Rauber-Luthy C, Kupferschmidt H, Kullak-Ublick GA, Ceschi A (2011). Moderate toxic effects following acute zonisamide overdose. *Epilepsy and Behavior* 21, 91–93.

Holyoak AL, Fraser TA, Gelperowicz P (2011). Cooling in the tropics: Ethylene glycol overdose. *Critical Care and Resuscitation* 13, 28–32.

Hopson J, Holmes J (2011). Through the wasteland: Chronic depression. *BMJ: British Medical Journal* 342, d93.

Huston B, Mills K, Froloff V, McGee M (2011). Bladder rupture after intentional medication overdose. *American Journal of Forensic Medicine and Pathology.* Published online: 2 September 2011. doi: 10.1097/PAF.0b013e31822c8f0a

Iacopini F, Scozzarro A, Romagnoli A, Grossi C, Elisei W, Bonabello F (2011). Over-the-scope-clip (otsc) successful closure of an acute phanryngeal perforation following throat stabbing for suicide proposal. *Digestive and Liver Disease* 43, S233.

Ishitobi M, Shukunami Ki, Murata T, Wada Y (2011). Hypomanic switching during influenza infection without intracranial infection in an adolescent patient with bipolar disorder. *Pediatric Emergency Care* 27, 652–653.

Jafferany M, Silverman MA (2011). Suicidal ideation associated with asenapine use: A report of 2 cases. *Journal of Clinical Psychopharmacology* 31, 534–535.

Jewsbury H, O'Duffy D (2011). The best treatment can be no treatment: Retained retro-orbital air gun pellet following attempted suicide. *BMJ Case Reports*. Published online: 9 June 2011. doi:10.1136/ bcr.02.2011.3826

Jones AW (2011). Fatality from drinking denatured alcohol and hypothermia. *Journal of Analytical Toxicology* 35, 316–318.

Jones R, Jones J, Causer J, Ewins D, Goenka N, Joseph F (2011). Yew tree poisoning: A near-fatal lesson from history. *Clinical Medicine (London, England)* 11, 173–175.

Jungmann L, Grosse Perdekamp M, Bohnert M, Auwarter V, Pollak S (2010). Complex suicide by ethanol intoxication and inhalation of fire fumes in an old lady: Interdisciplinary elucidation including post-mortem analysis of congener alcohols. *Forensic Science International* 209, 11–15.

Kang SH, Park SW, Moon KY (2011). Postoperative systemic dissemination of injected elemental mercury. *Journal of Korean Neurosurgical Society* 49, 245–247.

Khoharo HK, Ansari S, Abro A, Qureshi F (2009). Suicidal isoniazid poisoning. *Journal of Ayub Medical College, Abbottabad: JAMC* 21, 178–179.

Kim SY, Oh TH, Kang HM, Jeon TJ, Seo DD, Shin WC, Choi WC, Choi JH (2011). A case of corrosive injury-induced pharyngeal stricture treated by endoscopic adhesiolysis using an electrosurgical knife. *Gut and Liver* 5, 383–386.

Kirschner RI, Poterucha JT, Reilly DA (2011). Suicide attempt by injection of mercuric chloride. *Clinical Toxicology* 49, 615–616.

Kodikara S (2011). Suicide by electrocution- A case report. *Indian Journal of Forensic Medicine and Toxicology* 5, 109–110.

Kodikara S, Alagiyawanna R (2011). Accidental hanging by a T-Shirt collar in a man with morphine intoxication: An unusual case. *American Journal of Forensic Medicine and Pathology* 32, 260–262.

Kondo DG, Sung YH, Hellem TL, Delmastro KK, Jeong EK, Kim N, Shi X, Renshaw PF (2011). Open-label uridine for treatment of depressed adolescents with bipolar disorder. *Journal of Child and Adolescent Psychopharmacology* 21, 171–175.

Kondziella D, Danielsen ER, Arlien-Soeborg P (2009). Fatal encephalopathy after an isolated overdose of cocaine. *BMJ Case Reports* 78, 437–438.

Kumar S, Chatterjee I, Kumar N, Kumari A (2011). Management of flaccid dysarthria in a case of attempted suicide by hanging. *Eastern Journal of Medicine* 16, 66–71.

Kutluhan S, Baydar CL, Sezgin BY, Demirci S, Ozden A, Yavuz L (2011). Cerebral infarction due to thrombosis of ICA in a near hanging case. *Nobel Medicus* 7, 109–111.

Letsky MC, Zumwalt RE, Seifert SA, Benson BE (2011). Cause of death conundrum with methadone use a case report. *American Journal of Forensic Medicine and Pathology* 32, 193–196.

Leung PSC, Tsui SH, Siu TS, Tam S (2011). Acquired 5-oxoprolinuria (Pyroglutamic acidaemia) as a cause of early high anion gap metabolic acidosis in acute massive paracetamol overdose. *Hong Kong Journal of Emergency Medicine* 18, 264–270.

Levine M, Truitt CA, O'Connor AD (2011). Cardiotoxicity and serotonin syndrome complicating a milnacipran overdose. *Journal of Medical Toxicology*. Published online: 7 July 2011. doi: 10.1007/s13181-011-0167-1

Lovejoy V (2011). Chinese in late nineteenth-century Bendigo: Their local and translocal lives in 'this strangers' country'. *Australian Historical Studies* 42, 45–61.

Lyness JR, Crane J (2011). Carbon monoxide poisoning from disposable charcoal barbeques. *American Journal of Forensic Medicine and Pathology* 32, 251–254.

Magdalan J, Zawadzki M, Sozaski T (2011). Fulminant hepatic failure in woman with iron and non-steroidal anti-inflammatory drug intoxication. *Human and Experimental Toxicology* 30, 1106–1111.

Marciki M, Vuksic Z, Dumencic B, Matuzalem E, Cacinovic V (2011). Double suicide. *American Journal of Forensic Medicine and Pathology* 32, 200–201.

Marks S, Heinrich TW, Rosielle D (2011). Case report: Are clinicians obligated to medically treat a suicide attempt in a patient with a prognosis of weeks? *Journal of Palliative Medicine.* Published online: 4 August 2011. doi:10.1089/jpm.2010.0530

Meel BL (2011). Aluminium phosphide (tank pill) poisoning in the Transkei region of South Africa: A case report. *Medicine, Science & the Law* 51, 116–118.

Meel DE (2011). On the edge: A case study and resources for mathematics teachers. *PRIMUS: Problems, Resources, and Issues in Mathematics Undergraduate Studies* 21(6): 485–511.

Merzagora I, Travaini G, Battistini A, Pleuteri L (2011). Murder-suicide in the province of Milan, Italy: Criminological analysis of cases 1990–2009. *Medicine, Science and the Law* 51, 87–92.

Middleton O (2011). Suicide by gabapentin overdose. *Journal of Forensic Sciences* 56, 1373–1375.

Miklavcic A (2011). Canada's non-status immigrants: Negotiating access to health care and citizenship. *Medical Anthropology: Cross Cultural Studies in Health and Illness* 30, 496–517.

Mohammed R, Norton J, Geraci SA, Newman DB, Koch CA (2010). Prolonged QTc interval due to escitalopram overdose. *Journal of the Mississippi State Medical Association* 51, 350–353.

Mork TA, Killeen CT, Patel NK, Dohnal JM, Karydes HC, Leikin JB (2011). Massive insulin overdose managed by monitoring daily insulin levels. *American Journal of Therapeutics* 18, E162–E166.

Mutluoglu M, Senol MG, Yildiz S, Aydinoz S, Ay H, Uzun G (2011). Affective disorder and suicide attempt in a child after carbon monoxide poisoning: Close follow-up is imperative. *Pediatric Emergency Care* 27, 451.

Nagesh KR, Menezes RG, Rastogi P, Naik NR, Rasquinha JM, Senthilkumaran S, Fazil A (2011). Suicidal plant poisoning with colchicum autumnale. *Journal of Forensic and Legal Medicine* 18, 285–287.

Neitzel AR, Gill JR (2011). Death certification of 'Suicide by Cop'. *Journal of Forensic Sciences.* Published online: 9 August 2011. doi: 10.1111/j.1556-4029.2011.01891.x

Newman J, Widera E, Kao H (2011). A case of suicide at the end of life illustrating risk factors and ethical decision-making. *Journal of the American Geriatrics Society* 59, S164.

Nussbaum A, Thurstone C, Binswanger I (2011). Medical marijuana use and suicide attempt in a patient with major depressive disorder. *American Journal of Psychiatry* 168, 778–781.

Pan L, McKain BW, Madan-Khetarpal S, Mcguire M, Diler RS, Perel JM, Vockley J, Brent DA (2011). GTP-cyclohydrolase deficiency responsive to sapropterin and 5-HTP supplementation: Relief of treatment-refractory depression and suicidal behaviour. *BMJ Case Reports.* Published online: 30 June 2011. doi:10.1136/bcr.03.2011.3927

Panda S, Singh UP (2011). A case of non fatal suicidal stab injury. *Medico-Legal Update* 11, 92–93.

Park JS, Min JH, Kim H, Lee SW (2011). Esophageal perforation and mediastinitis after suicidal ingestion of 4.5% sodium hydrochlorite bleach. *Clinical Toxicology.* Published online: 22 August 2011. doi:10.3109/15563650.2011.607168

Park SM, Sohn YD, Ahn JY (2011). Chemical burn caused by dermal injection of potassium chloride. *Clinical Toxicology* 49, 436–437.

Parker GB (2011). Bipolar II disorder — diagnostic and management lessons for health practitioners from a coronial inquest. *Medical Journal of Australia* 195, 81–83.

Patel F (2011). Pesticidal suicide: Adult fatal rotenone poisoning. *Journal of Forensic and Legal Medicine* 18, 340–342.

Pavelites JJ, Prahlow JA, Landrum JE, Zollinger D, Vermillion D (2011). An unusual case of lead snowstorm caused by fragmentation of buckshot. *American Journal of Forensic Medicine and Pathology* 32, 223–236.

Persico A, Bacis G, Uberti F, Panzeri C, di Lorenzo C, Moro E, Restani P (2011). Identification of taxine derivatives in biological fluids from a patient after attempted suicide by ingestion of yew (Taxus baccata) leaves. *Journal of Analytical Toxicology* 35, 238–241.

Petkovi S, Maletin M, Durendi -Brenesel M (2011). Complex suicide: An unusual case with six methods applied. *Journal of Forensic Sciences* 56, 1368–1372.

Pringsheim T (2011). Missed diagnosis of tardive dystonia in an adolescent girl treated with risperidone. *Journal of Child and Adolescent Psychopharmacology* 21, 191–194.

Proenca P, Franco JM, Mustra C, Marcos M, Pereira AR, Corte-Real F, Vieira DN (2011). An UPLC-MS/MS method for the determination of valproic acid in blood of a fatal intoxication case. *Journal of Forensic and Legal Medicine* 18, 320–324.

Rashid M, Gosai I (2011). The girl who swallows knives: Uncontrollable deliberate self-harm in a teenage girl with borderline personality disorder. *BMJ Case Reports*. Published online: 25 January 2011. doi: 10.1136/bcr.07.2010.3136

Roberts DM, Smith MWH, Gopalakrishnan M, Whittaker G, Day RO (2011). Extreme gamma-butyrolactone overdose with severe metabolic acidosis requiring hemodialysis. *Annals of Emergency Medicine* 58, 83–85.

Sakoda C, Kusaba T, Adachi T, Sonomura K, Kimura T, Nakayama M, Kishimoto N, Nakagawa H, Okigaki M, Hatta T, Matsubara H, Mori Y (2011). A case of Goodpasture syndrome positive for anti-GBM antibody and MPO-ANCA complicated by a variety of serious infections. *Clinical Nephrology* 75, 384–388.

Salomone A, Di Corcia D, Gerace E, Vincenti M (2011). A fatal case of simultaneous ingestion of mirtazapine, escitalopram, and valproic Acid. *Journal of Analytical Toxicology* 35, 519–523.

Sawyer A (2011). Let's talk: A narrative of mental illness, recovery, and the psychotherapist's personal treatment. *Journal of Clinical Psychology* 67, 776–778.

Scheinin L, Rogers CB, Sathyavagiswaran L (2011). Familicide-suicide: A cluster of 3 cases in Los Angeles county. *American Journal of Forensic Medicine and Pathology*. Published online: 1 August 2011. doi: 10.1097/PAF.0b013e31821a555a

Schmid AM, Truog AW, Damian FJ (2011). Care of the suicidal pediatric patient in the ED: A case study. *The American Journal of Nursing* 111, 34–43.

Senthilkumaran S, Balamurgan N, Menezes RG, Thirumalaikolundusubramanian P (2011). An unusual case of attempted suicide by rectal administration of parathion. *Journal of Forensic and Legal Medicine*. Published online: 11 August 2011. doi:10.1016/j.jflm.2011. 07.002

Shahadi J (2011). Burn: The radical disappearance of Kathy Change. *TDR — The Drama Review — A Journal of Performance Studies* 55, 52–72.

Sharma A (2011). Acute copper sulphate poisoning: A case report and review of literature. *Medico-Legal Update* 11(2):11–12.

Sheshadri S, Sudhir U, Kumar S, Kempegowda P (2011). DORMEX® -hydrogen cyanamide poisoning. *Journal of Emergencies, Trauma and Shock* 4, 435–437.

Song JH, Yu BH, Lee D, Yoon SC, Jeon HJ (2011). Uncontrolled self-medication with venlafaxine in a patient with major depressive disorder. *Psychiatry Investigation* 8, 74–76.

Sorokin V, Persechino F, Deroux SJ, Greenberg MJ (2011). Suicidal ligature strangulation utilizing cable ties: a report of three cases. *Forensic Science, Medicine & Pathology*. Published online: 8 September 2011. doi: 10.1007/s12024-011-9277-y

Soumagne N, Chauvet S, Chatellier D, Robert R, Charriere JM, Menu P (2011). Treatment of yew leaf intoxication with extracorporeal circulation. *The American Journal of Emergency Medicine* 29, 354.

Spencer L, Lyketsos CG, Samstad E, Dokey A, Rostov D, Chisolm MS (2011). A suicidal adult in crisis: An unexpected diagnosis of autism spectrum disorder. *The American Journal of Psychiatry* 168, 890–892.

Sporkert F, Brune C, Augsburger MP, Mangin P (2010). Fatal tolperisone poisoning: Autopsy and toxicology findings in three suicide cases. *Forensic Science International.* Published online: 17 June 2011. doi:10.1016/j.forsciint.2011.05.025

Talebi S (2011). WHO is behind the name? A story of violence, loss, and melancholic survival in post-revolutionary Iran. *Journal of Middle East Women's Studies* 7, 39–69.

Teske J, Weller JP, Albrecht UV, Fieguth A (2011). Fatal intoxication due to brucine. *Journal of Analytical Toxicology* 35, 248–253.

Thierauf A, Lutz-Bonengel S, Sanger T, Vogt S, Rupp W, Perdekamp MG (2011). Suicide by multiple blunt head traumatisation using a stone. *Forensic Science International.* Published online: 9 September 2011. doi:10.1016/j.forsciint.2011.08.014

Thompson M (2011). A soldier's tragedy. *Time* 177, 46–51.

Tilney P (2011). Carbon monoxide poisoning in a 55-year-old man after a suicide attempt. *Air Medical Journal* 30, 112–115.

Ullrich HE (2011). The impact of cultural evolution on the ego ideal, depression, psychosis, and suicide: A South India community study of the widow. *Journal of the American Academy of Psychoanalysis and Dynamic Psychiatry* 39, 453–469.

Usumoto Y, Hifumi T, Kiriu N, Kato H, Koido Y, Nishida M, Namera A (2010). Survival case of colchicine intoxication following ingestion of a lethal dose. *The Japanese Journal of Toxicology* 23, 303–308.

Vaks YK, Nandu B (2011). A 34-year-old woman with depression, suicidal ideation. *Psychiatric Annals* 41, 367–369.

Wachtel LE, Jaffe R, Kellner CH (2011). Electroconvulsive therapy for psychotropic-refractory bipolar affective disorder and severe self-injury and aggression in an 11-year-old autistic boy. *European Child & Adolescent Psychiatry* 20, 147–152.

Webb KB (2011). Care of others and self: A suicidal patient's impact on the psychologist. *Professional Psychology: Research and Practice* 42, 215–221.

Zganjer V, Zganjer M, Cizmi A, Pajid A, Zupanci B (2011). Suicide attempt by swallowing sponge or pica disorder: A case report. *Acta Medica (Hradec Kralove)* 54, 91–93.

Zygowicz W, Grill M (2011). A quiet epidemic: how suicides affect patients & providers. *JEMS: Journal of Emergency Medical Services* 36, 40–46.

# MISCELLANEOUS

Adeeko A (2011). Okonkwo, textual closure, colonial conquest. *Research in African Literatures* 42, 72–86.

Anand R, Binukumar BK, Gill KD (2011). Aluminum phosphide poisoning: An unsolved riddle. *Journal of Applied Toxicology*. Published online: 24 May 2011. doi: 10.1002/jat.1692

Anonymous (2011). Mental health resources. *Australian Nursing Journal* 18, 59.

Anonymous (2011). Unite challenges NI policy on suicides. *Mental Health Nursing* 31, 4.

Anonymous (2011). Spate of suicides roils university, jeopardizing academic reforms. *Science* 332, 410.

Anonymous (2011). Serious mental ill health shortens lives. *Mental Health Nursing* 31, 5.

Appelbaum PS (2011). Law & psychiatry: SSRIs, suicide, and liability for failure to warn of medication risks. *Psychiatric Services* 62, 347–349.

Augustin D, Fagan TJ (2011). Roles for mental health professionals in critical law enforcement incidents: An overview. *Psychological Services* 8, 166–177.

Auxemery Y (2011). The mass murderer. *Annales Medico-Psychologiques* 169, 237–242.

Baars MY, Müller MJ, Gallhofer B, Netter P (2011). Depressive and aggressive responses to frustration: Development of a questionnaire and its validation in a sample of male alcoholics. *Depression Research and Treatment*. Published online: 17 March 2011. doi:10.1155/2011/352048

Bell R (2011). In Werther's thrall: Suicide and the power of sentimental reading in Early National America. *Early American Literature* 46, 93–120.

Bennell C, Jones NJ, Taylor A (2011). Determining the authenticity of suicide notes: Can training improve human judgment? *Criminal Justice and Behavior*. Published online: 25 April 2011. doi: 10.1177/ 0093854811405146

Berger O, Chamberlain JR (2011). Suicide by cop mental health expert testimony meets daubert standards. *Journal of the American Academy of Psychiatry and the Law* 39, 270–272.

Bigelow D (2011). The tender cut: Inside the hidden world of self-injury. *Library Journal* 136, 96.

Blanchflower DG, Oswald AJ (2011). International happiness: A new view on the measure of performance. *Academy of Management Perspectives* 25, 6–22.

Borschmann R, Hogg J, Phillips R, Moran P (2011). Measuring self-harm in adults: A systematic review. *European Psychiatry*. Published online: 21 June 2011. doi:10.1016/j.eurpsy. 2011.04.005

Boscarino JA, Kirchner HL, Hoffman SN, Sartorius J, Adams RE, Figley CR (2011). A brief screening tool for assessing psychological trauma in clinical practice: Development and validation of the New York PTSD Risk Score. *General Hospital Psychiatry* 33, 489–500.

Bossarte RM, He H, Claassen CA, Knox K, Tu X (2011). Development and validation of a 6-day standard for the identification of frequent mental distress. *Social Psychiatry & Psychiatric Epidemiology* 46, 403–411.

Boyce N (2011). Profile Alys Cole-King: A pioneer of suicide mitigation in the UK. *The Lancet* 378, 561.

Brian KM (2011). The reclamation of Anna Agnew: Violence, victimhood, and the uses of 'cure'. *Journal of Literary & Cultural Disability Studies* 5, 279–302.

Bromilow P (2011) Rereading Lucretia in the Angoysses douloureuses qui procedent d'amours (1538). *Renaissance Studies*. Published online: 27 April 2011. doi: 10.1111/j.1477-4658. 2011.00739.

Brown JV (2011). Book review: Lost to the collective: Suicide and the promise of soviet socialism, 1921–1929. *American Historical Review* 116, 902–903.

Bucolo C, Drago F (2011). Carbon monoxide and the eye: Implications for glaucoma therapy. *Pharmacology & Therapeutics* 130, 191–201.

Byard RW (2011). Ned Kelly tattoos — Origins and forensic implications. *Journal of Forensic and Legal Medicine* 18, 276–279.

Callaghan S, Ryan CJ (2011). Refusing medical treatment after attempted suicide: Rethinking capacity and coercive treatment in light of the Kerrie Wooltorton case. *Journal of Law & Medicine* 18, 811–819.

Cantor CH (2011). Reasonable practice is not defensive practice. *Medical Journal of Australia* 195, 55.

Casey P, Bailey S (2011). Adjustment disorders: The state of the art. *World Psychiatry* 11, 11–18.

Cersovsky SB (2011). Fighting the war within: Suicide as an individual and public health challenge in the U.S. army. *Psychiatry* 74, 110–114.

Chaney S (2011). A hideous torture on himself: Madness and self-mutilation in Victorian literature. *Journal of Medical Humanities*. Published online: 12 August 2011. doi: 10.1007/s10912-011-9152-6

Chaney S (2011). Self-control, selfishness and mutilation: How 'medical' is self-injury anyway? *Medical History* 55, 375–382.

Chao RC, Green KE (2011). Multiculturally sensitive mental health scale (MSMHS): Development, factor analysis, reliability, and validity. *Psychological Assessment*. Published online: 25 April 2011. E-publication.

Clemens CAL (2011). 'Suicide Girls': Orhan Pamuk's snow and the politics of resistance in contemporary Turkey. *Feminist Formations* 23, 138–154.

Cosh J (2011). Suburban sanctuary. *Mental health today (Brighton, England)*, 10–11.

Crutcher LM (2011). Finding the Keats family. *Keats-Shelley Review* 25, 9.

Cusack J, Deane FP, Wilson CJ, Ciarrochi J (2011). Who influence men to go to therapy? Reports from men attending psychological services. *International Journal for the Advancement of Counselling* 26, 271–283.

Dadour IR, Almanjahie I, Fowkes ND, Keady G, Vijayan K (2011). Temperature variations in a parked vehicle. *Forensic Science International* 207, 205–211.

Davis JW, Sise MJ, Albrecht R, Kuhls DA (2011). American association for the surgery of trauma prevention committee topical updates: Getting started, fall prevention, domestic violence, and suicide. *Journal of Trauma-Injury Infection and Critical Care* 70, 996–1001.

Davis-Berman J (2011). Conversations about death: Talking to residents in independent, assisted, and long-term care settings. *Journal of Applied Gerontology* 30, 353.

Delgado-Gomez D, Blasco-Fontecilla H, Alegria AA, Legido-Gil T, Artes-Rodriguez A, Baca-Garcia E (2011). Improving the accuracy of suicide attempter classification. *Artificial Intelligence in Medicine* 52, 165–168.

Dennis JP, Ghahramanlou-Holloway M, Cox DW, Brown GK (2011). A guide for the assessment and treatment of suicidal patients with traumatic brain injuries. *Journal of Head Trauma Rehabilitation* 26, 244–256.

Deryol R (2011). Suicide by cop: Police shooting as a method of self-harming. *Policing — An International Journal of Police Strategies & Management* 34, 364–365.

Devi S (2011). Mental health care for US veterans heavily criticised. *The Lancet* 377, 2071–2072.

Dewall CN, Anderson CA, Bushman BJ (2011). The general aggression model: Theoretical extensions to violence. *Psychology of Violence* 1, 245–258.

Dick T (2011). Death wish. Is your conversation someone's last chance? *EMS World* 40, 22.

Donnelly TT, Hwang JJ, Este D, Ewashen C, Adair C, Clinton M (2011). If I was going to kill myself, I wouldn't be calling you. I am asking for help: Challenges influencing immigrant and refugee women's mental health. *Issues in Mental Health Nursing* 32, 279–290.

du Plessis M, Hlaise KK (2011). Homicide-suicide (dyadic death): A case study of double hanging. *American Journal of Forensic Medicine and Pathology*. Published online: 26 July 2011. doi: 10.1097/ PAF.0b013e3182186f67.

Ferlauto MJ, Frierson RL (2011). The probate judge and involuntary civil commitment in South Carolina. *Journal of the American Academy of Psychiatry and the Law* 39, 209–216.

Fiori LM, Turecki G (2011). Epigenetic regulation of spermidine/spermine N1-acetyltransferase (SAT1) in Suicide. *Journal of Psychiatric Research* 45, 1229–1235.

Fleck DE, Kotwal R, Eliassen JC, Lamy M, Delbello MP, Adler CM, Durling M, Cerullo MA, Strakowski SM (2011). Preliminary evidence for increased frontosubcortical activation on a motor impulsivity task in mixed episode bipolar disorder. *Journal of Affective Disorders* 133, 333–339.

Folly WSD (2011). The threshold bias model: A mathematical model for the nomothetic approach of suicide. *PLoS ONE* 6, e24414.

Franzen AG, Gottzen L (2011). The beauty of blood? Self-injury and ambivalence in an Internet community. *Journal of Youth Studies* 14, 279–294.

Freckelton I (2011). Psychotherapy, suicide and foreseeable risks of decompensation by the vulnerable. *Journal of Law & Medicine* 18, 467–477.

Gassmann-Mayer C, Jiang K, McSorley P, Arani R, DuBrava S, Suryawanshi S, Webb DM, Nilsson M (2011). Clinical and statistical assessment of suicidal ideation and behavior in pharmaceutical trials. *Clinical Pharmacology and Therapeutics* 90, 554–560.

Gates BT (2011). Histories of suicide: International perspectives on self-destruction in the modern world. *University of Toronto Quarterly* 80, 250–251.

Geppert CMA (2011). Saving life or respecting autonomy: The ethical dilemma of DNR orders in patients who attempt suicide. *Internet Journal of Law, Healthcare and Ethics* 7, 1.

Glaesmer H, Grande G, Braehler E, Roth M (2011). The german version of the Satisfaction With Life Scale (SWLS): Psychometric properties, validity, and population-based norms. *European Journal of Psychological Assessment* 27, 127–132.

Goeschel C (2011). Lost to the collective: Suicide and the promise of soviet socialism, 1921–1929. *Journal of Social History* 44, 1241–1242.

Gontier E, Prigent Y (2011). Therapeutic alliance and commitment: A reflection about the ethics of taking care of patients who have attempted suicide in a psychoanalytical psychotherapy framework. *Annales Medico-Psychologiques* 169, 319–322.

Goodkind JR, Ross-Toledo K, John S, Hall JL, Ross L, Freeland L, Coletta E, Becenti-Fundark T, Poola C, Roanhorse R, Lee C (2011). Rebuilding trust: A community, multiagency, state, and university partnership to improve behavioral health care for American Indian youth, their families, and communities. *Journal of Community Psychology* 39, 452–477.

Grah M, Mihanovic M, Svrdlin P, Pisk SV, Restek-Petrovic B (2011). Serotonin and cortisol as suicidogenic factors in patients with PTSD. *Collegium Antropologicum* 34, 1433–1439.

Hamby S (2011). The second wave of violence scholarship: Integrating and broadening theories of violence. *Psychology of Violence* 1, 163–165.

Hammig B, Ogletree R, Wycoff-Horn MR (2011). The relationship between professional preparation and class structure on health instruction in the secondary classroom. *The Journal of School Health* 81, 513–519.

Harter TD (2011). Reconsidering Kant on suicide. *Philosophical Forum* 42, 167–185.

Hasselberg N, Grawe RW, Johnson S, Ruud T (2011). An implementation study of the crisis resolution team model in Norway: Are crisis resolution teams fulfilling their role? *BMC Health Services Research* 11, 96.

Healey D (2011). Book review: Lost to the Collective: Suicide and the promise of Soviet Socialism, 1921–1929. *Bulletin of the History of Medicine* 85, 312–313.

Hill DJ (2011). What is it to commit suicide? *Ratio* 24, 192–205.

Hon KL (2011). Dying with parents: An extreme form of child abuse. *World Journal of Pediatrics* 7, 266–268.

Hjelmeland H (2010). Cultural research in suicidology: Challenges and opportunities. *Suicidology Online* 1, 34–52.

Hjelmeland H, Knizek BL (2011). Methodology in suicidological research: Contribution to the debate. *Suicidology Online* 2, 8–10.

Hope T, McMillan J (2011). The art of medicine: Advance decisions, chronic mental illness, and everyday care. *The Lancet* 377, 2076–2077.

Hunter E (2011). Contextualizing Indigenous suicide. *Australia and New Zealand Journal of Psychiatry* 45, 601–602.

Huscher CG, Mingoli A, Mereu A, Sgarzini G (2011). Laparoscopy can be very effective in reducing mortality rate for caustic ingestion in suicide attempt. *World Journal of Surgery* 35, 2363–2364.

Inder KJ, Berry H, Kelly BJ (2011). Using cohort studies to investigate rural and remote mental health. *Australian Journal of Rural Health* 19, 171–178.

Jones R, Sharkey S, Smithson J, Ford T, Emmens T, Hewis E, Sheaves B, Owens C (2011). Using metrics to describe the participative stances of members within discussion forums. *Journal of Medical Internet Research* 13, e3.

Karoski S (2011). Has the health system failed men? The perceptions of the men's movement on men's health in Australia. *International Journal of Men's Health* 10, 45–64.

Kato TA, Shinfuku N, Fujisawa D, Tateno M, Ishida T, Akiyama T, Sartorius N, Teo AR, Choi TY, Wand APF, Balhara YPS, Chang JPC, Chang RYF, Shadloo B, Ahmed HU, Lerthattasilp T, Umene-Nakano W, Horikawa H, Matsumoto R, Kuga H, Tanaka M, Kanba S (2011). Introducing the concept of modern depression in Japan: An international case vignettes survey. *Journal of Affective Disorders*. Published online: 20 July 2011. doi:10.1016/j.jad.2011.06.030

Khan SS, Benger J (2011). SADPERSONS scale in assessing self harm risk. *Emergency Medicine Journal* 28, 335–336.

Kibayashi K, Shimada R, Nakao KI (2011). Frequent detection of stomach contents in accidental drowning. *Medicine, Science & the Law* 51, 161–163.

Kingston J, Clarke S, Ritchie T, Remington B (2011). Developing and validating the 'composite measure of problem behaviors'. *Journal of Clinical Psychology* 67, 736–751.

Kishi Y, Kurosawa H, Morimura H, Hatta K, Thurber S (2011). Attitudes of Japanese nursing personnel toward patients who have attempted suicide. *General Hospital Psychiatry* 33, 393–397.

Kozicz T, Sterrenburg L, Xu L (2011). Does midbrain urocortin 1 matter? A 15-year journey from stress (mal)adaptation to energy metabolism. *Stress* 14, 376–383.

Krenzelok EP, Mrvos R (2011). Friends and foes in the plant world: A profile of plant ingestions and fatalities. *Clinical Toxicology* 49, 142–149.

Kroner DG, Kang T, Mills JF, Harris AJR, Green MM (2011). Reliabilities, validities, and cutoff scores of the depression hopelessness suicide screening form among women offenders. *Criminal Justice and Behavior* 38, 779–795.

Lagresa E (2011). Narcissism and suicide in Shakespeare and his contemporaries. *Comitatus — A Journal of Medieval and Renaissance Studies* 42:259–261.

Lavigne JE, Mathews J, Knox KL (2010). The pharmacology and epidemiology of post-market surveillance for suicide: The case of gabapentin. *Journal of Pharmaceutical Health Services Research* 1, 47–51.

Leenaars AA (2010). Edwin S. Shneidman on Suicide. *Suicidology Online* 1, 5–18.

Lester D, Mcswain S, Gunn III JF (2011). A test of the validity of the IS PATH WARM warning signs for suicide. *Psychological Reports* 108, 402–404.

Lester D (2010). Qualitative research in suicidology: Thoughts on Hjelmeland and Knizek's 'Why we need qualitative research in suicidology'. *Suicidology Online* 1, 76–78.

Leventhal AM, Zvolensky MJ, Schmidt NB (2011). Smoking-related correlates of depressive symptom dimensions in treatment-seeking smokers. *Nicotine & Tobacco Research* 13, 668–676.

Lipczynska S (2011). Communication and collaboration in the treatment of mental disorders. *Journal of Mental Health* 20, 315–318.

Luxton DD, Rudd MD, Reger MA, Gahm GA (2011). A psychometric study of the suicide ideation scale. *Archives of Suicide Research* 15, 250–258.

Madianos MG, Sarhan AL, Koukia E (2011). Major depression across West Bank: A cross-sectional general population study. *International Journal of Social Psychiatry*. Published online: 25 March 2011. doi: 10.1177/0020764010396410

Marr L (2011). Breaking the Silence on suicide and mental illness: The brethren in Christ, 1968–1989. *Journal of Mennonite Studies* 29, 121.

Martinez RO, Santiago OJ, Espino D (2011). Comparison of attitudes toward suicide and physician-assisted suicide in chronic pain scenarios between elderly Whites and Hispanics. *Journal of the American Geriatrics Society* 59, S114.

Matsubayashi T, Ueda M (2011). Government partisanship and human well-being. *Social Indicators Research*. Published online: 29 March 2011. doi: doi.org/10.1007/s11205-011-9831-8

Mattei G, Ferrari S, Rigatelli M (2011). Economic recession in Italy: A review of short-term effects on health. *Journal of Psychosomatic Research* 70, 612.

Miguel-Hidalgo JJ, Overholser JC, Jurjus GJ, Meltzer HY, Dieter L, Konick L, Stockmeier CA, Rajkowska G (2011). Vascular and extravascular immunoreactivity for intercellular adhesion molecule 1 in the orbitofrontal cortex of subjects with major depression: Age-dependent changes. *Journal of Affective Disorders* 132, 422–431.

Moreno E (2011). The society of our 'out of Africa' ancestors (I): The migrant warriors that colonized the world. *Communicative and Integrative Biology* 4, 163–170.

Hammig B, Ogletree R, Wycoff-Horn MR (2011). The relationship between professional preparation and class structure on health instruction in the secondary classroom. *The Journal of School Health* 81, 513–519.

Mulder R (2011). Problems with suicide risk assessment. *Australia and New Zealand Journal of Psychiatry* 45, 605–607.

Munk-Jorgensen P, Ostergaard SD (2011). Register-based studies of mental disorders. *Scandinavian Journal of Public Health* 39, 170–174.

Musilek K, Dolezal M, Gunn-Moore F, Kuca K (2011). Design, evaluation and structure-Activity relationship studies of the AChE reactivators against organophosphorus pesticides. *Medicinal Research Reviews* 31, 548–575.

Musumeci C (2011). The suicide of the bad. *PONTE* 67, 20–21.

Myer T (2011). Inside intentional self-injury. *Nursing* 41, 26–31.

Nam M, Heo DS, Jun TY, Lee MS, Cho MJ, Han C, Kim MK (2011). Depression, suicide, and Korean society. *Journal of the Korean Medical Association* 54, 358–361.

Nielssen O, Large M (2011). Dangerous myths about suicide. *Australasian Psychiatry* 19, 269.

Nikolic S, Zivkovi V, Babic D, Jukovi F (2011). Cervical soft tissue emphysema in hanging-a prospective autopsy study. *Journal of Forensic Sciences*. Published online: 16 September 2011. doi: 10.1111/j.1556-4029.2011.01911.x

Nikunen M (2011). Murder-suicide in the news: Doing the routine and the drama. *European Journal of Cultural Studies* 14, 81–101.

Normile D (2011). Higher education. Spate of suicides roils university, jeopardizing academic reforms. *Science* 332, 410.

Oaklander AL (2011). Neuropathic itch. *Seminars in Cutaneous Medicine and Surgery* 30, 87–92.

Oberleitner LMS, Tzilos GK, Zumberg KM, Grekin ER (2011). Psychotropic drug use among college students: Patterns of use, misuse, and medical monitoring. *Journal of American College Health* 59, 658–661.

Ogden RD, Hassan S (2011). Suicide by oxygen deprivation with helium: A preliminary study of British Columbia coroner investigations. *Death Studies* 35, 338–364.

Okumura Y, Higuchi T (2011). Cost of depression among adults in Japan. *Primary Care Companion to the Journal of Clinical Psychiatry* 13, e1–e9.

Osafo J, Knizek BL, Akotia CS, Hjelmeland H (2011). Influence of religious factors on attitudes towards suicidal behaviour in Ghana. *Journal of Public Health*. Published online: 6 May 2011. doi: 10.1007/s10943-011-9487-3

Osterman LL, Brown RP (2011). Culture of honor and violence against the self. *Personality and Social Psychology Bulletin*. Published online: 15 August 2011. doi:10.1177/01461672 11418529

Ott P (2011). Murder in the Alpenglow: Swiss crime writing in the german language. *World Literature Today* 85, 24–25.

Parent R (2011). The police use of deadly force in British Columbia: Mental illness and crisis intervention. *Journal of Police Crisis Negotiations* 11, 57–71.

Pautex S, Zulian GB (2011). End-of-life care in elderly cancer patients. *Aging Health* 7, 469–475.

Peschel O, Kunz SN, Rothschild MA, Muetzel E (2011). Blood stain pattern analysis. *Forensic Science, Medicine & Pathology* 7, 257–270.

Petermann F (2011). Self-harming behavior or suicidal intent. *Deutsches Arzteblatt International* 108, 432.

Philippe FL, Laventure S, Beaulieu-Pelletier G, Lecours S, Lekes N (2011). Ego-resiliency as a mediator between childhood trauma and psychological symptoms. *Journal of Social and Clinical Psychology* 30, 583–598.

Poethke HJ, Dytham C, Hovestadt T (2011). A metapopulation paradox: Partial improvement of habitat may reduce metapopulation persistence. *American Naturalist* 177, 792–799.

Pompili M, Baldessarini RJ, Berman AL, Lester D, Wasserman D, De Leo D, Girardi P (2011). Integration of suicidology with general medicine: An obligation to society. *Patient Education and Counselling* 85, 127–128.

Powledge TM (2011). Behavioral epigenetics: How nurture shapes nature. *Bioscience* 61, 588–592.

Prakash R (2011). Suicidal behavior. *Journal of Clinical Psychiatry* 72, 264–264.

Pridmore S, Ahmadi J, Majeed ZA (2011). Suicide in old Norse and Finnish folk stories. *Australasian Psychiatry* 19, 321–324.

Pridmore S, Pridmore W (2011). The suicidal desire of Tolstoy. *Australasian Psychiatry* 19, 211–214.

Prince A, Nelson K (2011). Educational needs of practice nurses in mental health. *Journal of Primary Health Care* 3, 142–149.

Randall JR, Colman I, Rowe BH (2011). A systematic review of psychometric assessment of self-harm risk in the emergency department. *Journal of Affective Disorders* 134, 348–355.

Reddy K, Lowenstein EJ (2011). Forensics in dermatology: Part II. *Journal of the American Academy of Dermatology* 64, 811–824.

Reddy MS (2011). Suicide incidence and epidemiology. *Indian Journal of Psychological Medicine* 32, 77–82.

Rees G (2011). Is sex worth dying for? Sentimental-homicidal-suicidal violence in theological discourse of sexuality. *Journal of Religious Ethics* 39, 261–285.

Rezaeian M, Dunn G, St Leger S, Appleby L (2011). Application of commercial software to the classification of suicide cases: A brief report. *Violence and Victims* 26, 533–540.

Rhee YE (2011). Methodology of Humanities Therapy. *Universitas — Monthly Review of Philosophy and Culture* 38, 59–72.

Rhodes R, Aggarwal S, Schiano TD (2011). Overdose with suicidal intent: Ethical considerations for liver transplant programs. *Liver Transplantation* 17, 1111–1116.

Rhondali W, Perceau E, Saltel P, Girard R, Filbet M (2011). Translation and validation of Brief Edinburgh Depression Scale (BEDS) in French. *Bulletin du Cancer* 98, 199–208.

Riedel M (2011). Homicide- Suicides in the United States: A review of the literature. *Sociology Compass* 4, 430–441.

Rissanen ML, Kylma J, Laukkanen E (2011). Self-mutilation among Finnish adolescents: Nurses' conceptions. *International Journal of Nursing Practice* 17, 158–165.

Robinson MD, Gordon KH (2011). Personality dynamics: Insights from the personality social cognitive literature. *Journal of Personality Assessment* 93, 161–176.

Rogan RG (2011). Linguistic style matching in crisis negotiations: A comparative analysis of suicidal and surrender outcomes. *Journal of Police Crisis Negotiations* 11, 20–39.

Rogers JR, Apel S (2010). Revitalizing suicidology: A call for mixed methods designs. *Suicidology Online* 1, 92–94.

Ronningstam E (2011). Narcissistic personality disorder: A clinical perspective. *Journal of Psychiatric Practice* 17, 89–99.

Rosenberg L (2011). Addressing trauma in mental health and substance use treatment. *Journal of Behavioral Health Services & Research* 38, 428–431.

Ruwanpura R, Ariyaratne C (2011). A homicide by suspension. *Medicine, Science & the Law* 50, 224–227.

Sado M, Yamauchi K, Kawakami N, Ono Y, Furukawa TA, Tsuchiya M, Tajima M, Kashima H (2011). Cost of depression among adults in Japan in 2005. *Psychiatry and Clinical Neurosciences* 65, 442–450.

Saiz PA, García-Portilla P, Paredes B, Corcoran P, Arango C, Morales B, Sotomayor E, Alvarez V, Coto E, Flórez G, Bascaran MT, Bousoño M, Bobes J (2011). Role of serotonergic-related systems in suicidal behavior: Data from a case-control association study. *Progress in Neuro-psychopharmacology and Biological Psychiatry* 35, 1518–1524.

Sakurai K, Nishi A, Kondo K, Yanagida K, Kawakami N (2011). Screening performance of K6/K10 and other screening instruments for mood and anxiety disorders in Japan. *Psychiatry and Clinical Neurosciences* 65, 434–441.

Santosh PJ, Sattar S, Canagaratnam M (2011). Efficacy and tolerability of pharmacotherapies for attention-deficit hyperactivity disorder in adults. *CNS Drugs* 25, 737–763.

Sauvageau A, Laharpe R, King D, Dowling G, Andrews S, Kelly S, Ambrosi C, Guay JP, Geberth VJ (2011). Agonal sequences in 14 filmed hangings with comments on the role of the type of suspension, ischemic habituation, and ethanol intoxication on the timing of agonal responses. *American Journal of Forensic Medicine and Pathology* 32, 104–107.

Sauvaget A, Guitteny-Collas M, Volkaert M, Rouaud T, Francois S, Raoul S, N'Guyen JP, Derkinderen P, Damier P, Vanelle JM (2011). Consultation-liaison psychiatry for the assessment of suicidal risk following deep brain stimulation of the subthalamic nucleus in Parkinson's disease: The PPSAQ. *Journal of Psychosomatic Research* 70, 623–623.

Schulz F, Buschmann C, Braun C, Püschel K, Brinkmann B, Tsokos M (2011). Haemorrhages into the back and auxiliary breathing muscles after death by hanging. *International Journal of Legal Medicine*. Published online: 21 September 2011. doi: 10.1007/s00414-011-0622-1

Scourfield J, Roen K, Mcdermott E (2011). The non-display of authentic distress: Public-private dualism in young people's discursive construction of self-harm. *Sociology of Health and Illness* 33, 777–791.

Shorter E (2011). A sadly troubled history: The meanings of suicide in the modern age. *American Historical Review* 116, 162–163.

Shrubb R (2011). A problem shared. *Mental health today (Brighton, England)* 14–15.

Stirman SW, Brown GK, Ghahramanlou-Holloway M, Fox AJ, Chohan MZ, Beck AT (2011). Participation bias among suicidal adults in a randomized controlled trial. *Suicide and Life-Threatening Behavior* 41, 203–209.

Stone SA, Frost LE, Van Norman JR, Casey KA (2011). Creating a mentally healthy community through the use of behavioral health indicators. *Applied Research in Quality of Life* 5, 273–285.

Takahashi T (2011). Neuroeconomics of suicide. *Neuroendocrinology Letters* 32, 400–404.

Takahashi Y, Moiseyev G, Chen Y, Farjo K, Nikolaeva O, Ma JX (2011). An enzymatic mechanism for generating the precursor of endogenous 13-cis retinoic acid in the brain. *FEBS Journal* 278, 973–987.

Thupayagale-Tshweneagae G, Benedict S (2011). The burden of secrecy among South African adolescents orphaned by HIV and AIDS. *Issues in Mental Health Nursing* 32, 355–358.

Van Orden KA, Witte TK, Holm-Denoma J, Gordon KH, Joiner TE (2011). Suicidal behavior on Axis VI. *Crisis* 32, 110–113.

Varghese P, Gray BP (2011). Suicide assessment of adolescents in the primary care setting. *Journal for Nurse Practitioners* 7, 186–192.

Villalba MM, Slater S, Davis J (2009). Laser treated carbon composites for the determination of suicide biomarkers: Development of a forensic diagnosis device. *ECS Transactions* 19, 49–60.

Vodovosoff A (2011). 'I have always thought about death, a death that I might give myself'. *Journal of Theoretical and Philosophical Psychology* 31, 140–150.

Walter G, Pridmore S (2011). The suicide of Adam Czerniakow. *Australasian Psychiatry*. Published online: 15 Setember 2011. doi:10.3109/10398562.2011.619267

Wanberg CR, Wanberg CR (2011). The individual experience of unemployment. *Annual Review of Psychology*. Published online: 8 December 2010. doi: 10.1146/annurev-psych-120710-100500

Warren LJ, Mullen PE, Ogloff JR (2011). A clinical study of those who utter threats to kill. *Behavioral Sciences and the Law* 29, 141–154.

Wray M, Colen C, Pescosolido B (2011). The sociology of suicide. *Annual Review of Sociology* 37, 505–528.

Yang B, Lester D (2010). Is there an economic argument for suicide prevention? A response to Doessel and Williams. *Suicidology Online* 1, 88–91.

Zausner T (2011). Chaos, creativity, and substance abuse: The nonlinear dynamics of choice. *Nonlinear Dynamics, Psychology and Life Sciences* 15, 207–227.

www.ingramcontent.com/pod-product-compliance
Lightning Source LLC
Chambersburg PA
CBHW080237270326
41926CB00020B/4282